The Parenting Skills Treatment Planner, with DSM-5 Updates

Practice*Planners*® Series

Treatment Planners

The Complete Adult Psychotherapy Treatment Planner, Fifth Edition
The Child Psychotherapy Treatment Planner, Fifth Edition
The Adolescent Psychotherapy Treatment Planner, Fifth Edition
The Addiction Treatment Planner, Fifth Edition
The Continuum of Care Treatment Planner
The Couples Psychotherapy Treatment Planner, with DSM-5 Updates, Second Edition
The Employee Assistance Treatment Planner
The Pastoral Counseling Treatment Planner
The Older Adult Psychotherapy Treatment Planner, with DSM-5 Updates, Second Edition
The Behavioral Medicine Treatment Planner
The Group Therapy Treatment Planner, with DSM-5 Updates, Second Edition
The Gay and Lesbian Psychotherapy Treatment Planner
The Family Therapy Treatment Planner, with DSM-5 Updates, Second Edition
The Severe and Persistent Mental Illness Treatment Planner, with DSM-5 Updates, Second Edition
The Mental Retardation and Developmental Disability Treatment Planner
The Social Work and Human Services Treatment Planner
The Crisis Counseling and Traumatic Events Treatment Planner, with DSM-5 Updates, Second Edition
The Personality Disorders Treatment Planner
The Rehabilitation Psychology Treatment Planner
The Special Education Treatment Planner
The Juvenile Justice and Residential Care Treatment Planner
The School Counseling and School Social Work Treatment Planner, with DSM-5 Updates, Second Edition
The Sexual Abuse Victim and Sexual Offender Treatment Planner, with DSM-5 Updates
The Probation and Parole Treatment Planner
The Psychopharmacology Treatment Planner
The Speech-Language Pathology Treatment Planner
The Suicide and Homicide Risk Assessment and Prevention Treatment Planner, with DSM-5 Updates
The College Student Counseling Treatment Planner
The Parenting Skills Treatment Planner, with DSM-5 Updates
The Early Childhood Intervention Treatment Planner
The Co-occurring Disorders Treatment Planner, with DSM-5 Updates
The Complete Women's Psychotherapy Treatment Planner
The Veterans and Active Duty Military Psychotherapy Treatment Planner, with DSM-5 Updates

Progress Notes Planners

The Child Psychotherapy Progress Notes Planner, Fifth Edition
The Adolescent Psychotherapy Progress Notes Planner, Fifth Edition
The Adult Psychotherapy Progress Notes Planner, Fifth Edition
The Addiction Progress Notes Planner, Fifth Edition
The Severe and Persistent Mental Illness Progress Notes Planner, Second Edition
The Couples Psychotherapy Progress Notes Planner, Second Edition
The Family Therapy Progress Notes Planner, Second Edition
The Veterans and Active Duty Military Psychotherapy Progress Notes Planner

Homework Planners

Couples Therapy Homework Planner, Second Edition
Family Therapy Homework Planner, Second Edition
Grief Counseling Homework Planner
Group Therapy Homework Planner
Divorce Counseling Homework Planner
School Counseling and School Social Work Homework Planner, Second Edition
Child Therapy Activity and Homework Planner
Addiction Treatment Homework Planner, Fifth Edition
Adolescent Psychotherapy Homework Planner, Fifth Edition
Adult Psychotherapy Homework Planner, Fifth Edition
Child Psychotherapy Homework Planner, Fifth Edition
Parenting Skills Homework Planner
Veterans and Active Duty Military Psychotherapy Homework Planner

Client Education Handout Planners

Adult Client Education Handout Planner
Child and Adolescent Client Education Handout Planner
Couples and Family Client Education Handout Planner

Complete Planners

The Complete Depression Treatment and Homework Planner
The Complete Anxiety Treatment and Homework Planner

PracticePlanners®

Arthur E. Jongsma, Jr., Series Editor

The Parenting Skills Treatment Planner with DSM-5 Updates

Sarah Edison Knapp

Arthur E. Jongsma, Jr.

WILEY

This book is printed on acid-free paper. ♾

Published by John Wiley & Sons, Inc., Hoboken, New Jersey.

Published simultaneously in Canada.

For general information on our other products and services please contact our Customer Care Department within the United States at (800) 762-2974, outside the United States at (317) 572-3993 or fax (317) 572-4002.

Wiley also publishes its books in a variety of electronic formats. Some content that appears in print may not be available in electronic books. For more information about Wiley products, visit our Web site at www.wiley.com.

Library of Congress Cataloging-in-Publication Data:

ISBN 1-119-07312-X
1-119-07484-3 (ePDF)
1-119-07487-8 (ePub)

Printed in the United States of America.

10 9 8 7

To parents worldwide who have undertaken the most joyful, difficult, challenging, heartbreaking, rewarding, and never-ending job of raising their children; and to my own parents, Marion and Richard Edison, who made this manuscript possible.

—S.E.K.

To Kendra and Erwin, Michelle and Dave who patiently, prayerfully, and positively parent my delightful grandchildren, Tyler, Kaleigh, Justin, and Carter.

—A.E.J.

CONTENTS

PRACTICE*PLANNERS*® SERIES PREFACE

Accountability is an important dimension of the practice of psychotherapy. Treatment programs, public agencies, clinics, and practitioners must justify and document their treatment plans to outside review entities in order to be reimbursed for services. The books in the Practice*Planners*® series are designed to help practitioners fulfill these documentation requirements efficiently and professionally.

The Practice*Planners*® series includes a wide array of treatment planning books including not only the original *Complete Adult Psychotherapy Treatment Planner*, *Child Psychotherapy Treatment Planner*, and *Adolescent Psychotherapy Treatment Planner*, all now in their fifth editions, but also *Treatment Planners* targeted to specialty areas of practice, including:

- Addictions
- Co-occurring disorders
- Behavioral medicine
- College students
- Couples therapy
- Crisis counseling
- Early childhood education
- Employee assistance
- Family therapy
- Gays and lesbians
- Group therapy
- Juvenile justice and residential care
- Mental retardation and developmental disability
- Neuropsychology
- Older adults
- Parenting skills
- Pastoral counseling
- Personality disorders
- Probation and parole
- Psychopharmacology
- Rehabilitation psychology
- School counseling and school social work

- Severe and persistent mental illness
- Sexual abuse victims and offenders
- Social work and human services
- Special education
- Speech-language pathology
- Suicide and homicide risk assessment
- Veterans and active military duty
- Women's issues

In addition, there are three branches of companion books that can be used in conjunction with the *Treatment Planners*, or on their own:

- ***Progress Notes Planners*** provide a menu of progress statements that elaborate on the client's symptom presentation and the provider's therapeutic intervention. Each *Progress Notes Planner* statement is directly integrated with the behavioral definitions and therapeutic interventions from its companion *Treatment Planner*.
- ***Homework Planners*** include homework assignments designed around each presenting problem (such as anxiety, depression, substance use, anger control problems, eating disorders, or panic disorder) that is the focus of a chapter in its corresponding *Treatment Planner*.
- ***Client Education Handout Planners*** provide brochures and handouts to help educate and inform clients on presenting problems and mental health issues, as well as life skills techniques. The handouts are included on CD-ROMs for easy printing from your computer and are ideal for use in waiting rooms, at presentations, as newsletters, or as information for clients struggling with mental illness issues. The topics covered by these handouts correspond to the presenting problems in the *Treatment Planners*.

The series also includes adjunctive books, such as *The Psychotherapy Documentation Primer* and *The Clinical Documentation Sourcebook*, contain forms and resources to aid the clinician in mental health practice management.

The goal of our series is to provide practitioners with the resources they need in order to provide high-quality care in the era of accountability. To put it simply: We seek to help you spend more time on patients, and less time on paperwork.

ARTHUR E. JONGSMA, JR.
Grand Rapids, Michigan

ACKNOWLEDGMENTS

Writing this planner has been an effort of joy and dedication for me. I am aware that parenting is the most difficult job assumed by human beings. I thank my own children Michael Knapp and Heather Werkema for teaching me this lesson throughout their childhood years. They are now lovingly and graciously repaying my efforts with their own amazing life journeys.

I am immensely grateful to co-author Art Jongsma who has worked diligently with me on this treatment planner ever since its inception. Further special thanks go to Jennifer Byrne who applied her transcription gifts to make this planner consistent, well organized, and user-friendly. Peggy Alexander, David Bernstein, Cris Wojdylo, Judi Knott, and Micheline Frederick at Wiley are the final links in a collaborative chain that produced this book in its final form.

—S.E.K.

As we try to collect our thoughts and ideas and commit them to paper in writing a book, we are confronted with gaps in our knowledge. I am grateful for Sarah Knapp who has been most competent in providing the background and knowledge to allow me to help her write this book. She has been very professional in her approach and very responsible about completing this project with high-quality work. Thank you Sarah. You have made a fine contribution to the literature that will surely assist many people for years to come.

I also continue to be grateful to my support staff at Wiley, most of whom have already been named above by Sarah. This crew is the best around.

—A.E.J.

ACKNOWLEDGMENTS

INTRODUCTION

PLANNER FOCUS

The *Parenting Skills Treatment Planner* is designed for all adult and family therapists, family life educators, clergy, pediatric doctors and nurses, and other mental health professionals who provide guidance, counseling, and therapeutic support to parents and their children. The contents incorporate an extensive representation of the social-emotional, behavioral, academic, and interpersonal challenges faced by families as their children grow into adulthood.

Interventions have been designed to offer the family counselor a variety of workable, constructive, and meaningful strategies to improve the parent's ability to relate to the child in a positive, loving manner while setting limits and encouraging responsible behavior using various techniques of positive discipline. The emphasis is always on enhancing the independence and personal competency of the child, regardless of the type or intensity of the treatment issue. The interventions target the parent's and the child's functioning in the family, social settings, and the community. Reality-based therapeutic interventions are offered to strengthen the parent's role in directing the child's growth in social skills development, personal responsibility, self-esteem, self-control, academic achievement, and preparation for future independence.

The writing of quality therapeutic treatment plans based on specific, targeted areas of need can offer the family counselor an essential tool in identifying meaningful and effective interventions for parents and their children with social-emotional challenges. Further, it is our belief, that following an individualized treatment plan can significantly enhance the process of overcoming difficult parent/child relationships and discipline issues.

HISTORICAL BACKGROUND

Our research and brainstorming determined that pediatric health care providers, family counselors, family life educators, clergy, family mental health agencies, family courts, adoption agencies, child protection services, day care programs, foster parent programs, private and public school programs, and numerous other mental health care providers who support parents and their children would view a treatment guide focusing on techniques of developing positive parent/child relationships as invaluable.

Throughout more than a decade of teaching parent education classes, parents frequently ask for recommendations or referrals to independent counselors who would provide ongoing guidance or therapy consistent with the principles taught in the parenting classes. We have aspired to incorporate numerous treatment interventions that will allow the family counselor to offer the same positive and effective strategies for positive discipline, limit setting, effective communication, relationship building, character enhancement, parental modeling, and responsibility training incorporated in several of the most popular and effective parenting programs that are presented by dedicated parent educators worldwide. References to several of these recommended parent programs are listed in Appendix A.

TREATMENT PLAN UTILITY

Detailed, written treatment plans can benefit the family therapist and other mental health professionals working with parents and their children to address problems interfering with positive parent/child relationships, effective discipline, and the functional operation of the family unit. The parents are served by a written plan because it stipulates the issues that are the focus of the treatment process. The treatment plan is a guide that structures the focus of the therapeutic interventions that are essential for the parents and the identified child to progress toward their goals. Since issues can change as the family's circumstances or needs change, the treatment plan must be viewed as a dynamic document that can, and must be, updated to reflect any major change of problem, definition, goal, objective, or intervention.

The parents and the mental health service provider also benefit from the treatment plan because it forces careful and direct consideration of the desired treatment outcomes. Behaviorally stated, observable objectives clearly focus the treatment endeavor. The parents no longer have to wonder what the counseling is trying to accomplish. Clear objectives also allow the parents to channel their efforts into specific changes that will lead to the long-term goal of problem resolution and/or improved functioning. Both the parents and the counselor are concentrating on specifically stated objectives using carefully coordinated interventions to achieve those objectives.

The process of developing an effective treatment plan assists the mental health specialist to consider analytically and critically which therapeutic interventions are best suited for objective attainment of the parent's goal. Goals are developed and interventions are implemented based on the professional service provider's attention to the unique qualities and circumstances of each parent/child relationship and other existing family dynamics.

A well-crafted treatment plan that clearly stipulates the presenting problems and intervention strategies facilitates the treatment process carried out by the mental health provider during individual or group counseling sessions with the parents alone or conjointly with the parents and other family members. Good communication with the parents, the child, and other family members about what approaches are being implemented and who is responsible for which intervention is important. A thorough treatment plan stipulates in writing the details of the established objectives and the varied interventions, and can identify who will implement them.

Family life educators, counselors, and other family therapists will also benefit from the use of more precise, measurable objectives to evaluate success between the parents, their children, and other family members. With the advent of detailed treatment plans, outcome data can be more easily collected for interventions that are effective in achieving specific goals.

DEVELOPING A TREATMENT PLAN

The process of developing a treatment plan involves a logical series of steps that build on each other much like constructing a house. The foundation of any effective treatment plan is the data gathered in a comprehensive evaluation. As part of the process prior to developing the treatment plan, the family counselor must sensitively listen to and understand what the parents struggle with in terms of family dynamics, cognitive abilities, current stressors, social network, physical health and physical challenges, coping skills, self-esteem, extended family support, and so on. It is imperative that assessment data be drawn from a variety of sources that could include family background and social history, physical and mental health evaluations, clinical interviews, psychological testing, psychiatric evaluation/consultation, and assessment of the child's school history and records. The integration of the data by the mental health care provider or team is critical for understanding the parent/child relationship and discipline needs. We have identified five specific steps for developing an effective treatment plan based on assessment data.

Step One: Problem Selection

Although the parents may discuss a variety of issues during the assessment, the family counselor must ferret out the most significant problems on which to focus the treatment process. Usually a primary problem will surface, although secondary problems may also be evident. Some other problems may have to be set aside as not urgent enough to require treatment at this time. An effective treatment plan can deal only with a few selected problems or treatment will lose its direction. A variety of problems are presented as chapter titles representing specific social/emotional issues within the *Parenting Skills Treatment Planner*. The mental health professional may select those that most accurately represent the parents and child's current needs.

As the problems to be selected become clear to the family counselor or team, it is important to consider opinions from the parents, and the child's perspective in determining the prioritization of social/emotional concerns. The identified child's motivation to participate with the parents and cooperate with the treatment process depends, to some extent, on the degree to which treatment addresses his or her greatest needs, particularly in circumstances with adolescent children who may have strong feelings as to what should be emphasized.

Step Two: Problem Definition

Each parent presents with unique nuances as to how a problem behaviorally reveals itself in his or her life. Therefore, each problem that is selected for treatment focus requires a specific definition about how it is evidenced in the particular family. The symptom pattern is associated with diagnostic criteria similar to those found in the *Diagnostic and Statistical Manual of Mental Disorders-Fourth Edition (DSM-5).* The *Planner* offers behaviorally specific definition statements to choose from or to serve as a model for your own personally crafted statements. You will find several behavior symptoms or syndromes listed that may characterize one of the 31 presenting problems identified in the *Planner.* Turn to the chapter that identifies the presenting problem being experienced by parents or their child. Select from the listed behavioral definitions the statements that best describe the observable behavior directly interfering with the parent/child relationship.

Step Three: Goal Development

The next step in treatment plan development is that of setting broad goals for the resolution of the target educational problem. These statements need not be crafted in measurable terms but can be global, long-term goals that indicate a desired positive outcome to the treatment procedures. The *Planner* suggests several possible goal statements for each problem, but one statement is all that is required in a treatment plan.

Step Four: Objective Construction

In contrast to long-term goals, short-term objectives must be stated in behaviorally observable language. It must be clear when the parents and the identified child have achieved the objectives; therefore, vague, subjective objectives are not acceptable. Various alternatives are presented to allow construction of a variety of treatment plan possibilities for the same presenting problem. The family specialist must exercise professional judgment as to which objectives are most appropriate for a given family.

Each objective should be developed as a step toward attaining the broad instructional goal. In essence, objectives can be thought of as a series of steps that, when completed, will result in the achievement of the long-term goal. There should be at least two objectives for each problem, but the mental health professional may construct as many as are necessary for goal achievement. Target attainment dates may be listed for each objective. New objectives should be added to the plan as the family's treatment progresses. When all the necessary objectives have been achieved, the parents should have resolved the target problem successfully.

Step Five: Intervention Creation

Interventions are the therapeutic actions of the counselor designed to help the parents and the child to complete the objectives. There should be at least one intervention for every objective. If the parents do not accomplish the objective after the initial intervention has been implemented, new interventions should be added to the plan.

Interventions should be selected on the basis of the family's needs and the mental health specialist's full instructional and/or therapeutic repertoire. The *Parenting Skills Treatment Planner* contains interventions from a broad range of approaches including cognitive, behavioral, academic, dynamic, medical, and family-based. Other interventions may be written by the provider to reflect his or her own training and experience. The addition of new problems, definitions, goals, objectives, and interventions to those found in the *Planner* is encouraged to add to the database for future reference and use.

Some suggested interventions listed in the *Planner* refer to specific books, journals, or Internet sites where specific methodologies can be located for the counselor to look for a more lengthy explanation or discussion of the intervention. Appendix A offers a list of bibliotherapy references that may be helpful to families, referenced by the problem focused on within each chapter.

Step Six: Diagnosis Determination

The determination of an appropriate diagnosis is based on an evaluation of the client's complete clinical presentation. The clinician must compare the behavioral, cognitive, emotional, and interpersonal symptoms that the client presents to the criteria for diagnosis of a mental illness condition as described in *DSM-5*. The issue of differential diagnosis is admittedly a difficult one that has rather low inter-rater reliability. Psychologists have also been trained to think more in terms of maladaptive behavior than in disease labels. In spite of these factors, diagnosis is a reality that exists in the world of mental health care and it is a necessity for third-party reimbursement. However, recently, managed care agencies are more interested in behavioral indices that are exhibited by the client than in the actual diagnosis. It is the clinician's thorough knowledge of *DSM-5* criteria and a complete understanding of the client assessment data that contribute to the most reliable, valid diagnosis. An accurate assessment of behavioral indicators will also contribute to more effective treatment planning. If the parents are being seen in a family therapy mode, along with a child or children, there may be separate diagnoses given for different members of the family. Appendix B contains all of the suggested diagnoses cited in this book, sorted by presenting problems and chapter titles.

HOW TO USE THIS PLANNER

The *Parenting Skills Treatment Planner* was developed as a tool to aide family-oriented mental health professionals in writing a treatment plan in a rapid manner that is clear, specific, and highly individualized according to the following progression:

1. Choose one presenting problem/disability (Step One) you have identified through your assessment process. Locate the corresponding page number for that problem/disability in the Planner's table of contents.
2. Select two or three of the listed behavioral definitions or symptoms of the problem (Step Two) and record them in the appropriate section on your treatment plan form. Feel free to add your own defining statement if you determine that your client's behavioral manifestation of the identified problem is not listed.
3. Select one or more long-term goals (Step Three) and again write the selection, exactly as it is written in the *Planner* or in some appropriately modified form, in the corresponding area of your Treatment form.
4. Review the listed objectives for this problem and select the ones that you judge to be clinically indicated for your client (Step Four). Remember, it is recommended that you select at least two objectives for each problem. Add a target date allocated for the attainment of each objective, if necessary.
5. Choose relevant interventions (Step Five). The *Planner* offers suggested interventions related to each objective in the

parentheses following the objective statement. But do not limit yourself to those interventions. Just as with definitions, goals, and objectives, there is space allowed for you to enter your own interventions into the *Planner*. This allows you to refer to these entries when you create a plan around this problem in the future. You may have to assign responsibility to a specific person for implementation of each intervention if the treatment is being carried out by a team.

Congratulations! You should now have a complete, individualized, treatment plan that is ready for immediate implementation and presentation to the parents. It should resemble the format of the "Sample Treatment Plan" presented on page 9.

A FINAL NOTE

One important aspect of effective treatment planning is that each plan should be tailored to the individual problems and needs of parents and their children. The family's strengths and weaknesses, unique stressors, social network, circumstances, and symptom patterns *must* be considered in developing a treatment strategy. Drawing on our own years of parent education and clinical experiences, we have put together a variety of treatment choices. These statements can be combined in thousands of permutations to develop detailed treatment plans. Relying on their own good judgment, family mental health professionals can easily select the statements that are appropriate for the parents and children on their caseload. In addition, we encourage readers to add their own definitions, goals, objectives, and interventions to the existing samples. It is our hope that the *Parenting Skills Treatment Planner* will promote effective, creative treatment planning—a process that will ultimately benefit the parents, the identified child, the family, and the greater community.

SAMPLE TREATMENT PLAN

PROBLEM: STRATEGIES FOR CHILDREN (AGE 7 TO 12)

Definitions: Lack effective parenting strategies and the ability to set reasonable limits for the child.

Verbalize unclear boundary definitions and fail to differentiate between the parent and the child's needs, interests, and problems.

Maintain low expectations of and fail to reinforce the child's abilities and achievements.

Goals: Acquire positive discipline strategies that set limits and encourage independence.

Agree to form a united parental front and cooperate on all issues of discipline and child management.

OBJECTIVES	INTERVENTIONS
1. List the essential needs of an elementary school child and create a plan for accommodating those needs.	1. Brainstorm with the parents the essential requirements for the healthy development of their child (e.g., food, shelter, affirmation, discipline, character development); determine how these needs are being met.
	2. Assist the parents in creating a definition of unconditional love (e.g., complete and constant love given regardless of personal attributes or performance); brainstorm methods of sharing this most nurturing form of love with all family members.

2. Establish limits for the child using "I" statements, choices, positive conditions, and time out.

    1. Instruct the parents in using "Controlled Choices" (see *Parent Talk* by Moorman) to limit options according to the child's level of responsibility (e.g., "Would you like pizza or grilled cheese?" versus "What would you like to eat?").
    2. Advise the parents to use a short time out when the child's behavior becomes defiant or overly emotional and to require that the child remain excluded from family interaction until the child adopts a cooperative attitude.

3. Utilize natural and logical consequences to redirect behavior.

    1. Define natural (e.g., naturally occurring in the environment) and logical (e.g., created by the parents) consequences and outline their effectiveness as part of a positive disciplinary strategy.
    2. Assist the parents in designing several logical consequences to deal with chronic, inappropriate behavior (e.g., child forgets to make bed before school, child is not allowed after school activities until the bed is made).

4. Differentiate between adult problems and those that belong to the child.

    1. Teach the parents to differentiate problems that belong to the child (e.g., friends, homework) from problems that belong to the parents (e.g., messy kitchen, misplaced belongings of the parent).

2. Guide the parents in using proactive strategies (e.g., "I" statements, consequences, limit setting, choices) to modify behavior that is creating a problem for them and supportive interventions (e.g., active listening, empathy, encouragement, brainstorming, problem solving) to assist when the problem belongs to the child.

5. Report a reduction in power struggles resulting from strategies designed to enlist the child's cooperation.

1. Ask the parents to practice methods of sidestepping power struggles (e.g., broken record, "I" statements, choices, refusing to argue).

Diagnosis: Z62.820 Parent-Child Relational Problem

ABUSIVE PARENTING

BEHAVIORAL DEFINITIONS

1. Fail to provide the minimum care, supervision, emotional support, and nurturing required for normal childhood development.
2. Lack the emotional stability, cognitive ability, and/or knowledge base to perform appropriate parenting behaviors.
3. Report the generational cycle of abuse and neglect present in the parent's childhood.
4. Tolerate, condone, or ignore abuse, neglect, or maltreatment from the spouse or another caregiver.
5. Demands and expectations exceed the child's maturity and ability level.
6. Value, promote, and demand family secrecy and isolation.
7. Refuse to cooperate with the school, medical care facilities, private agencies, or child protection services that offer treatment programs for abused children and their families.
8. The child is the recipient of physical, sexual, or emotional aggression, resulting in injury or emotional trauma from a parent or caregiver.
9. The child incorporates aggressive and dysfunctional parental characteristics into own behavior patterns through internalization and modeling.

—. ____

____

LONG-TERM GOALS

1. Terminate all abusive treatment of the child.

2. Accept responsibility for the abusive treatment of the child, express remorse, and commit to using positive parenting strategies.
3. Adopt reasonable expectations for the child's behavior, abilities, and level of maturity.
4. Establish a compassionate, loving relationship with the child and establish appropriate parent/child boundaries.
5. Access social and mental health services for self, the child and other family members.
6. Reduce personal and family isolation and increase family, faith-based, and community support systems.

—. ____

____

SHORT-TERM OBJECTIVES

1. Outline the family history and disclose all incidents and circumstances involving child mistreatment, neglect and/or sexual or physical abuse. (1, 2, 3, 4)

THERAPEUTIC INTERVENTIONS

1. Explore the parent's perceptions and concerns about improper treatment of the child and offer assurance that disclosure is the first step in getting help to terminate the abuse.
2. Elicit a pledge from the parents to terminate all abuse immediately; establish a process to monitor the child's welfare.
3. Gather enough information to categorize the type of abuse and contact an investigative child protection agency if one is not already actively involved with the family.
4. Explore the family history with the parents to determine if chronic abuse or maltreatment is present or if the mistreatment of the child is an isolated incident.

2. Communicate with the child protection agency and report all known facts and suspicions of abuse. (5, 6, 7)

3. Cooperate with the child protection authorities to ensure the termination of the abuse and the safety and emotional well-being of the child. (8, 9)

5. Assist the parents in contacting the proper child protection authorities and completing the required forms if they suspect abuse from another caregiver or support them to disclose their own involvement.

6. Instruct the parents to report any suspected abuse by another caregiver to the state authorized child protection services (CPS) agency or local police department and to keep notes on behaviors, physical marks, or other suspicious evidence in regard to the child.

7. Review with the parents the therapist's obligation regarding the reporting of child abuse and notify them that any information about mistreatment of the child will be communicated to the appropriate CPS agency as required by law.

8. Encourage the parents to cooperate with the CPS caseworkers during the investigative process; request that they permit an exchange of information between the CPS caseworker and their private therapist.

9. Help the parents and the child deal with the legal aspects associated with disclosure of the abuse by providing information about the process and acquiring legal assistance.

4. Cooperate with the legal process and community agencies to acquire long or short-term living arrangements for the child that are safe and promote the development of love, trust, and healthy self-esteem. (10, 11, 12)

10. Instruct the parents to provide background and personal information to the CPS caseworkers to facilitate placement of their child in foster care, if deemed necessary to protect the child.

11. Assist the parents and the child in adjusting to the new living arrangements by addressing the adjustment issues and identifying the positive aspects of the child living in a healthy, abuse-free environment while the family prepares to reunite with the child.

12. Assign the parents to initiate immediate contact with the child's foster parents to plan for a smooth transition.

5. Share feelings about the abuse and dysfunctional family relationships. (13, 14)

13. Advise the parents that disclosure of abusive behavior is extremely difficult and painful for both them and the child; encourage the expression and processing of associated feelings.

14. Assign the parents to complete the "Our Family's Secret Story" activity from the *Parenting Skills Homework Planner* (Knapp) to portray their family's history of abuse.

6. Verbalize an awareness of the problems created for the child by overly punitive, abusive, inappropriate, and inconsistent parenting. (15, 16, 17)

15. Assign parents to listen to the audiotape *Helicopters, Drill Sergeants and Consultants* (Fay) to identify their own style of parenting and recognize the advantages of

encouraging the child to problem-solve independently.

16. Brainstorm with the parents a list of problems created in the family by overly punitive parenting and discuss how these problems are manifested in their family.

17. Instruct the parents to identify and address areas where the child is using triangulation to divide and control the environment (e.g., creating conflict between family members).

7. Promote positive character development through family discussions, analyzing literature and media examples, loving interactions, spiritual training, and community involvement. (18, 19, 20)

18. Assign the parents to read stories from *Where the Heart Is* (Moorman) or *Chicken Soup for the Soul* (Canfield, Hansen, and Kirberger) to stress family togetherness and the important role played by each family member.

19. Encourage family viewing of television or video programs that are consistent with their family values and to hold discussions that allow each family member to react without criticism.

20. Discuss with the parents the significance of regular family attendance at the spiritual organization of their choice for character development, moral training, and family cohesion.

8. Establish appropriate parent/child boundaries and

21. Assist the parents in differentiating parental and adult

differentiate between adult problems and those that belong to the child. (21, 22, 23)

problems from problems that belong to and should be solved by the child.

22. Guide the parents in using pro-active discipline strategies (e.g., I-statements, reasonable and logical consequences) to modify behavior that is creating a problem for them and supportive interventions (e.g., active listening, encouragement) to assist when the problem belongs to the child.

23. Encourage the parents to allow the child to seek solutions with guidance even if it requires some struggle and learning from mistakes; recommend that they listen to the child's problems with empathy and give assistance only when requested.

9. Arrange for the child to begin individual counseling focusing on the emotional reactions to the abuse and reconstructing feelings of trust, love, support, and empowerment. (24, 25, 26)

24. Assign the parents to schedule regular counseling appointments for the child to ensure psychological support throughout the abuse reporting, investigation, and intervention process.

25. Assign the parents to make a daily emotional assessment of how they and the child are coping with the ramifications of the abuse (or complete the "Measuring Our Feelings" activity in the *Parenting Skills Homework Planner* by Knapp).

26. Assign the parents and child to meet weekly to review

progress, note continuing concerns, and keep a written progress report to share with the child's private therapist.

10. Attend parent education classes and read parenting literature that teaches techniques of positive discipline. (27, 28)

27. Refer the parents to a parenting class (e.g., *Systematic Training for Effective Parenting* by Dinkmeyer and McKay) to help them replace abusive parent-child interactions with techniques of positive discipline.

28. Assign the parents to read literature about implementing strategies of positive discipline in their family (e.g., *Kids Are Worth It!* by Coloroso, *Children: The Challenge* by Dreikurs).

11. Grant specific freedoms consistent with the child's maturity and level of self-control. (29, 30)

29. Recommend that the parents grant privileges and choices consistent with the child's level of maturity and responsible behavior.

30. Teach the parents to use the phrase "Soon you'll be on your own" to encourage the child to earn freedom from parental monitoring by demonstrating independent and responsible behavior (see *Parent Talk* by Moorman).

12. Report a reduction in power struggles resulting from strategies designed to enlist the child's cooperation. (31, 32)

31. Teach the parents methods of sidestepping power struggles (e.g., using a broken record response, choices, refusing to argue); ask them to record the results in a discipline journal.

32. Assist the parents and the child in establishing a verbal or nonverbal cue to signal the need to break the cycle of negative behavior or abusive reaction by implementing a prearranged strategy (e.g., time out, change the location of the behavior, or switch activities).

13. Single parents seek respite, support, and encouragement from co-parent, family, and friends. (33, 34, 35)

33. Brainstorm with the single parent a list of support people who can be called on to babysit, console, and help out in case of emergency.

34. Identify with the single parent several community agencies available to offer assistance and support (e.g., respite care, single parent support groups).

35. Discuss with the single parent or separated parents the importance of cooperation in the co-parenting process and offer to mediate any current roadblocks or refer them to an independent mediator.

14. Solicit assistance from social service agencies that provide support, guidance, and respite. (36, 37)

36. Refer the parents to community agencies and services designed to support families struggling with parent/child or abuse issues (e.g., Visiting Nurses, family abuse counseling services) or refer them to a national support resource (e.g., Childhelp, U.S.A.: (800) 422-4453).

37. Assist the parents in listing their personal and family

resources for respite from the demands of managing the family (e.g., friends, family, church members); urge them to utilize the resources on a regular basis.

15. Increase the family's and the child's social interaction with the school, classmates, and friends. (38, 39)

38. Assign the parents to encourage the child to join a social group or club by brainstorming options and helping the child make a selection.

39. Encourage the family to become involved with social activities at school (e.g., PTA, sports events, concerts).

16. Invite extended family members to parenting classes and/or counseling sessions. (40)

40. Suggest that the parents invite the grandparents to parenting classes or a counseling session to help them understand their newly acquired discipline strategies.

__. ____________________

__. ____________________

DIAGNOSTIC SUGGESTIONS:

ICD-9-CM	*ICD-10-CM*	*DSM-5* Disorder, Condition, or Problem
309.81	F43.10	Posttraumatic Stress Disorder
300.4	F34.1	Persistent Depressive Disorder
995.53	T74.22XA	Child Sexual Abuse, Confirmed, Initial Encounter
995.53	T74.22XD	Child Sexual Abuse, Confirmed, Subsequent Encounter
300.14	F44.81	Dissociative Identity Disorder
______	______	____________
______	______	____________

ATTENTION-DEFICIT/HYPERACTIVITY DISORDER (ADHD)

BEHAVIORAL DEFINITIONS

1. Child is identified by the family, school, or physician as having symptoms of ADHD.
2. Lack understanding of ADHD and its effects on children.
3. Reluctant to accept the possibility of ADHD in their child and are resistant to allowing medical intervention.
4. Feel guilty and responsible for their child's ADHD symptoms.
5. Blame child for inattentive, distractible, hyperactive, and/or irresponsible behavior.
6. Increasing frustration with the child's behavior and its overall negative effects on the family.
7. Child becomes increasingly manipulative, irresponsible, resistant, and develops symptoms of low self-esteem.
8. Family members are conflicted over how to help the child with ADHD.
9. Siblings are confused and resentful over child's ADHD behavior.

—. ____
____

LONG-TERM GOALS

1. Gain a comprehensive understanding of ADHD and its effects on children and families.
2. Recognize ADHD as a condition that impairs a child's ability to control behavior and attention.
3. Seek out and utilize available resources for managing ADHD including medical treatment, behavioral therapy and family support.

4. Learn skills to cope with the challenges of ADHD and acquire strategies to deal with the family's fatigue and frustration.
5. Engage in activities that build harmony, support, and unity among family members.

—. ____

____

SHORT-TERM OBJECTIVES

1. Acquire current and credible information about ADHD and its effects on families by reading pertinent literature, attending informational forums, and seeking professional guidance. (1, 2, 3)

2. Attend regular consultations with the child's doctor and/or a family therapist to discuss ADHD and its effects on children and their families. (4, 5)

THERAPEUTIC INTERVENTIONS

1. Review basic information about ADHD with the parents and begin the process of educating them concerning the implications of ADHD.
2. Advise the parents to read current literature that defines ADHD, its effects, and treatment. (See *Driven to Distraction* by Hallowell and Ratey or *Taking Charge of ADHD* by Barkley.).
3. Refer the parents to Web sites or informational resources that distribute credible and current information about ADHD and its effects on families (e.g., Children with Attention Deficit Disorders [CHADD] (301) 306-7070 or www.chadd.org, The National Attention Deficit Disorder Association (440) 350-9595 or www.add.org).
4. Assign the parents to meet with the ADHD child's doctor to review pharmacological interventions available for treatment.
5. Schedule a time-limited series of family counseling sessions

with the parents and other family members to continue their educational process, resolve specific areas of frustration and conflict, and offer support in their efforts to cope with the effects of ADHD on the family.

3. Read and discuss current law pertaining to children's disabilities and available accommodations in the school and the community. (6, 7)

6. Assist the parents to become familiar with the laws pertaining to ADHD and related disabilities by providing them with copies of the law and/or literature that summarize it (e.g., Section 504 of the Rehabilitation Act of 1973, The Americans with Disabilities Act, Title II, and the Individuals with Disabilities Education Act [IDEA]).
7. Instruct the parents to contact their state and district education departments to obtain information about educational programs and accommodations available to the ADHD student; discuss the applicability of these programs to the success of their child in school.

4. Advocate for the child's right to accommodations and support in school and in the community. (8, 9, 10)

8. Assist the parents in preparing a written statement for those educators and others working closely with their ADHD child who would benefit from specific information regarding ADHD and its effects on the child.
9. Brainstorm with the parents to create a list of accommodations, programs, and support strategies that would assist the child in the

school or community (or assign the "ADHD Accommodations Request Form" from the *Parenting Skills Homework Planner* by Knapp).

10. Role-play interviews with the parents that they will have with educators and other adults working directly with their child; guide the parents to develop assertive and cooperative skills for advocating for their child at school and in the community.

5. Join a local support group for families dealing with ADHD. (11, 12)

11. Refer the parents to a local support group that assists families and children coping with ADHD; or contact the national office of Children with Attention Deficit Disorders (CHADD), (301) 306-7070 or www.chadd.org, for a list of support groups in the community.

12. Refer the parents to a parenting class (e.g., *Becoming a Love and Logic Parent* by Fay, Cline, and Fay) to acquire techniques of positive discipline to use with their ADHD child.

6. Build a system of support that includes school personnel, extended family members, medical and/or mental health professionals, and community members. (13, 14)

13. Assist the parents in developing a list of resources available to provide day care and occasional relief from the intensity of parenting an ADHD child (e.g., after school programs, summer programs, respite programs, community activities).

14. Ask the parents to identify areas where family assets are lacking (e.g., housing, financial, medical, school-related, extended family, or social outlets) and help them build a list of advocates and supportive resources.

7. Implement recommended strategies for parenting and disciplining the ADHD child. (15, 16)

15. Ask the parents to assume the role of a Parent Coach when directing and disciplining their child by determining the skill they wish the child to develop and initiating practice sessions to help their ADHD child acquire that skill; suggest the parents develop or purchase a series of Parent Coaching Cards (see www.parent-coachcards.com/home1.html and *Parent Coaching Cards* by Richfield) that colorfully illustrate the skill to be developed on one side of the card and offer self-talk coping messages for skill development on the other side.

16. Brainstorm with the parents a list of proactive strategies they can implement that will help them cope with the frustration, stress, and intensity created by the ADHD child (e.g., humor, redirection, classical music, physical activity, relaxing baths or showers, and healthy snack food).

8. Avoid power struggles and set limits using controlled choices and logical consequences. (17, 18)

17. Assign the parents to use limited choices with the ADHD child by giving two options either one of which is acceptable

(e.g., "Would you like to go to bed with your blue or red pajamas on?") to teach responsible decision making and to allow the child to experience some limited control.

18. Instruct the parents to use logical consequences that are related to the rules infraction (e.g., the child whines and cries for half an hour at bedtime and therefore must go to bed half an hour earlier the next night).

9. Use structure, consistency, and a combination of kindness and firmness to promote appropriate and responsible behavior in the ADHD child. (19, 20, 21)

19. Emphasize to the parents the importance of close supervision and a structured environment that allows little opportunity for problematic behavior to go unnoticed until the ADHD child has demonstrated an adequate degree of self-control and responsibility.

20. Encourage the parents to tackle behavior problems one at a time and to approach the ADHD child with a combination of empathy, kindness, and firmness in order to maintain a supportive and loving relationship while setting limits.

21. Assign the parents to predict potential problems that may occur during the following week and determine methods of averting a negative outcome (e.g., bedtime resistance—allow more time to prepare for bed); ask the parents to record the results of their planning for

discussion at the next counseling session.

10. Create a total family treatment plan for managing the ADHD child and collateral family issues. (22, 23, 24)

22. Assign the ADHD child and siblings to read children's literature that describes the syndrome (e.g., *Jumpin' Jake Settles Down* by Shapiro) to gain a better understanding of ADHD from a child's perspective.

23. Brainstorm with the parents and other family members five to ten problem issues they are experiencing as a result of ADHD and prioritize them in order of need to resolve (or assign the "Family Problem Resolution Worksheet" from the *Parenting Skills and Discipline Homework Planner* by Knapp).

24. Assign the parents to begin a journal that documents the family's efforts in coping with ADHD and related family issues.

11. Develop a system for recognizing and focusing on the positive attributes of each family member. (25, 26)

25. Assign all family members to remain watchful for positive behavior from one another and to recognize and reinforce it by identifying the specific behavior and describing how it benefits the family or the person involved.

26. Encourage the parents to initiate weekly family meetings where family issues are discussed and time is designated for stories reflecting the positive contributions of each family member.

12. Child and parents implement the use of planners and organizing strategies to assist the child in completing tasks successfully. (27, 28, 29)

27. Assign the ADHD child and the parents to develop a management system for schoolwork by designating a specific color for each academic subject and color coding all information and related resources.

28. Instruct the ADHD child and other family members in the use of calendars, organizers, and written reminders to assist the child in the daily organization of tasks and activities.

29. Assign the ADHD child to use a planner to list all assignments, record working time, and check off when completed; instruct the parents to monitor the student's assignment planner daily and give encouragement and direction as needed.

13. Give instructions to the child in a clear, direct, and calm manner. (30)

30. Discuss with the parents strategies for assisting the child to successfully complete tasks and assignments (e.g., maintain eye contact when delivering calm instructions, encourage questions, offer guidance on an as needed basis).

14. Child and siblings accept responsibility for developing resolutions to their conflicts. (31)

31. Assign the ADHD child and the siblings to identify five to ten issues of conflict in their relationships and to brainstorm possible methods of resolving these conflicts (e.g., take turns, play separately, share, write a plan).

15. Engage the child in positive extracurricular activities that develop self-confidence, empathy, responsibility, and independent functioning. (32, 33)

32. Advise the parents to encourage participation in activities that develop self-confidence, social skills, persistence, and offer positive role modeling (e.g., team-sports, karate, Tae Kwon Do); assign the parents to enroll the ADHD child in one positive extracurricular activity.

33. Instruct the parents and the ADHD child to avoid or substantially reduce the time spent in activities that are passive, reduce productive brain activity, and involve long periods of inactivity (e.g., TV, videos); encourage the parents to promote quiet activities that stimulate logical thinking and problem solving (e.g., reading, board games).

16. Plan for leisure activities the whole family can participate in and enjoy. (34, 35)

34. Assign the family members to take turns planning family meals and sharing the work involved in the preparation and clean up; the meals should include all family members seated at a table with no TV or loud music playing.

35. Instruct family members to plan for a bimonthly family fun night when individual family members are responsible for providing the at-home entertainment (e.g., live music or drama, video, reading from a book aloud, or a special TV program followed by family discussion) and refreshments.

17. Celebrate each accomplishment, milestone, and success achieved by the ADHD child and the family unit. (36, 37)

36. Teach the parents and other family members the importance of giving frequent affirmations to the ADHD child for progress noted in a private, low-key manner.

37. Assign the parents, the ADHD child, and the siblings to affirm themselves and one another for each victory, large or small, in managing both personal and family challenges.

DIAGNOSTIC SUGGESTIONS:

ICD-9-CM	*ICD-10-CM*	*DSM-5* Disorder, Condition, or Problem
314.01	F90.2	Attention-Deficit/Hyperactivity Disorder, Combined Presentation
314.01	F90.1	Attention-Deficit/Hyperactivity Disorder, Predominately Hyperactive /Impulsive Presentation
314.01	F90.9	Unspecified Attention-Deficit/ Hyperactivity Disorder
314.01	F90.8	Other Specified Attention-Deficit/ Hyperactivity Disorder
312.9	F91.9	Unspecified Disruptive, Impulse Control, and Conduct Disorder
312.89	F91.8	Other Specified Disruptive, Impulse Control, and Conduct Disorder
313.81	F91.3	Oppositional Defiant Disorder
309.24	F43.22	Adjustment Disorder, With Anxiety
______	______	______________________
______	______	______________________

ATTENTION-SEEKING BEHAVIOR

BEHAVIORAL DEFINITIONS

1. Child continually demands attention from parents and siblings in negative and irritating ways.
2. Waver between giving the child attention for negative behavior and reacting with anger and frustration.
3. Confused, frustrated, and exhausted by the constant demands by the attention-seeking child on the family's resources.
4. Lack the positive strategies, disciplinary techniques, and confidence necessary to deal effectively with the attention-seeking child.
5. Siblings resent and reject the attention-seeking child.
6. The attention-seeking child feels unimportant and unrecognized and escalates the negative attention-seeking behaviors in an attempt to satisfy unmet needs.
7. Parents and siblings are embarrassed by the attention-seeking child's behavior in public. The attention-seeking child is viewed as different or not fitting in with acceptable patterns of family behavior or family values.
8. The family is demoralized due to the stress and conflict resulting from living with an attention-seeking child.

—. ____

____

—. ____

____

—. ____

____

LONG-TERM GOALS

1. Acquire and use effective strategies and disciplinary techniques for dealing with inappropriate attention-seeking behavior.
2. Recognize each child in family for unique strengths and abilities.
3. Siblings express acceptance and affection toward the attention-seeking child.
4. The attention-seeking child views self as an essential and valued member of the family.
5. All family members understand and accept that recognition and affection are family resources that are given in response to appropriate, respectful behavior.
6. Quality time and activities are experienced and appreciated by all family members.

—. ____
____

—. ____
____

—. ____
____

SHORT-TERM OBJECTIVES

1. Acquire and verbalize an understanding of the causes underlying negative attention-seeking behavior. (1, 2, 3, 4)

THERAPEUTIC INTERVENTIONS

1. Meet with the family as a whole to observe and assess the family dynamics that may contribute to the child's negative attention-seeking behavior.
2. Explain to the parents and/or the family as a whole that some children and adults seek attention through misbehavior because they lack the skills to acquire necessary recognition using positive strategies and behavior.
3. Assign the parents to read literature that explains

negative attention-seeking behavior (e.g., Children: The Challenge by Dreikurs and Stoltz or Raising a Responsible Child by Dinkmeyer and McKay).

4. Refer the parents to a class that focuses on helping children develop self-confidence and responsible behavior (e.g., *Systematic Training for Effective Parenting (STEP)* by Dinkmeyer and McKay or The Parent Talk *System: The Language of Responsible Parenting* by Moorman and Knapp).

2. Arrange for testing to identify causes for low self-esteem in the attention-seeking child. (5, 6)

5. Administer a normed, self-reporting assessment scale to the child (e.g., The Coopersmith Self- Esteem Inventory or The Youth Self-Report by Achenbach) to determine specific areas of social/emotional concern.

6. Assist the parents to identify the child's current misperceptions that may be motivating inappropriate behavior according to Dreikurs' theory of misbehavior (see *Children: The Challenge* by Dreikurs).

3. Use reflective listening techniques with the attention-seeking child to encourage expression of feelings and opinions concerning unmet needs for recognition. (7, 8)

7. Process the results from the child's self-assessment scales with the parents and the child to begin the task of reframing and building a more positive self-image in the child.

8. Help the parents to remain open and nondefensive when listening to the concerns of the

attention-seeking child by teaching them the strategies of reflective listening (e.g., engaged listening without judgment as explained in Parent Effectiveness Training by Gordon).

4. Implement strategies for recognizing and reinforcing positive attempts to seek attention. (9, 10, 11)

9. Instruct the parents to implement "special time," a short, 10 to 20 minutes, child-directed play activity between parent and child at least once a day (see *When Your Child Craves Attention—A Parenting Strategy* from www.educational-psychologist.co.uk).

10. Ask the parents to brainstorm with the attention-seeking child various positive methods of seeking attention and recognition (e.g., complete homework, clean room, assist in a household chore).

11. Assign the parents to develop a plan with the attention-seeking child that satisfies the child's need for recognition using positive strategies (e.g., build a model car, learn to play the guitar) which involve an interactive activity between parent and child.

5. Implement strategies for extinguishing negative attention-seeking behavior. (12, 13, 14)

12. Use role play to help the parents prepare for ignoring negative behavior; emphasize that this behavior may escalate during initial attempts to ignore it; however, it will diminish as the result of consistent and sustained lack of reinforcement.

6. Assist the attention-seeking child in developing and implementing positive strategies for gaining recognition. (15, 16)

7. Determine and list the individual strengths and special talents of each family member. (17, 18)

13. Instruct the parents to prepare the attention-seeking child for being ignored while engaging in negative behavior episodes by explaining to the child that positive behavior is the most successful method of gaining recognition.

14. Assist the parents in listing their reactions that may be reinforcing negative attention-seeking behavior in their children (e.g., responding to whining, allowing tears to influence a decision). Help them to develop techniques that diffuse the negative attempts to gain recognition.

15. Meet with the attention-seeking child alone to explore any dynamics in the family situation and relationship with parents that may contribute to the need to gain attention in desperate ways.

16. Brainstorm positive statements of encouragement that the family members could use to affirm one another during the following week.

17. Discuss the theory of Multiple Intelligences with the parents (e.g., every person has unique abilities and talents in specific areas of functioning as explained in *Intelligence Reframed: Multiple Intelligences for the 21st Century* by Gardner); indicate that recognizing and affirming these talents in their child is the key to the development of mature,

appropriate behavior and healthy self-esteem.

18. Instruct the family members to brainstorm a list of the various strengths and abilities of each family member and to record the list in a family journal.

8. Implement strategies for affirming the talents of each family member. (19, 20)

19. Help the parents to develop and implement strategies for recognizing the personal strengths of their children and each other on a regular, ongoing schedule (e.g., verbally recognize accomplishments using the words, "I noticed that you . . . [fill in the personal strength]," discuss proud feelings within earshot of the child, write a note of affirmation and give it to the child).

20. Encourage the parents to acknowledge the accomplishments of the attention-seeking child and other family members by arranging a family celebration.

9. Acknowledge the siblings' positive attempts to interact with the attention-seeking child. (21, 22)

21. Instruct the parents to verbally express to the siblings their desire for family harmony and positive interaction among all family members.

22. Assign the parents to watch for positive sibling interaction and to acknowledge it verbally by saying, "that's cooperation" or "I'm seeing some real collaboration," or "It's so good to see you guys getting along well" when it occurs.

10. Articulate, prioritize, and implement family values that emphasize empathy, inclusion, and appreciation. (23, 24)

23. Assist the family in creating a family mission statement that lists all of the family's values and prioritizes the merits of inclusion, empathy, and appreciation of/for one another.

24. Instruct the parents to read stories and select movies and TV programs for the family that emphasize the values of family cooperation, inclusion, and appreciation and encourage them to initiate a family discussion of how love and support was demonstrated in each case.

11. Develop a family plan for mutual support and encouragement. (25, 26)

25. Ask each family member to list several personal jobs or obligations that would benefit from assistance from another family member (or assign the "Family Job Support Checklist" activity from the *Parenting Skills Homework Planner* by Knapp).

26. Instruct the family members to begin writing notes of appreciation for support and assistance in meeting personal challenges and monitor the notes written and received by the attention-seeking child to ensure participation in this process.

12. Implement strategies that encourage the attention-seeking child to become self-reliant, organized, and self-confident. (27, 28, 29)

27. Request that the parents use the phrase "Act as if" to encourage the attention-seeking child to make an effort despite fear of failure (e.g., "Act as if you know how to draw that tree;" "Pretend you

can jump rope;" "Play like you've done this before;" or "Fake it till you make it" when attempting to bake a cake). (See *Parent Talk: Words That Empower, Words That Wound* by Moorman).

28. Ask the parents to substitute the phrase "Next Time" for "don't" in order to shape positive future efforts from the attention-seeking child (e.g., "Next time you make your bed, make sure the sheets are flat and smooth," versus "Don't pull up the blankets when the sheets are such a wrinkled mess.") (See *Parent Talk: Words That Empower, Words That Wound* by Moorman.)

29. Encourage the parents to give age-appropriate chores and responsibilities to the attention-seeking child and to implement a consequence when the job is not completed satisfactorily and to use affirmations when the responsibility has been accomplished.

13. Attention-seeking child, siblings, and parents identify significant others who communicate love and care. (30, 31)

30. Ask the attention-seeking child to make a list of significant others and rate the degree of support given (or assign the "My Love and Trust Support Network" activity from the *Parenting Skills Homework Planner* by Knapp).

31. Assist the family members in writing a definition of unconditional love (e.g., complete

and constant love given regardless of personal attributes, attitude, behavior, or performance) and list significant others who give their love unconditionally.

14. Keep a written record of all family members' progress toward engaging in positive attention-seeking behavior. (32, 33)

32. Instruct the family to create a family journal that will contain the family's counseling worksheets and serve as a record of progress and suggest that the attention-seeking child be the family secretary.

33. Help the parents to develop a chart that records the child's negative attention-seeking interactions compared to the number of positive attention-seeking interactions during the week and implement a reward each week when the positive interactions exceed the negative ones.

15. Model positive attention-seeking behavior for all family members. (34)

34. Ask the parents to review their own family interactions and identify those behaviors that model positive attention-seeking behavior and those that are negative examples to their children; encourage the parents to target one or two negative behaviors to be eliminated from their repertoire.

16. Engage in inclusive activities currently enjoyed by all family members. (35, 36)

35. Brainstorm with the family a list of activities that are currently enjoyed and participated in by all family members.

36. Instruct the attention-seeking child to paste pictures of positive family interactions in the family journal.

17. Research additional options for positive family interaction and goal attainment. (37, 38)

37. Instruct family members to develop a plan for a major family project or quality time experience (e.g., family vacation, home project completion, visit to or from relatives) by choosing a specific activity and assigning each family member a specific task or responsibility to ensure its successful completion.

38. Each month assign one family member to assess the family's progress toward achieving its goals of empathy, inclusion, and mutual appreciation by writing a short paragraph or drawing a picture in the family journal.

__. ____________________

__. ____________________

__. ____________________

__. ____________________

DIAGNOSTIC SUGGESTIONS:

ICD-9-CM	*ICD-10-CM*	*DSM-5* Disorder, Condition, or Problem
312.9	F91.9	Unspecified Disruptive, Impulse Control, and Conduct Disorder
312.89	F91.8	Other Specified Disruptive, Impulse Control, and Conduct Disorder
313.81	F91.3	Oppositional Defiant Disorder
314.01	F90.2	Attention-Deficit/Hyperactivity Disorder, Combined Presentation
309.21	F93.0	Separation Anxiety Disorder
V61.20	Z62.820	Parent-Child Relational Problem
______	______	____________________
______	______	____________________

BLENDED FAMILY

BEHAVIORAL DEFINITIONS

1. Breakup of the nuclear family has resulted in feelings of sadness, grief, guilt, fear, and confusion.
2. Creation of the blended family unit results in significantly altered roles and responsibilities of all family members that are vague and poorly defined.
3. Spouses differ in their approach to their own and the other's children and do not assume equal responsibility for discipline and childcare.
4. Legal, emotional, and financial conflict with former spouses impacts the family's ability to form a self-directed cohesive unit.
5. Custody and visitation arrangements interfere with the family's activities and create feelings of divided loyalty.
6. Conflict or inappropriate relationships among the stepsiblings living together in the blended family.
7. Stepparents and the stepchildren view one another as obstacles or competition to intimate relationships with their spouse or natural parents.

__. ____

____

__. ____

____

LONG-TERM GOALS

1. Form a united front and work together to develop effective parenting skills and discipline in the blended family.

2. Accept a range of feelings and conflicting emotions as a natural part of adjustment to change.
3. Clearly define family roles, rules, and responsibilities.
4. Focus on the best interests of the children while working to resolve emotional, financial, and legal issues.
5. Invest in the blended family with personal time, energy, and commitment to creating a loving and supportive family unit.
6. Recognize that attaining family harmony and positive relationships within the blended family takes effort, time, and patience.

—. ____

____

—. ____

____

SHORT-TERM OBJECTIVES

1. All family members share feelings about and reactions to the formation of the blended family at family meetings. (1, 2)
2. List strategies for coping with negative feelings related to adjusting to a blended family. (3, 4, 5)

THERAPEUTIC INTERVENTIONS

1. Assign the family to hold weekly family meetings where open and considerate discussion of individual feelings and reactions to the blended family is encouraged.
2. Review issues discussed in the family meetings during family or couple counseling sessions; offer congratulations for resolved issues and guidance in areas that remain of concern.
3. Provide strategies for the family to cope effectively with contentious issues (e.g., listen with empathy, discuss problems when calm, brainstorm for possible solutions).
4. Invite each family member to record in a journal incidents of successful strategies used to

cope with negative or hurt feelings (or ask the family to complete the "Healing Hurt Feelings" activity from the Parenting Skills Homework Planner by Knapp).

5. Assist the family in establishing ground rules for the arguments and disagreements that will inevitably occur (e.g., listen to the other's point of view, stay with the current issue, avoid name-calling).

3. Implement techniques of effective communication that involve empathetic listening and clearly stated points of view. (6, 7)

6. Teach each family member to clearly state individual points of view using the "I statement" format (e.g., "I feel . . . When . . . Because . . .") which expresses personal feelings and reactions to a situation rather then blaming personal feelings upon another person (see Parent Effectiveness Training by Gordon).

7. Present the technique of active listening (e.g., listening with empathy and understanding) and role play how to use it during family discussions.

4. Verbalize realistic expectations for the newly formed blended family. (8, 9)

8. Discuss common myths about blended families (e.g., new family will quickly adjust, the blended family will be the same as the first family, stepparent will be immediately accepted,) and help the family set more realistic expectations.

9. Invite the family to set short-term goals that are specific and attainable (e.g., eat dinner together three times per week,

hold a one-hour family meeting once per week) in order to avoid unrealistic expectations.

5. Negotiate and define family roles and responsibilities during a family meeting. (10, 11)

10. Instruct the family to list all the jobs and duties necessary for effective functioning of the blended family at their weekly meeting and indicate the person responsible for each assignment.

11. Assign the family to define family roles by listing each family member and describing in writing the role they play (or complete the "Unique Roles in Our Blended Family" activity from the *Parenting Skills Homework Planner* by Knapp).

6. Identify and establish family rules and procedures with input from all family members. (12, 13)

12. Assist the family in establishing basic procedures that are essential for efficient family functioning (e.g., the morning routine, family meals, laundry); encourage the family to spend time practicing these procedures until they become routine.

13. Assist the family in formulating household rules (e.g., curfew, table manners, homework, dress code) using the process of brainstorming all regulations necessary for harmonious co-existence, consolidating the ideas into a few general limits, stating each rule in a positive form, obtaining consensus on the final list of rules, and agreeing that rules can be changed only at family meetings.

7. Resolve custody, visitation, and other legal issues affecting the family. (14, 15)

14. Encourage the parents and stepparents to work together to establish custody and visitation arrangements that are conducive to the emotional stability of the children involved.

15. Agree to mediate disputes and differences between former spouses to reduce the level of conflict and hostility and increase the spirit of cooperation.

8. Agree to prioritize the children's welfare when making decisions which affect the family. (16, 17)

16. Encourage the adult couple to reassure the children about their personal security and to express awareness and empathy for their fears, feelings, and reactions to change.

17. Ask the parents to share any immediate plans for change involving custody, visitation, or possible moves with all affected family members.

9. Support each other in child management issues and eliminate resistance, manipulation, and competition from children and former spouse(s). (18, 19, 20)

18. Advise the parents to avoid power struggles in the blended family by setting limits with controlled choices (e.g. "Would you rather clean your room on Saturday or Sunday?") and using contingency management strategies that make privileges dependent on responsible behavior (e.g., "You may watch television as soon as you homework is completed.").

19. Teach the parents the importance of reinforcing children's positive behavior,

administering discipline to all children in an even-handed and logical manner, and defusing manipulative efforts from children or former spouses.

20. Help the parents to avoid overparenting and to encourage independent functioning by determining who owns a problem and allowing that person to solve the problem alone or with guidance if necessary.

10. Seek information or professional guidance in the area of child management in the context of a blended family. (21, 22)

21. Refer parents to a child management parenting class (e.g., *Becoming a Love and Logic Parent* by Fay, Cline, and Fay).

22. Assign parents and stepparents to read *Living in Step* (Roosevelt and Lofas) for an understanding of how various family members react to the formation of a blended family.

11. Negotiate and agree on strategies for cooperative disciplining all of the children in the blended family. (23, 24, 25)

23. Teach the parents to arrive at a mutually satisfying approach to specific discipline issues by discussing the problem privately, sharing individual perspectives, brainstorming solutions, and determining an approach which is satisfying to both parties.

24. Instruct the parents to use logical consequences designed to teach their children a more appropriate behavior and to eliminate overly punitive reactions to negative behavior; explain that consequences can be delayed briefly to allow the

couple to discuss and agree upon an appropriate intervention.

25. Encourage the parents to refrain from interfering when a natural consequence (e.g., refusing to eat lunch results in getting hungry before dinner) will teach their children to be more responsible.

12. Utilize techniques of positive discipline to address all child behavior concerns. (26, 27, 28)

26. Teach the parents to offer frequent encouragement and descriptive praise when recognizing positive behavior and to use constructive feedback and guidance when behavior requires redirection.

27. Encourage the parents to prioritize the discipline issues of concern to the family and to address them one by one rather than trying to solve all the behavior problems at once.

28. Advise parents to remain alert and intimately involved in the lives and activities of all of their children living or not living in the blended family; explain that careful monitoring of the children's behavior, although not always appreciated, is an essential responsibility of parents and stepparents.

13. Encourage positive and appropriate relationships among the stepsiblings. (29, 30)

29. Instruct the adult couple to promote positive interaction among the siblings and stepsiblings by initiating family games, recognizing attempts to engage in mutual activities, and encouraging discussions during meals and family gatherings.

30. Caution the adult couple to avoid pushing the stepsiblings to constantly interact before they have been given time to adjust to the newly formed family unit.

14. The stepsiblings engage in activities that create affection for and bonding with one another. (31, 32)

31. Instruct the stepsiblings to brainstorm activities appropriate for family interaction, choose one or more activities, and report on the process at the next family meeting or counseling session.

32. Help the stepsiblings plan for doing a personal favor that expresses love and caring for parent(s) and/or stepparent(s) (e.g., cooking a meal, baby-sitting for a younger sibling).

15. Set clear boundaries for privacy and sexual taboos among the blended family members. (33, 34)

33. Advise the parents to set up appropriate sleeping and activity centers so that all siblings have privacy and a place for their personal belongings.

34. Assign the family to discuss appropriate intersibling behavior and respect for one another at a family meeting requesting input from all family members.

16. Participate in activities that involve both total family and one to one interactions among family members. (35)

35. Encourage the family to plan for a weekly family outing at each family meeting and to enlist the participation of each family member in the preparation.

17. Model positive, supportive interaction with all family members. (36, 37)

36. Discuss with the adult couple the negative impact on the children of their demonstrative romantic or sexualized

interactions in the children's presence (e.g., jealousy, embarrassment, loyalty conflicts) and encourage them to respect the siblings' sensitivity to this behavior.

37. Stress to the adult couple the importance of modeling regard and respect for one another and for the children; role play appropriate interactions during sensitive or stressful circumstances (e.g., stepchild's refusal to cooperate).

18. Express and record progress in the development of positive feelings toward all members of the blended family. (38, 39)

38. Ask each family member to list the benefits of developing close positive relationships within the blended family in a personal journal and identify methods of improving family interactions.

39. Assign each family member to describe their family prior to the formation of the blended family, currently, and five years in the future; share these descriptions during a family meeting or a counseling session.

—. ____________________

—. ____________________

DIAGNOSTIC SUGGESTIONS

ICD-9-CM	*ICD-10-CM*	*DSM-5* Disorder, Condition, or Problem
309.0	F43.21	Adjustment Disorder, With Depressed Mood
309.3	F43.24	Adjustment Disorder, With Disturbance of Conduct
309.24	F43.22	Adjustment Disorder, With Anxiety
______	______	____________________
______	______	____________________

BONDING/ATTACHMENT ISSUES

BEHAVIORAL DEFINITIONS

1. One or more children in the family have had an interruption in the initial bonding process with their primary caretaker due to abuse, neglect, illness, separation, or adoption.
2. Lack of parenting skills and strategies to deal with the severe nature of the unattached child's rage, distrust, and inability to function within the family structure.
3. Family is in a constant state of crisis due to the outrageous and demanding behavior of the unattached child.
4. Doubts about their ability to cope with the disrupted family situation lead to feelings of hopelessness and despair.
5. Feelings of unreasonable anger and frustration toward the unattached child.
6. Lack of an effective and unified child management strategy leads to parental frustration, conflict, triangulation, and potentially eventual separation and/or divorce.
7. Siblings who are mistreated and/or abused by the unattached child develop fear and anxiety reactions and try to distance themselves from their threatening sibling.

__. ____

____

__. ____

____

__. ____

____

LONG-TERM GOALS

1. Gain confidence, expertise, and effectiveness in ability to manage discipline issues resulting from the early lack of attachment and bonding.
2. Combine affection, nurturing, and highly structured discipline to set limits and help the unattached child to function appropriately within the family unit.
3. Understand the underlying causes and options for coping with and treating attachment disorder.
4. Work together to eliminate divisive influences and form a cohesive family unit.
5. Siblings develop strategies to relate appropriately while protecting selves from threats, intimidation, and abusive behavior.

—. ____
____

—. ____
____

—. ____
____

SHORT-TERM OBJECTIVES

1. Verbalize an accurate understanding of the dynamics of and constructive approaches to coping with childhood attachment disorder. (1, 2)

THERAPEUTIC INTERVENTIONS

1. Refer the parents to organizations, literature or Web sites that describe attachment disorder and offer support for affected families (e.g., Attachment Center at Evergreen, (303) 674-1910, www.attachmentcenter.org; Families by Design, (970) 984-2222, www.attachment.org.
2. Assign the parents to read books focusing on parenting children with attachment disorder (e.g., *When Love Is Not Enough* by Thomas or *The Whole Life Adoption Book* by Schooler.

2. Describe the unattached child's behavior and its affect on the family. (3, 4)

3. Assign parents to complete a normed behavior scale describing the child with symptoms of unattachment from their perspective (e.g., Child Behavior Checklist by Achenbach, or the Randolph Attachment Disorder Questionnaire [RADQ] by Randolph).

4. Ask the family members to describe in behavioral terms how the unattached child impacts the functioning of individuals and the family as a whole.

3. Define goals for addressing the problematic behavior of the unattached child. (5, 6)

5. Help the family members define short-, mid- and long-term goals for successful family functioning; caution them that expectations should be clearly stated and obtainable.

6. Assign the parents to list immediate and midterm goals for their unattached child (or assign them the "Steps to Responsible Behavior" activity from the *Parenting Skills Homework Planner* by Knapp).

4. Attend parenting classes, workshops, and seminars that teach strategies for parenting troubled children. (7, 8)

7. Refer the parents to a parenting class (e.g., *Systematic Training for Effective Parenting (STEP)* by Dinkmeyer and McKay) to acquire basic techniques of positive discipline to use with their children.

8. Help the parents initiate parenting strategies of positive discipline learned in parenting classes, seminars, and from recommended parenting books or tapes (e.g., *Your Defiant*

Child: Eight Steps to Better Behavior by Barkley).

5. Structure the household environment to reduce the opportunity for the unattached child's disruptive and problematic behavior. (9, 10, 11, 12)

9. Assist the parents in planning to structure the home environment to reduce the unattached child's disruptive and destructive behavior (e.g., put locks on bedroom doors, food, and toy cabinets; create a safe and sparse time-out area).

10. Encourage the parents to buy healthy food for the home and model healthy eating habits for the children.

11. Advise the parents to establish areas where food is allowed and not allowed, and to require that eating take place in designated areas only.

12. Instruct the parents to "establish respect through speech patterns" (see *When Love Is Not Enough* by Thomas) by maintaining eye contact, engaging in listening exercises, using firm directions, and insisting on a polite, correct response.

6. Formulate a system of discipline that identifies clear boundaries, establishes household rules, and promotes responsible behavior. (13, 14, 15, 16)

13. Teach the parents how to implement relevant consequences to help the child learn more appropriate behavior patterns (e.g., chores not done leads to loss of television time, late for curfew or bedtime leads to earlier time next night).

14. Assign the parents to create a list of privileges that the unattached child must earn by

demonstrating appropriate behavior (e.g., watching television, playing in yard, having toys in bedroom).

15. Instruct the parents to describe the specific positive behavior they want to see (e.g., "Please hand me the book.") rather than the negative behavior they want to eliminate (e.g., "Don't throw the book at me.") when correcting their child.

16. Advise the parents to use very restricted choices to share control with the unattached child (e.g., popcorn or an apple, red shirt or blue shirt, hold mom's hand or dad's hand); explain that unlimited choices (e.g., "What do you want to eat or wear?") confuse and frustrate the unattached child.

7. Devise strategies for administering love, support and nurturing in the face of resistance and rejection from the unattached child. (17, 18, 19)

17. Encourage the parents to engage the unattached child in activities which promote attachment (e.g., snuggle time, playing games that require interaction, nightly prayers) for a designated period of time each day.

18. Assign the parents to read *Holding Time* (Welch) to understand the technique of personal touch in promoting the bonding process.

19. Ask the parents to promote feelings of continuity with the unattached child's past by sharing baby and family pictures, telling early childhood stories, recounting the child's first few years of life

and connecting with significant others from the past if appropriate.

8. Siblings implement limit-setting and structured rules for coping with the unattached child. (20, 21)

20. Teach the siblings to set limits with the unattached child (e.g., share only unbreakable toys, game over when rules are broken, seek adult assistance when behavior becomes threatening.

21. Discuss problematic sibling interactions with the unattached child and siblings and brainstorm solutions (e.g., time-limit interactions; set up a bathroom schedule; keep possessions in safe, designated areas).

9. Siblings verbalize their successes in establishing a positive relationship with their unattached sibling. (22, 23)

22. Instruct the siblings to log interactions with their unattached brother or sister and record interventions that lead to a successful outcome.

23. Assign the unattached child and siblings to keep an ongoing list of activities that create a feeling of attachment and kinship (e.g., one-to-one chats, high fives, daily greetings).

10. Monitor the frequency of the unattached child engaging in positive, target behaviors. (24, 25)

24. Caution the parents against trying to correct too many behaviors at once and instruct them to identify one or two negative behaviors and prioritize them for change.

25. Help the parents to create a color graph to monitor the progress made by the unattached child in several behavioral areas (or assign the parents to complete "The

Behavior Progress Chart" in the *Parenting Skills Homework Planner* by Knapp).

11. Engage in pleasurable, relaxing activities and interests apart from the problematic family issues. (26, 27)

26. Encourage the parents to give themselves and each other time and permission to pursue personal interests and hobbies apart from work and family obligations as a respite from family stress.

27. Assign the parents to engage in, as a couple, at least one social activity apart from their child or children per week.

12. Establish a network of support and respite based on understanding family, friends, and professionals. (28, 29, 30)

28. Instruct the parents to list their personal and family resources for respite from the unattached child (e.g., friends, family, church members) and to utilize them on a regular basis.

29. Encourage the parents to educate their support groups on the specific strategies recommended for dealing with an unattached child and the essential need for respite.

30. Help the parents access community resources for respite from the unattached child (e.g., social services, support groups, community mental health agencies, Head Start, preschool programs, special education programs).

13. Agree to work together to solve all family problems. (31, 32)

31. Advise the parents of the importance of a unified front when dealing with the unattached child; encourage them to discuss all areas of disagreement privately or during counseling sessions and

to develop a mutually acceptable plan before addressing the problem.

32. Instruct the parents to identify and address areas where the unattached child uses triangulation to divide and control the environment (e.g., lying, asking permission from other parent after being told no, creating conflict between parents and school, relatives, or siblings).

14. Implement strategies for coping with the stress associated with living with an unattached family member. (33, 34, 35)

33. Encourage the parents to remain in counseling for personal and family support while coping with the stress and constant trauma of living with an unattached child.

34. Assign the parents to engage in one or more affective strategies for stress reduction (e.g., journaling, assertiveness training, using humor, giving personal or mutual affirmations).

35. Instruct the parents to pursue faith options that offer guidance and support during times of trauma (e.g., attending faith based services, spiritual readings, prayer, healing rituals, quiet meditation).

15. Celebrate family progress and successes in overcoming the trauma of attachment disorder. (36, 37, 38)

36. Instruct the parents to remain alert to the signs of progress in their unattached child and to record them in the family journal.

37. Caution the parents that overreaction to the unattached child's positive behavior can

cause regression; instruct them to recognize positive behavior with low-key affirmations given to the child and to celebrate the progress wildly in their own hearts.

38. Assign the unattached child and siblings to recognize progress in behavior or relationships by entering a photo, drawing or paragraph in the family journal.

__. ____________________

__. ____________________

__. ____________________

__. ____________________

__. ____________________

__. ____________________

DIAGNOSTIC SUGGESTIONS:

ICD-9-CM	*ICD-10-CM*	*DSM-5* Disorder, Condition, or Problem
319.89	F94.1	Reactive Attachment Disorder
314.01	F90.9	Unspecified Attention-Deficit/Hyperactivity Disorder
314.01	F90.8	Other Specified Attention-Deficit/Hyperactivity Disorder
296.xx	F32.x	Major Depressive Disorder, Single Episode
296.xx	F33.x	Major Depressive Disorder, Recurrent Episode
309.81	F43.10	Posttraumatic Stress Disorder
313.81	F91.3	Oppositional Defiant Disorder
______	______	____________________
______	______	____________________

CAREER PREPARATION

BEHAVIORAL DEFINITIONS

1. Lack of awareness of various career pathways and options available to the children for future employment.
2. Under-involvement in the career choices of the children or a tendency to push too hard toward a specific career pathway.
3. Failure to emphasize academic excellence and to associate school curriculum with the future career goals of the children.
4. Display a negative attitude toward work and model a poor work ethic and undesirable personal work habits.
5. View work and employment opportunities as limited by gender, socioeconomic status, and ethnicity.
6. Absence of an early childhood and ongoing emphasis on literacy, communication, and social skills in the family setting.
7. Lack of availability of or an interest in work-related technology (e.g., computers, Internet, distance learning, educational television).
8. Failure to make the necessary plans for the children's college and/or postgraduation training and to assist them in the school to work transition.

__. ____

____

__. ____

____

LONG-TERM GOALS

1. Become actively involved in each child's interests, aptitudes, and abilities and explore their possible link to future careers and lifestyles.

2. Verbalize an awareness of various career pathways available to the children and their educational or training prerequisites.
3. Expose the children to career opportunities that broaden their goals beyond the limitations of stereotypical gender, status, and ethnic roles.
4. Participate as a family in work, school, and community-sponsored career awareness programs.
5. Involve family members in the use of career-based technology.
6. Actively promote and explore with the children, opportunities for post high school, career-oriented training (e.g., college, work-study programs, armed services, internships).

—. ____

____

—. ____

____

SHORT-TERM OBJECTIVES

1. Regularly hold family discussions that focus on different jobs and professions available in the community, nation, and world. (1, 2, 3)

THERAPEUTIC INTERVENTIONS

1. Ask the parents to brainstorm with their children the various reasons why they and other adults work and assign the children to discuss their ideas with several employed family members.
2. Advise the parents to raise their children's career awareness by holding discussions about various career opportunities citing examples from television, books, magazines, and newspapers.
3. Instruct the parents to enlist their children's help in creating an occupational family history (or complete the "Career Family Tree" activity from the *Parenting Skills Homework Planner* by Knapp).

2. Positively involve the children in the parents' own career experiences through discussion and modeling. (4, 5, 6)

4. Advise the parents of their position as primary teacher and career role model and encourage them to relate personal stories and work experiences that will positively shape their children's knowledge and attitudes toward their own future career decisions.

5. Assign the parents to participate in a "Take Your Child to Work Day" or job-shadowing opportunity and to actively engage their child in the experience by allowing them to create a product, wear a uniform, or be involved in an actual work process.

6. Assign the parents to take several actual or virtual parent-child field trips to explore community, national, or worldwide businesses.

3. Verbalize the connection between regular attendance, academic progress, social skill development and excellent work habits in school and in extra-curricular activities and future success in the workplace. (7, 8, 9)

7. Encourage the parents to emphasize the crucial connection between school performance and future success in their child's career choices by detailing how specific curriculum is used in the workplace (e.g., math facilitates money management, reading facilitates following directions, writing facilitates communication).

8. Instruct the parents to relate personal experiences detailing how education played an important role in their own career paths.

9. Assign the parents to brainstorm with their children the personal qualities required to work cooperatively with

others (e.g., speaking and listening with respect, problem solving, promptness).

4. Arrange for aptitude and interest testing for the child and discuss the results with the child. (10, 11)

10. Advise the parents to consult the school regarding aptitude and interest tests available at various grade levels and discuss how the test results may relate to the child's future career decisions.

11. Assign the parents to explore Web sites with their children that offer career information (e.g., Education World: Great Sites for Teaching About . . . Preparing for the Future, http://www.education-world.com/a_sites/sites076.shtml.

5. Establish future life goals and expectations with each child. (12, 13)

12. Encourage the parents to begin a journal or portfolio for each child in the family that details important demographic and personal data (e.g., early childhood information, health history, school information) and to actively involve the child in its maintenance.

13. Ask the parents to work with each child to create an ongoing list of future goals and aspirations to be entered in the child's career journal or portfolio.

6. Regularly affirm each child for his/her special interests and abilities. (14, 15, 16)

14. Encourage the parents to focus on the individual interests and abilities of each child and to emphasize personal best achievement rather than competition to prevent sibling and peer rivalry.

15. Assign the parents to engage each child in at least one extracurricular activity that

supports and promotes that child's special interest or ability.

16. Instruct the parents to help each child to develop self-awareness through discussions of feelings, special interests and abilities, or to participate with the child in an Internet survey that helps assess their personal traits, values, and the effects of their personal choices on their future (e.g., Making Choices for Life, http://library.thinkquest.org/J001709).

7. Maintain regular contact with the school while monitoring and reinforcing the children's academic progress. (17, 18)

17. Assign the parents to monitor their children's school attendance, punctuality, and academic achievement, to recognize progress and achievement in these areas and to offer guidance, encouragement, and discipline where necessary.

18. Instruct the parents to discuss progress reports, grade cards, conference input, and the results of tests and evaluations with the children immediately to understand their perspective and to emphasize the family's focus upon quality education.

8. Participate in and promote career awareness programs for youth of all ages at school and in the community. (19)

19. Assign the parents to become involved in the career awareness program at their children's school by volunteering to participate in field trips to area businesses, or by developing a career awareness day.

9. Encourage responsible behavior in the home by assigning age-appropriate jobs and chores to each child. (20, 21)

20. Emphasize the important connection between responsible behavior at home and success at school and in future

occupations by instructing the parents to assign age-appropriate tasks and chores to the children at home.

21. Assign the parents to promote responsible decision making from their children by asking each child to decide for themselves when an issue is noncritical and to decide within the limitations and guidance provided by the parents for more important issues.

10. Attend school, church, and community programs that celebrate ethnic, cultural, and socioeconomic diversity. (22, 23)

22. Encourage the parents to prepare their children for the diversity they will experience in their future workplaces by participating in multicultural events sponsored by various social, cultural, and ethnic groups in the community.

23. Assign the parents to expose their children to multilingual diversity by learning a foreign language as a family project.

11. Create a list of a wide variety of jobs and careers and emphasize their unique contribution to the society as a whole. (24, 25, 26)

24. Advise the parents to create a list in a family career journal of the many careers that draw each child's interest and to define these careers by listing their educational and training prerequisites and indicating their contribution to society.

25. Assign the parents to join their child in playing the *Career Interest Game* (Holland, (http://career.missouri.edu/holland/) to match interests and skills with similar careers.

26. Introduce the concept of career pathways by having the parents view a career cluster

chart of broad occupational categories (e.g., *Career Pathways* by the Michigan Occupational Information System [MOIS] or The Occupational Cluster Packet from the *Missouri Comprehensive Guidance Model* [Gysbers]); ask the parents to review the career categories with their children, eliciting areas of interest.

12. Encourage the children through discussion and observation to explore various jobs previously designated to a specific gender, culture, or socioeconomic group.(27, 28)

27. Advise the parents to reduce biases and job discrimination by encouraging their children to consider jobs previously considered specific to a particular gender, culture, or socioeconomic group (e.g., doctor, engineer, pilot, nurse, firefighter).

28. Assist the parents in assessing their hidden biases that might translate into stereotyping their children into prescribed gender roles and to guard against this type of negative classification by involving the children in household tasks, activities, and outings based on interest and age-appropriateness, rather than gender.

13. Read about, discuss, and utilize career-based technology in the home, school, and community. (29, 30, 31)

29. Advise the parents to remain current in their knowledge of work-related technology (e.g., computers, Internet, distance learning, robotics) and to share their expertise with their children.

30. Encourage the parents to enroll their children in after school or summer programs offered by area schools,

colleges, and businesses that teach technical skills, use of office machines, and other occupational tools.

31. Ask the parents to strongly encourage their high school children to enroll in core curriculum and recommended electives to acquire skills in technical areas of career preparation.

14. Develop an ongoing plan with each child for a successful school to career transition. (32, 33, 34)

32. Encourage the parents to begin career planning with their children at a young age (or invite the parents to complete the "School to Career Diary" activity in the *Parenting Skills Homework Planner* by Knapp).

33. Assign the parents to explore available career-based instruction (CBI) programs with their children that offer school credit for actual work experience.

35. Instruct the parents of non-college bound high school children to encourage participation in a career/technical curriculum to acquire entry level job skills in a trade, technical, medical technician, or business employment cluster.

15. Assist the college-bound child in selecting an appropriate college. (35, 36, 37)

35. Advise parents of high school children who have completed core requirements to earn college credit by taking advanced placement classes from local colleges or by using online resources or distance learning facilities.

36. Assign the parents to work with their college-bound child to complete a search of colleges using an Internet tool (e.g., *My Dream Explorer* created by MOIS) to identify several colleges or training programs which meet specific career, financial, and geographical requirements.

37. Ask the parents to collaborate with their college-bound child to select several colleges that meet the personal goals and career criteria from a college resource guide (e.g., *The Fiske Guide to Colleges 2005* by Fiske).

16. Verbalize and model the importance of lifelong learning to ensure continuous employment and enhance the quality of life. (38)

38. Assign the parents to attend with their children a community- or school-sponsored class designed to explore the future of careers and the world of work; ask them to discuss how future occupations will vary from today's careers.

__. ____________________ __. ____________________

__. ____________________ __. ____________________

DIAGNOSTIC SUGGESTIONS:

ICD-9-CM	*ICD-10-CM*	*DSM-5* Disorder, Condition, or Problem
309.0	F43.21	Adjustment Disorder, With Depressed Mood
309.24	F43.22	Adjustment Disorder, With Anxiety

CHARACTER DEVELOPMENT

BEHAVIORAL DEFINITIONS

1. The values of trustworthiness and honesty are not prioritized and modeled in the home.
2. Family members neither give nor expect respect as a basic human entitlement.
3. Personal biases overrule tolerance of diversity, community cooperation and support for the principles of justice and equality.
4. Failure to verbalize and demonstrate the principle of integrity results in the children's lack of appropriate conscience development.
5. Responsible behavior fails to develop in the children as a result of the parents' poor example and low expectations.
6. The child's egocentric attitudes and behavior restrict the expression of empathy, compassion, and kindness toward others.
7. The child tends to give up or take shortcuts when a task or goal becomes difficult to achieve.
8. The child is easily influenced or tempted to engage in behavior considered immoral, dishonest, or socially unacceptable.
9. Rules are bent or broken by the children when there is no eminent threat of a consequence.

—. ____

____

—. ____

____

—. ____

____

LONG-TERM GOALS

1. Verbalize the importance of integrity, trustworthiness, and moral courage in everyday life.
2. Demonstrate consistent respect through polite and tolerant actions and deeds and expect that respect will be reciprocated.
3. Teach responsibility by expecting each family member to complete chores, follow rules, and exercise self-control.
4. Promote the feelings of self-worth by expressing appreciation for each family member's unique qualities and administering fair and impartial affection and treatment.
5. Model the character values of consideration, compassion, empathy, and unconditional love.
6. Teach good citizenship by demonstrating family, community, and national pride and showing respect for societal rules and customs.

—. ____

____

—. ____

____

—. ____

____

SHORT-TERM OBJECTIVES

1. Verbalize and record a family code of values and post for easy reference. (1, 2)

THERAPEUTIC INTERVENTIONS

1. Assign the parents to brainstorm a list of family values (e.g., compassion, kindness, honesty, truthfulness, tolerance) with their children and post for easy reference; ask them to refer to the list when disciplining questionable behavior.

2. Advise the parents to choose a family value to discuss as a regular part of the weekly family meeting and give examples of how this value was demonstrated by family

members during the previous week.

2. Regularly cite examples of behaviors that demonstrate integrity, trustworthiness, and moral courage in everyday life. (3, 4, 5)

3. Encourage the parents to use examples from the media, school, church, workplace, and community to engage their children in a discussion of behavior that does and does not reflect the values of integrity and moral courage.

4. Instruct the parents to read and discuss with their children stories that support their family values (e.g., *A Call to Character* by Greer and Kohl).

5. Council the parents to refer verbally to their own ethical actions (e.g., "I phone ahead if I'm going to be late; I let the car merge in front of us because she needed to turn left.") to set a positive example of character in daily life.

3. Facilitate the children's age-appropriate conscience development by discussing behavior in terms of right and wrong or ethical and unethical. (6, 7)

6. Advise the parents to emphasize the importance and long-term benefits of making the moral choice when tempted to engage in unethical behavior and to cite examples involving lying, cheating, stealing, and causing harm.

7. Encourage the parents to model trustworthiness and accountability by keeping promises, fulfilling obligations and being on time, and to insist that the children do the same.

4. Teach and model active listening. (8, 9)

8. Advise the parents that listening and thoughtful conversation are the greatest

gift they can give to their child and ask them to re-program their daily behavior so that listening to each other and the children becomes a top priority.

9. Teach the parents to use the process of active listening (see *Teaching Children Self-Discipline* by Gordon); assign them to use this process with each other and with the children daily.

5. Treat each child with respect and offer discipline and guidance when child-parent respect is not shown. (10, 11, 12)

10. Encourage the parents to build regard and respect within the family by treating one another with love and compassion; explain that discipline administered in a loving yet firm manner will enhance rather than diminish the bond between parent and child.

11. Teach the parents the critical difference between responding to a child's poor behavior using anger, guilt, and shame and using compassionate, logical discipline; instruct them to respond firmly when a child behaves in a disrespectful manner by identifying the behavior (e.g., "That's disrespect!") and describing a more acceptable response (e.g., "Please explain your concern without using putdowns or profanity.").

12. Teach the parents to extinguish disrespectful statements by stating that they will only listen to messages delivered in a respectful

language and tone of voice and then totally ignoring any further unacceptable statements made by the child.

6. Establish a zero tolerance policy for putdowns and teasing. (13, 14)

13. Instruct the parents to address teasing and putdowns by verbalizing a strong family value of kindness and personal dignity and implementing discipline strategies (e.g., time-out, apologizing, loss of a privilege, paying restitution to the harmed party) when respect is not shown.

14. Advise the parents to teach their children an assertive response to teasing and harassment using the bug-wish statement (e.g., "It bugs me when you take my toys. I wish you would stop.").

7. Assign chores and responsibilities to each family member. (15, 16)

15. Instruct the parents to develop a family chore list (or assign the "Division of Family Labor" activity from the *Parenting Skills Homework Planner* by Knapp).

16. Assign the parents to use chores and tasks to teach responsibility to each child using the four-step process described in *Parenting with Love and Logic* (Cline and Fay): (1) Give the child an age-appropriate task, (2) Hope that the child "blows it," (3) Let the resulting consequences and empathy do the teaching, and (4) Give the same task again.

8. Verbally affirm children for positive behavior that demonstrates the exercise

17. Instruct the parents to continually watch for their child's behavior that emulates ethical

of self-control and positive character development. (17, 18)

and moral character and recognize it verbally.

18. Assign the parents to frequently name a commendable behavior that has been demonstrated by the child and connect the behavior to the list of core family values (e.g., "That's punctuality. It's one of our family values.").

9. Promote independence by allowing children to make decisions and live with the consequences. (19, 20, 21)

19. Teach the parents to use a problem-solving process to help their children become more independent and responsible problem solvers (e.g., listen with empathy; if invited, explore possible solutions together, choose a strategy, and meet later to discuss the outcome).

20. Instruct the parents to build their children's decision-making skills and sense of responsibility by offering them many choices in their daily lives (e.g., complete homework before or after dinner, join the hockey team or the football team).

21. Teach the parents the role that natural and logical consequences play in fostering independence and character development in their children (e.g., responsible decision making, problem ownership, self-reliant behavior).

10. Explore issues of justice and fairness by discussing with the family examples from the media,

22. Advise the parents to use examples from the news media or their personal experiences that reflect justice or injustice

community issues, and personal examples. (22, 23)

in our society and to hold discussions with the children eliciting their opinions.

23. Encourage the parents to invite their children to discuss moral dilemmas they have encountered or wondered about from their experiences at home, school, church, or in the neighborhood.

11. Promote the principles of equality and personal uniqueness by administering love, attention, material resources, discipline and guidance in a caring and impartial manner. (24, 25)

24. Instruct the parents to check their own behavior and relationships with their children to insure that each child is given adequate love, attention, material resources, and discipline and guidance.

25. Help the children and parents list their personal needs and wants and realize the extent to which they are met in the family (or assign the "Sharing the Family Resources" activity from the *Parenting Skills Homework Planner* by Knapp).

12. Verbally affirm each person's unique contribution to the family and larger community. (26, 27)

26. Advise the parents to recognize each child for their unique contribution to the family and community (e.g., Jimmy is dependable and does many chores without being asked, Darnell listens with an empathetic ear) to help the children internalize their developing character assets.

27. Encourage the parents to celebrate the character accomplishments of each family member (e.g., attendance records, good sportsmanship certificates,

citizenship awards) with a family outing or recognition at the weekly family meeting.

13. Enlist the help of the children in assisting family members with needed jobs and projects. (28, 29)

28. Ask each family member to list several personal jobs or obligations which would benefit from assistance from another family member (or assign the "Family Job Support Checklist" activity from the *Parenting Skills Homework Planner* by Knapp).

29. Encourage the parents to promote consideration and helpfulness toward extended family members and friends by involving the children in activities that offer needed assistance and support (e.g., shoveling show, cooking a meal, running errands).

14. Separate the deed from the doer when disciplining by using empathy and compassion while focusing on the problem, not the person. (30, 31)

30. Instruct the parents to discipline problem behavior without attacking the character of the child by focusing upon and dealing with the problem rationally while assuring the child of being a loved and cared for member of the family.

31. Advise the parents that empathy and compassion when combined with a logical consequence (e.g., "You spilled the milk, that's too bad. Please get a cloth and clean it up.") is significantly more powerful and effective than anger combined with punishment (e.g., "You spilled the milk. What a mess!").

15. Teach social skills by describing expected behavior and practicing during meal times, family outings, and activities. (32, 33)

32. Instruct the parents to create a list of manners and social behaviors they want their children to acquire and to teach and correct the behavior during family activities.

33. Advise the parents to keep their expectations for their children's social and character development realistic and age-appropriate and to offer support and encouragement when progress is being made and providing loving guidance when necessary.

16. Volunteer for an outreach project at school, church, or in the community. (34, 35)

34. Assign the parents to select a church, family, or school project to participate in with their children to demonstrate and experience the value of giving back to the community.

35. Counsel the parents to insist that the children volunteer for outreach projects at school or church and ask them to emphasize the personal benefits received from giving time and effort to others.

17. Participate in the development of family rules and relate them to laws and customs in the larger society. (36, 37)

36. Instruct the parents to create a list of family rules with input from all family members (e.g., curfew, table manners, homework, dress code) using the process of brainstorming all regulations necessary for harmonious co-existence and consolidating the ideas into a few general limits.

37. Assign the parents to discuss the family rules with their children and to determine how they compare to religious, school, and community rules and consider why rules are necessary in an ethical and moral society.

__. ____________________ __. ____________________

__. ____________________ __. ____________________

__. ____________________ __. ____________________

DIAGNOSTIC SUGGESTIONS:

ICD-9-CM	*ICD-10-CM*	*DSM-5* Disorder, Condition, or Problem
V61.20	Z62.820	Parent-Child Relational Problem
______	______	____________________
______	______	____________________

CHILDREN WITH PHYSICAL CHALLENGES

BEHAVIORAL DEFINITIONS

1. Child is diagnosed with a long-term chronic illness or a life-long disability.
2. Trauma, devastation and confusion result from awareness of the chronic nature of the child's physical challenges.
3. The stages of grief and loss (e.g., denial, bargaining, anger, despair, acceptance) are experienced as the family begins to cope with the child's illness or disability and the resulting special health needs.
4. Pervasive feelings of anger and disappointment interfere with normal loving relationships among family members.
5. Fear and anxiety regarding the future of the child with special health needs.
6. Guilt and blame over the cause of the illness or disability.
7. Confusion and feelings of powerlessness over how to best deal with the child's chronic condition.
8. Feelings of disappointment and resentment directed toward God, medical personnel, society, and the child with special health needs.
9. Siblings are kind and supportive toward their chronically ill or disabled brother or sister.
10. Siblings remain distant from, resentful of, and rejecting toward their brother/sister with special medical needs.
11. Overprotective parenting results in the child with physical challenges becoming depressed, anxious, fearful, overly dependent, and/or socially immature.

__. ____

____

__. ____

____

—. ____
____

LONG-TERM GOALS

1. Gain acceptance of the disability or condition, the child with physical challenges and resulting personal reactions and emotions.
2. Become fully informed about the child's illness or disability and advocate for services at school and in the community.
3. Create a realistic plan to deal with the challenges of parenting a child with special health needs.
4. Parent the child with physical challenges to facilitate the achievement of a personal best level of independence, responsibility, social skills, and character.
5. Recognize and attend to the needs of the other relationships in the family.
6. Maintain a realistically optimistic outlook for the future of the child with physical challenges and the family.

—. ____
____

—. ____
____

—. ____
____

SHORT-TERM OBJECTIVES

1. Describe the facts and feelings associated with parenting a child with physical challenges. (1, 2)

THERAPEUTIC INTERVENTIONS

1. Meet with the parents and other family members to gather background information and discuss the ramifications of the child's chronic illness or disability on the family.
2. Invite the parents to fully disclose and explore their

feelings and reactions to parenting a child with special health needs; explain that denial, anger, and fear are common reactions for parents with a child that has a chronic illness or disability.

2. Reframe negative thoughts and fears into a more positive and realistic perspective and attitude. (3, 4)

3. Brainstorm with the parents a list of concerns or potential problems they fear may occur (e.g., "Will my child be able to go to school?") and help them develop strategies for addressing their concern (e.g., talk to local school personnel about programs for special health needs children).

4. Ask the parents to complete the "Strategies for Supporting Our Child with Physical Challenges" activity from the *Parenting Skills Homework Planner* (Knapp).

3. Read materials written for parents of disabled or chronically ill children and seek information from medical personnel, educators, therapists, and other parents. (5, 6)

5. Assign the parents to gather information about their child's health issues from their family physician, the child's pediatrician, and other medical specialists and to share the information and related questions and concerns during their counseling sessions.

6. Encourage the parents to become more informed about the special health needs of their child by reading literature written specifically for parents of children with physical challenges (e.g., *Special Kids Need Special Parents* by Lavin).

4. Gather information regarding services from the school, government, and community available for children with physical challenges. (7, 8)

7. Assist the parents in establishing a database of services available for their child with physical challenges by accessing information available from National Information Center for Children and Youth with Disabilities (NICHCY; Web: www.nichcy.org; e-mail: nichcy@aed.org; phone: (800) 695-0285).

8. Assign the parents to contact their local school district, the state board of education, and community health organization to seek information about early intervention and ongoing programs available for children with physical challenges.

5. Become actively involved in planning for the treatment of and interventions recommended for the child with physical challenges. (9, 10, 11)

9. Inform the parents about the federally mandated services that seek to include the parents in the planning for the child and encourage them to actively participate and advocate for their child.

10. Suggest that the parents keep a notebook which contains an ongoing account of their child's medical history, professional instructions, diagnostic information, prescribed medications, and therapeutic suggestions.

11. Review with the parents the worksheet "When Your Child with Special Health Needs Goes to School" provided by the Seattle Children's Hospital and Regional Medical Center (www.cshcn.org or (866) 987-2500) to assist them in

requesting necessary special services and accommodations from their child's school.

6. Share feelings, set goals, and create realistic expectations for the child with physical challenges. (12, 13)

12. Ask the parents to clarify their expectations for their child with physical challenges by creating a list of short- and long-term goals which realistically consider the child's age, medical condition, ability level, and interests.

13. Encourage the parents to clarify and disclose their inner feelings through journaling and refer them to a list of topics suggested in the article "Journaling Your Way Through Stress: Finding Answers Within Yourself" by Naseef.

7. Enroll the child with physical challenges in programs designed to help him/her cope with the illness or disability. (14, 15)

14. Assign the parents to access information for children with special health needs from the Internet (e.g., www.kidshealth.org/kid/, *Band-aides and Blackboards for Kids,* www.faculty.fairfield.edu/fleitas/contkids.html, or *Chronic Illness Resources for Teens,* www.dartmouth.edu/dms/koop/resources/chronicillness/chronic.shtml]).

15. Discuss with the parents the various early intervention services provided through the 1997 Individuals with Disabilities Education Act (IDEA) legislation (e.g., assistive technology devices, nutrition services, psychological services); help them determine which services are

appropriate for their child with physical challenges.

8. Join a support group for help in addressing the child's special health needs. (16, 17)

16. Assign the parents to join a group supporting parents of special needs children provided by their church, school, medical facility, or community.

17. Encourage the parents to seek friendship, support and guidance from other parents of children with physical challenges by connecting often with compatible parents met at support groups, school, church, and community meetings.

9. Seek respite help from family members, friends, or community agencies. (18, 19)

18. Assign the parents to explore available respite care from community agencies or to access a list of respite facilities from ARCH National Respite Network and Resource Center (800) 773-5433 or www.archrespite.org.

19. Help the parents to create a list of respite support possibilities from family members, church groups, and friends and encourage them to use this help to avoid burnout.

10. Implement strategies of positive discipline to help the child with physical challenges develop self-confidence and responsibility. (20, 21, 22)

20. Instruct the parents to use choices to set limits for the child while at the same time developing a sense of independence and helping the child acquire problem-solving abilities (e.g., "Would you like to take your medication before or after lunch?").

21. Guide the parents to encourage responsible behavior in their child by using

natural and logical consequences (e.g., loss of privileges when chores or homework aren't completed, free time delayed until exercises are done).

22. Encourage the parents to enhance self-esteem and self-reliance by using questions to allow the child to be an essential part of the decision-making and problem-solving process (e.g., "When is the best time to schedule your doctor's appointment?").

11. Arrange for the child with physical challenges to participate in social groups and play or leisure time activities with children with similar conditions. (23, 24)

23. Stress the importance of maintaining peer relationships for the child with physical challenges and encourage the parents to arrange play groups for younger children, work with the school to develop a circle of friends for a school-aged child, and involve their child in groups of children with similar conditions.

24. Direct the parents to gather information about camps for children with physical challenges provided by the Federation for Children with Special Needs (see www.fcsn.org/camps/2003/resources.html or (800) 331-0688) or from the American Camping Association (http://find.acacamps.org/finding_a_camp.cgi or (765) 342-8456).

12. Promote the values of integrity and personal best achievement in all of the

25. Assign the parents to use the concept of unique rather than equal to address the

children by verbalizing and supporting the attainment of age- and ability-appropriate, individualized goals for each child. (25, 26)

distribution of love, attention, and meeting their children's physical needs (e.g., "I love and parent you each uniquely. You need my help with homework and soccer, your sister needs my help with taking medication and physical therapy.").

26. Encourage the parents to teach, model, and affirm the positive behaviors they hope to bring out in each of their children (e.g., persistence, responsibility, empathy) using the criteria of age, ability, and personal best rather than comparing one child to another.

13. Help the siblings of the child with physical challenges resolve feelings of resentment through focused discussion and general family activities. (27, 28)

27. Alert the parents to watch for reactions of anger, resentment, jealousy, and depression in the child's siblings and encourage them to seek counseling and support for them when necessary.

28. Instruct the parents to schedule time to have fun together as a family engaging in activities that do not involve or focus upon the illness or disability (e.g., a family overnight at a motel with a pool, family movie or video night).

14. Schedule quality time and relationship enhancing activities with the spouse. (29, 30, 31)

29. Advise the parents of the importance of nurturing and supporting their personal relationship by taking time to share feelings and thoughts and backing each other up in times of crisis.

30. Assign the parents to read *The Five Love Languages*

(Chapman) to gain understanding of how to express love and gratitude to one another in meaningful ways.

31. Advise the parents to participate as a couple in a nonwork and nonfamily-related social or church activity, or other entertainment to reduce stress and become reacquainted with the fun-loving aspects of their personalities.

15. Schedule personal time to renew energy and regain balance. (32)

32. Instruct the parents to carve out personal time for themselves each day to relax and renew their energy for the demands of parenting a child with physical challenges.

16. Involve the grandparents and other extended family members in the care and activities of the child with physical challenges. (33, 34)

33. Encourage the parents to include grandparents and extended family members in the lives of all of their children by sharing problems, setbacks, progress, and achievements.

34. Assign the parents to solicit help from extended family members with doctor visits, occupational therapy appointments, physical therapy sessions, transportation to activities and special classes, and babysitting to forge a loving relationship between the child with physical challenges and the helpful family member and to bring great relief to them as the primary caregivers.

17. Involve the child with physical challenges in the plans for coping with the illness or disability. (35, 36)

35. Describe to the parents the importance of involving the child with physical challenges in the plans for coping with the

illness or disability and setting long-term goals and short-term objectives for progress toward these goals.

36. Assign the parents to work with their special needs child to complete the "Working Together to Create a Plan" activity from the *Parenting Skills Homework Planner* (Knapp) to structure a cooperative effort in solving the daily and long-term problems of living with a serious physical illness or disability.

18. Define hopes and dreams, and express optimism for the future of the child with physical challenges and the family. (37)

37. Encourage the parents to remain hopeful and realistically optimistic about the future of the child with physical challenges and the family as a whole and help them to recognize the contributions the child has made to the family.

__. ____________________________

__. ____________________________

__. ____________________________

__. ____________________________

__. ____________________________

__. ____________________________

DIAGNOSTIC SUGGESTIONS:

ICD-9-CM	*ICD-10-CM*	*DSM-5* Disorder, Condition, or Problem
316	F54	Psychological Factors Affecting Other Medical Conditions
______	______	____________________
______	______	____________________

CONDUCT DISORDER/ DELINQUENT BEHAVIOR

BEHAVIORAL DEFINITIONS

1. Child is diagnosed with a conduct disorder and seriously violates family, school, and community rules.
2. Child is physically aggressive and cruel to people and/or animals.
3. Child deliberately destroys property at home, school, and/or in the community.
4. Child is deceitful, lies, steals, and exhibits antisocial behavior without apparent remorse or consideration of the consequences.
5. Fear for personal safety and the safety of others as the result of the child's aggressive behavior.
6. Predominant use of demeaning, neglectful, and/or abusive parenting methods during the child's developmental years.
7. Emotional instability and volatile interpersonal conflict contribute to the chaos within the family.
8. Abuse of drugs and/or alcohol permeates the family lifestyle.
9. Others blame the child's socially maladjusted behavior on poor parenting.
10. Siblings in family develop psychological or behavioral difficulties as a result of living with an aggressive and socially maladjusted brother or sister.
11. Feelings of despair that the problem is so great that no agencies or professionals can or will help.

__. ____
____

__. ____
____

__. ____
____

LONG-TERM GOALS

1. Replace abusive, neglectful parenting with consistent limit-setting within a context of respect and caring for the child.
2. Develop a highly structured and intensified level of discipline for the child with aggressive and antisocial behavior.
3. Stand together to form a united front with one another and other agencies and professionals working with the child with a conduct disorder.
4. Ensure the safety of the child with a conduct disorder and all other family members.
5. Seek medical, educational, behavioral, and psychological help for the child with a conduct disorder and other family members if necessary.
6. Maintain physical, mental, and emotional health and balance in order to cope with the monumental task of parenting a child with a conduct disorder.

—. ____

____

—. ____

____

—. ____

____

SHORT-TERM OBJECTIVES

1. Arrange for a complete medical and psychosocial evaluation of the child with a conduct disorder. (1, 2)

THERAPEUTIC INTERVENTIONS

1. Meet with the parents to gather a developmental history and review their concerns about maladaptive behavior, academic, and social-emotional problems presented by the child.
2. Assist the parents in arranging for their child to receive a comprehensive psychosocial, medical, and educational evaluation completed by a mental health clinic, hospital,

or agency and the child's school.

2. Eliminate abusive and neglectful parent/child interactions. (3, 4)

3. Explore for incidents of abuse, neglect, volatile, or overly punitive parenting that may have contributed to the formation of the child's aggressive and antisocial behavior.

4. Initiate either a verbal or written commitment from the parents to substitute positive forms of consequential discipline for punitive, volatile, or abusive discipline.

3. Adopt a parenting approach that is compassionate yet very firm and highly structured and takes the emotionality out of the discipline. (5, 6, 7, 8)

5. Assign the parents to use the technique of broken record when the child questions an instruction or challenges parental authority (e.g., "You need to do your homework now"; "Probably so, but you need to do your homework now.").

6. Emphasize to the parents the crucial difference between firmness (holding to a disciplinary intervention and focusing on the child's inappropriate behavior) and harshness (attacking the child's personality and demeaning the self-esteem).

7. Advise the parents to use tightly controlled choices when allowing the child to make some decisions and have some control in his/her life (e.g., "Would you prefer to feed the dog now or in 15 minutes?"); inform the parents that if the child refuses to

make a choice or manipulates the options then the parent must make the decision.

8. Assign the parents to create a plan for time out in their home when the child's behavior becomes negative or intolerable and to utilize this process as an opportunity for the child to calm down, regroup and regain appropriate behavior.

4. Create a behavior management plan that targets the problem behaviors, and provides structured and straightforward parental actions and consequences. (9, 10, 11, 12)

9. Assist the parents in prioritizing a few critical behaviors for modification and defining an alternate expected, appropriate behavior for the child.

10. Assign the parents to complete the "Replacing Noncompliance with Compliance and Cooperation" activity from the *Parenting Skills Homework Planner* (Knapp) to encourage the child to recognize and substitute appropriate actions for inappropriate behavior.

11. Advise the parents to be realistic in their expectations expressed in the behavior plan to increase the success level and avoid defeat.

12. Instruct the parents to plan ahead and prepare their responses to the chronic negative, oppositional, and defiant behavior exhibited by their child and to remain calm and extremely firm when implementing a predetermined intervention.

5. Participate in ongoing counseling sessions focusing on the multifaceted problems of parenting a child with a conduct disorder. (13, 14)

13. Discuss with the parents the emotionally draining nature of parenting a child with a conduct disorder and encourage them to participate in regularly scheduled counseling sessions to help them deal with the critical issues the child may present.

14. Advise the parents to arrange for ongoing counseling for the child at school or with a private therapist to deal with antisocial feelings and behaviors and to learn alternate behaviors and strategies for successful coping.

6. Seek information from professionals, mental health organizations, and by reading literature describing the diagnosis and treatment of conduct disorder in youth. (15, 16)

15. Assign the parents to read literature that describes conduct disorder in youth (e.g., *Your Defiant Child* by Barkley, *Parenting the Strong-Willed Child* by Forehand and Long, or *It's Nobody's Fault* by Koplewicz).

16. Instruct the parents to access information about conduct disorder from organizations that can provide help information and support (e.g., American Academy of Child and Adolescent Psychiatry (202) 966-7300 or www.aacap.org, Family Self-Help Group for Parents of Children and Adolescents (800) 950-6264 or www.nami.org, TOUGHLOVE® International (215) 348-7090 or www.toughlove.org).

7. Agree to share the parenting burden by seeking respite from community agencies, foster parent programs, hospitals, and trained extended family members. (17, 18)

17. Assign the parents to explore available respite care from community agencies or to access a list of respite facilities from ARCH National Respite Network and Resource Center (800) 773-5433 or www.archrespite.org).

18. Instruct the parents to place the child in a psychiatric hospital or a residential treatment center or wilderness school when the behavior becomes uncontrollable or the child becomes a threat to self or others.

8. Cooperate with the school to ensure that the child's conduct is not threatening to others. (19, 20)

19. Assist the parents and the school in establishing a time-out area or Student Responsibility Center where the child can go when disruptive or uncooperative to cool off and plan for more appropriate behavior before participating in routine classroom activities.

20. Recommend that the parents and the school consider special education or Section 504 accommodations to help the child participate successfully in the academic environment (e.g., smaller classroom, special classes, reduced school day).

9. Cooperate with the juvenile justice system to thwart continued criminal behavior from the child with a conduct disorder. (21, 22)

21. Advise the parents to enlist the help of local law enforcement immediately when the child attempts to break the law; stress that early intervention with criminal or pre-criminal behavior is essential to reduce

the occurrence of future attempts.

22. Instruct the parents to become familiar with programs offered by the juvenile justice system in their area and to enroll the child in any programs that could help control the antisocial behavior.

10. Agree to discuss feelings, issues, and personal concerns relating to the child with a conduct disorder regularly in face-to-face conversations. (23, 24)

23. Assign the parents to arrange private discussions so they can share feelings, anxieties, concerns, successes, and problems related to parenting a child with a conduct disorder.

24. Advise the parents to be aware of attempts at triangulation and manipulation by the child and support one another with all of their parenting strategies.

11. Meet with school personnel, other caregivers, and involved professionals regularly to review strategies for working with the child with a conduct disorder. (25, 26)

25. Assign the parents to meet with the child's teachers to access the child's academic potential and determine a mutually agreed upon level of academic performance that must be maintained to earn privileges at home or school.

26. Advise the parents to meet regularly with all caregivers of the child to coordinate behavior plans, address problem situations, and clarify the current level of adjustment.

12. Participate in parent training classes. (27, 28)

27. Refer the parents to a parenting class (e.g., *Systematic Training for Effective Parenting (STEP)* by

Dinkmeyer and McKay) to acquire techniques of positive discipline to use with the child.

28. Meet with the parents to help them initiate parenting strategies of positive discipline learned in parenting classes or from recommended parenting books or tapes (e.g., *Your Defiant Child* by Barkley or *Children: The Challenge* by Dreikurs and Stoltz).

13. Use privileges to shape the child's cooperation, compliance, and positive behavior. (29, 30)

29. Assist the parents in creating a list of privileges that can be used as rewards when the child behaves appropriately or withheld when the child does not adhere to the behavior plan.

30. Assign the parents to complete the "Using Privileges as Contingencies and Consequences" activity from the *Parenting Skills Homework Planner* (Knapp) to encourage the child to engage in more appropriate behavior.

14. Limit the child's exposure to television and violent computer or video games. (31)

31. Inform the parents that television, video, and computer games are filled with violence, drug and alcohol use, sexuality, and youth given unreasonable entitlements and advise them to limit all media use to no more than 1 to 2 hours per day.

15. Investigate the possibility of comorbid conditions that may be affecting the child with a conduct disorder. (32, 33)

32. Advise the parents that conduct disorder often exists with other neuropsychiatric disorders and review the child's psychiatric and psychological

evaluations with the parents to identify any other coexisting conditions.

33. Assign the parents to consult with the child's medical doctor to explore the possibility of medication to treat the symptoms of conduct disorder and other existing comorbid conditions.

16. Enroll the child with a conduct disorder in anger management and social skills classes provided by the school or a community mental health agency. (34)

34. Assist the parents in locating an anger management and a social skills program for the child with a conduct disorder offered by school, the juvenile justice system, or local community health agencies.

17. Adopt programs to eliminate alcohol and substance abuse from the lifestyle and enhance physical and mental fitness. (35, 36)

35. Assign the parents to adopt daily habits that will prepare them for the immensely challenging job of parenting a child with a conduct disorder (e.g., get enough sleep, exercise regularly, eat healthy foods, eliminate abuse of alcohol and illegal or restricted substances).

36. Encourage the parents to participate in strategies and programs designed to reduce stress and enhance emotional balance (e.g., reduce workload, keep a journal, build a support network).

18. Implement strategies to reduce the stress level within the family and between themselves. (37, 38)

37. Instruct the parents to implement a getaway evening every week to escape from the pressures of parenting and the demands of their children.

38. Advise the parents to enroll the siblings in counseling sessions at school or with a private therapist or agency to deal with the emotional stresses of living with a brother or sister with a conduct disorder.

—. ____________________

—. ____________________

—. ____________________

—. ____________________

—. ____________________

—. ____________________

DIAGNOSTIC SUGGESTIONS

ICD-9-CM	*ICD-10-CM*	*DSM-5* Disorder, Condition, or Problem
312.81	F91.1	Conduct Disorder, Childhood-Onset Type
313.81	F91.3	Oppositional Defiant Disorder
314.01	F90.1	Attention-Deficit/Hyperactivity Disorder, Predominately Hyperactive /Impulsive Presentation
V71.02	Z72.810	Child Antisocial Behavior
V61.20	Z62.820	Parent-Child Relational Problem
______	______	____________________
______	______	____________________

DEPENDENT CHILDREN/ OVERPROTECTIVE PARENT

BEHAVIORAL DEFINITIONS

1. Chronic and obsessive worry about the welfare of the child.
2. Restrict the normal and age-appropriate activities of the child.
3. Control all decision making, leaving the child little opportunity to make choices or solve problems independently.
4. Unrealistic belief that the child is fragile, incapable, and needs protection.
5. Fear that the child will be devastated by failure or mistakes.
6. Frustration that the child fails to demonstrate self-confidence, courage, and responsible behavior.
7. Remain close and overly involved while the child participates in activities that other children handle alone.
8. Child demonstrates dependent behavior and verbalizes feelings of inadequacy.
9. Child relies excessively on others for support, direction, and guidance.
10. Child is reluctant to take the initiative, attempt unfamiliar tasks, or assume a leadership role.

__. ____

____

__. ____

____

__. ____

____

LONG-TERM GOALS

1. Allow the child to participate independently in age-appropriate activities offering support and "can-do" encouragement.
2. Allow the child to learn from mistakes and react with empathy and support when the consequences are experienced.
3. Encourage the child to solve problems alone or with minimal guidance only when requested.
4. Utilize techniques of positive discipline to facilitate responsible behavior and independent thinking.
5. Offer unconditional love for the child that is not based on behavior or accomplishments.
6. Encourage the child to plan for the future by setting long- and short-term personal goals.

—. ____

____

—. ____

____

—. ____

____

SHORT-TERM OBJECTIVES

1. Identify inappropriate or excessive fears and anxieties held regarding the child's welfare and develop more positive and realistic expectations. (1, 2, 3)

THERAPEUTIC INTERVENTIONS

1. Review the parents' family histories, discuss their concerns about the child's dependency needs, and define their role in the parent-child relationship.
2. Ask the parents to list their fears, worries and concerns that may be contributing to overprotective parenting (or assign the "Overprotective Parent vs. Positive Parent" activity from the *Parenting Skills Homework Planner* by Knapp).
3. Assign the parents to listen to the audiotape *Helicopters, Drill*

Sergeants, and Consultants (Fay) and discuss the three different types of parenting styles at the next counseling session.

2. Express unconditional love for the child verbally and behaviorally. (4, 5)

4. Define unconditional love for the parents (e.g., complete and constant love given regardless of personal attributes, attitude, behavior, or performance) and discuss how this type of personal regard is essential to the development of feelings of adequacy and self-worth in children.

5. Brainstorm with the parents various ways that unconditional love can be given (e.g., frequently state, "I love you," play with the child, pay attention when the child speaks, hug the child, spend quality time with the child).

3. Encourage mutual respect by treating the child with respect and eliminating comments or behavior that would damage the child's self-concept. (6, 7, 8)

6. Explain to the parents that demeaning comments create feelings of dependency and inadequacy; assign them to observe their parent-child interactions for one week and list any of their behavior that may be considered demeaning by their child.

7. After reviewing the parent's list of demeaning interactions with their child, role play respectful and positive methods of handling these encounters.

8. Teach the parents to remain respectful when disciplining by focusing on the behavior and not the child and by letting the child know that although the

deed is not acceptable, love is given unconditionally.

4. Attend workshops and read literature focusing on teaching children to become responsible. (9, 10)

9. Refer the parents to a parenting class which focuses on helping children develop responsible behavior (e.g., *Becoming a Love and Logic Parent* by Fay, Cline, and Fay).

10. Assign the parents to read child development literature which addresses promoting responsibility in children (e.g., *Children: The Challenge* by Dreikurs and Stoltz or *Parent Talk* by Moorman).

5. Initiate interactions with the child that encourage more self-reliant, organized, and self-confident behavior. (11, 12, 13)

11. Ask the parents to substitute the phrase "Next Time" (see *Parent Talk* by Moorman) for "don't" to shape positive future efforts from the child (e.g., "Next time, please park your bike in the garage" versus "Don't leave your bike outside in the rain.").

12. Assign the parents to use "Act as if" (see *Parent Talk* by Moorman) to encourage the child to make an effort despite the fear of failure, (e.g., "Act as if you knew how to draw that tree"; "Pretend you can jump rope"; "Play like you've done this before"; or "Fake it until you make it.").

13. Instruct the parents to teach the child the skill of completing a large task by subdividing it into smaller more manageable tasks (e.g., making a bed: smooth the sheets, pull up the covers, place the pillow, put on the spread).

6. Implement strategies at home designed to foster responsible behavior. (14, 15)

14. Instruct the parents to implement "The Four Steps to Responsibility" (see *Parenting with Love and Logic* by Cline and Fay) by: (1) Giving the child a manageable task, (2) allowing any mistake to become a learning opportunity, (3) using consequences to teach appropriate behavior, and (4) giving the same task again to check for learning.

15. Ask the parents to use "Red Light, Green Light" (see *Parent Talk* by Moorman) to turn an irresponsible behavior into a responsible behavior by implementing the following: (1) Describing the inappropriate behavior to the child: red light (e.g., unmade bed, wet towels on floor) and (2) describing the expected behavior: green light (e.g., bed made before school, towels on rack).

7. Verbalize confidence in the child's ability to function independently. (16, 17, 18)

16. Advise the parents to offer encouragement when the child is acting overly dependent and asking for too much assistance and to help only in a supportive role by allowing the child to do the majority of the problem solving.

17. Ask parents to use the statement, "Check Yourself" (see *Parent Talk* by Moorman) (e.g., "This is sharing day at school, check yourself to make sure you have what you need when it's your turn to share.") to help the child develop the

ability to prepare successfully for upcoming events and personal experiences.

18. Assign the parents to assist the child in prioritizing key assigned tasks and to designate a target completion time.

8. Affirm the child for progress in assuming responsibility and acquiring independence. (19, 20)

19. Discuss with the parents the importance of giving frequent affirmations to the child for independent and responsible behavior in a private, low-key manner.

20. Assign the parents to acknowledge the child's independent and responsible behavior in the presence of the child.

9. Outline circumstances in which the child can safely learn from the consequences of a mistake or poor decision. (21, 22)

21. Brainstorm with the parents the various times they can allow the child to learn form the consequences of a poor decision without creating significant danger, destruction, or distress.

22. Assign the parents to identify the circumstances in which they have allowed their child to struggle with the consequences of a personal mistake or poor judgment.

10. List and discuss the benefits of allowing the child to gain wisdom from the experience of making mistakes. (23, 24)

23. Assist the parents in creating a list of the benefits to both the parent and the child of allowing the child to learn from mistakes (e.g., child learns to accept responsibility for the outcome of both good and bad decisions).

24. Instruct the parents to express empathy and understanding when the child struggles with

the result of poor judgment or irresponsible behavior without interfering to prevent the teaching value of the consequence.

11. Develop household rules that promote responsible behavior and are positive in expectation. (25, 26)

25. Advise the parents to establish household rules with the child by brainstorming necessary rules and framing them in positive rather than negative language (e.g., hang coats in closet, arrive on time for dinner, bedtime is 8:30 P.M.).

26. Assign the parents and child to complete the "Creating and Cooperating with the Family Rules" activity from the *Parenting Skills Homework Planner* (Knapp) to promote a cooperative effort in making the family rules work.

12. Use logical and natural consequences to teach the child responsibility. (27, 28)

27. Instruct the parents to allow natural consequences (e.g., getting hungry after failing to eat, feeling tired after lack of sleep) to teach the child about the results of poor decisions; advise them that natural consequences are powerful teachers when parents don't interfere with the lesson.

28. Assist the parents in creating a list of logical or parent-imposed consequences (e.g., restricted use of television when homework is not done, earlier bedtime when child is uncooperative with the bedtime routine) to use when no natural consequence is available to modify the child's behavior.

13. Offer choices and explicit limit-setting statements to teach the child responsible decision making. (29, 30)

29. Assign the parents to use limited choices to share control and facilitate responsible decision making by their child; advise them that choices should be framed so that either option is acceptable to them (e.g., "Would you like to wear your red shirt or green shirt today?"), should be limited to specific stated alternatives (e.g., "Would you like to eat a hamburger or a pizza tonight?"), and the parent should be prepared to choose if the child refuses to choose.

30. Instruct the parents to set reasonable limits for the child by using statements that make the child's desired privileges contingent upon the child's appropriate behavior and responsible decisions (e.g., "Feel free to go out with your friends as soon as your room is cleaned.").

14. Use a reality-based decision-making process to teach the child to solve problems independently or with minimal guidance. (31, 32)

31. Advise the parents to allow the child to solve as many problems as possible using a 5-step process that offers guidance when requested but doesn't take over for the child (e.g., (1) Ask the child to describe the problem; (2) Ask the child for plans to solve the problem; (3) Offer to brainstorm possible solutions with the child only if help is requested; (4) Discuss with the child which solution would work best; (5) Invite the child to share the results of the solution selected).

32. Advise the parents that providing empathetic listening to the child whenever the child is struggling with a personal dilemma is often all that is needed to help solve the problem.

15. Verbalize the special considerations required by a child with special needs and plan for any necessary accommodations. (33, 34)

33. Ask the parents to create a list of accommodations the child requires because of a special needs condition (e.g., physical or mental disability, chronic illness, ADHD, psychological disorder) and help them plan for providing these accommodations without overprotecting the child and creating unnecessary dependency.

34. Assign the parents to work cooperatively with the child's school staff and other professionals in the area of special needs to create a plan for necessary accommodations while encouraging personal growth and independent functioning.

16. Offer statements of encouragement when the child demonstrates feelings of inadequacy and low self-esteem. (35, 36)

35. Assign the parents to observe their child for two weeks and make a list of behaviors that indicate low self-esteem and feelings of inadequacy.

36. Instruct the parent to offer statements of encouragement when the child demonstrates feelings of inadequacy and role play positive statements they can use to support the child (e.g., "I think you can handle it"; "I see you as capable"; "I'll bet you can figure that out.").

17. Establish and maintain structured daily family mealtimes and weekly family meetings. (37, 38)

37. Assign the parents to establish a nightly family mealtime when the whole family sits at one table with the television and other media turned off and the conversation is focused on daily events and other items of interest.

38. Instruct the parents to initiate a weekly family meeting to allow each family member to discuss family business and concerns, household rules, give recognition for personal accomplishments, and plan for family events and activities.

18. Encourage the child to verbalize hopes for the future and long- and short-term goals that are important. (39)

39. Instruct the parents to work with their child to formulate long-term goals for the child's future education, lifestyle, and career and to record the short-term steps necessary to reach these goals.

—. ______________________________

—. ______________________________

—. ______________________________

—. ______________________________

—. ______________________________

—. ______________________________

DIAGNOSTIC SUGGESTIONS:

ICD-9-CM	*ICD-10-CM*	*DSM-5* Disorder, Condition, or Problem
314.01	F90.2	Attention-Deficit/Hyperactivity Disorder, Combined Presentation
300.02	F41.1	Generalized Anxiety Disorder
309.21	F93.0	Separation Anxiety Disorder
______	______	______________________
______	______	______________________

DEPRESSION

BEHAVIORAL DEFINITIONS

1. Child in family is diagnosed with depression, dysthymia, bipolar disorder, or suicidal ideation.
2. Child in family exhibits symptoms of depression (e.g., depressed or irritable mood, diminished interest in activities, fatigue, feelings of worthlessness, low energy, guilt) daily.
3. Child has taken prescribed medication or been hospitalized for treatment of depression.
4. One or both parents have a history of depression.
5. Chronic marital difficulties, separation, or divorce.
6. One or both parents have a history of drug or alcohol abuse.
7. Child's depression is a significant concern and interferes with normal family functioning.
8. Unstable family relationships, unrealistic expectations, and lack of stable parent/child emotional support.
9. Inconsistent parenting styles and erratic disciplinary strategies.
10. Chronic unemployment, poverty, lack of financial support, and volatile, unsafe living conditions.

—. ____

____

LONG-TERM GOALS

1. Seek medical and psychological treatment of the child's depression.
2. Create a positive and supportive parent/child relationship.
3. Improve and stabilize the relationship with the child's co-parent.
4. Establish mental health and emotional stability of all family members.

5. Treat drug and alcohol abuse.
6. Implement positive, effective, and consistent disciplinary strategies.

—. ____

____

SHORT-TERM OBJECTIVES

1. Describe the child's symptoms of depression and their effects on the family. (1, 2)
2. Arrange for the child to obtain a complete physical and psychological evaluation of the depth and causes for depression. (3, 4)
3. Review various treatment options for childhood depression and select a course of action to pursue. (5, 6)

THERAPEUTIC INTERVENTIONS

1. Meet with the parents to gather a family history and review their observations of the child's symptoms of depression and how this is affecting the family.
2. Gain permission from the parents to contact the school to acquire any information relevant to their child's symptoms of depression and how these symptoms have affected school adjustment.
3. Assign the parents to schedule a physical and neurological examination by the child's physician to rule out physical causes of the child's symptoms of depression.
4. Instruct the parents to arrange for a complete psychological evaluation of the child with a private therapist, mental health clinic, or a psychiatric hospital.
5. Review treatment options with the parents (e.g., no intervention, behavioral interventions, cognitive therapy, medication, hospitalization) and help them determine an initial plan based on the following considerations: (1) The age of the child, (2) the

severity of the illness, (3) existing comorbid conditions, and (4) parents and child's attitude toward medication.

6. Encourage the parents to obtain treatment for the existing depression of the child and other family members immediately and to remain alert to future episodes after the current problem has been successfully treated.

4. Gain a deeper understanding of depression, its causes, and treatment strategies by joining a support group, reading recommended literature, or viewing tapes about depression. (7, 8)

7. Direct the parents to informational resources offering best practice interventions and treatments for childhood and adolescent depression (e.g., American Academy of Child and Adolescent Psychiatry, www.aacap.org, Child and Adolescent Bipolar Foundation, www.bpkids.org, or the National Mental Health Association, www.nmha.org).

8. Assign the parents to read literature which describes depression, it's causes and coping strategies (e.g., *Survival Guide to Childhood Depression* by Dubuque or *'Help Me I'm Sad'* by Fassler and Dumas).

5. Teach the child to replace distorted, negative perceptions that contribute to the depression with positive, realistic thoughts. (9, 10)

9. Assign the parents to assist the child in identifying and eliminating negative thoughts and replacing them with positive perceptions (or ask them to complete with their child the "Creating Positive Self Talk" activity from the *Parenting Skills Homework Planner* by Knapp).

10. Instruct the parents to engage in mutual story telling with their child by letting the child initiate a story and using parental input to guide the script toward a positive or an optimistic conclusion.

6. Engage the child in age-appropriate, creative, or enjoyable activities and/or social events. (11, 12)

11. Advise the parents to insist that the depressed child participate in activities and social events on a daily basis and to make privileges desired by the child contingent upon engagement in these activities.

12. Assign the parents to enroll the child in age-appropriate activity groups to counter the tendency to perseverate about feelings of hopelessness.

7. Examine all relationships in the child's life to determine factors contributing to the depression. (13, 14)

13. Assign the parents to create a list of all the relationships in the child's life and rate each one as a positive, negative, or neutral influence on the child; instruct the parents to seek input from the child and to be especially alert to relationships which are manipulative, controlling, or abusive in nature.

14. Instruct the parents to promote positive relationships and eliminate or manage negative relationships in the child's life (or ask them to complete the "Managing Positive and Negative Relationships" activity from the *Parenting Skills Homework Planner* by Knapp).

8. Encourage the child to actively participate in school and school-

15, Instruct the parents to insist on regular school attendance and to strongly encourage and

sponsored activities. (15, 16, 17)

support the child's participation in school-related programs and activities.

16. Assign the parents to meet with the school social worker or counselor to enlist counseling support for the child and explore the child's participation in focused counseling groups at school.

17. Instruct the parents to meet with the school psychologist and other educational staff to explore the possibility of a learning disability or other identifiable problems that may be contributing to the child's depression and may qualify the child for special education or other academic accommodations.

9. Spend time alone with the depressed child's siblings to promote their self-esteem and reinforce their attempts to cope with their depressed sibling. (18, 19)

18. Encourage the parents to remain sensitive and empathetic to the needs of the depressed child's siblings and to schedule time for interaction and activities several times per week.

19. Meet with the child siblings to evaluate their feelings and frustrations of living with a depressed sister or brother and role play methods of engaging their sibling in positive interactions.

10. Commit to collaborate with all family members to help the child overcome his/her depression. (20)

20. Brainstorm with the couple or the single parent methods of enlisting the support of the noncustodial or estranged parent, or blended and extended family members in supporting the family's plan to treat the child's depression.

11. Engage in relationship counseling and couple-centered activities to strengthen the marital bond. (21, 22, 23)

21. Enlist the parent's commitment to support one another and avoid any manipulation or triangulation that may be contributing to the child's depression.

22. Explore with the couple how the child's depression is affecting their relationship and assist them in brainstorming methods of remaining loving and supportive toward one another.

23. Assign the parents to schedule "couple-time" daily for personal communication and weekly for activities of mutual interest.

12. Identify and replace any depressive, negative cognitions and distorted perceptions that may be affecting the emotional well-being of the child with depression and other family members. (24, 25)

24. Review with the parents their own history of depression and mental illness and refer them to a mental health professional for evaluation and treatment if there is any indication of psychopathology.

25. Explore with the parents any of their negative perceptions or attitudes that are contributing to the child's depression and brainstorm with the parents methods of modeling a more positive attitude.

13. Identify the negative consequences of financial instability on family functioning. (26)

26. Explore with the parents the effects of poverty on the family and the child (e.g., lack of nutritional meals or appropriate clothing, frequent geographic moves).

14. Increase family income through employment and/or community agency assistance. (27, 28)

27. Help the parents develop a plan for obtaining consistent employment and needed economic assistance and

services; note any roadblocks to achieving these goals.

28. Refer the family to agencies that provide social, financial, and economic services and help the family apply for these services.

15. Establish safe and stable housing for the family. (29, 30)

29. Assign the parents to assess their current housing and neighborhood in terms of safety, stability, and suitability and determine if poor and unsafe living conditions are contributing to family volatility and the child's depression.

30. Assist the parents in enlisting the help of community agencies (e.g., Habitat for Humanity, www.habitat.org, Department of Housing and Urban Development programs: (800) 569-4287) in finding safe and suitable housing.

16. Reassure the child about personal security, express an awareness of and empathy for the child's fears, and commit to maintaining a supportive and loving relationship. (31, 32)

31. Assign the parents to read How to Talk so Kids Will Listen and Listen so Kids Will Talk (Faber and Mazlish) to assist in opening the lines of positive communication with the child.

32. Instruct the parents to schedule a daily time for actively listening to the child, offering reassurance about personal security and expressing an awareness of and empathy for the feelings of fear, helplessness, and hopelessness.

17. Seek treatment for alcohol and drug dependency. (33, 34, 35)

33. Instruct the parent with a chemical dependence problem to participate in substance

abuse treatment program and to commit to the long-term termination of any abuse of substances.

34. Direct the parents to require drug and alcohol testing if there is a suspicion that the depressed child is using restricted substances.

35. Instruct the parents to enroll the child in a rehabilitation program if there is evidence that the child is using alcohol or drugs.

18. Utilize discipline strategies that teach responsibility and self-reliance. (36, 37)

36. Assign the parents to help the child develop responsible behavior by implementing the four steps to teaching responsibility: (1) assign chores and tasks to the child; (2) expect some noncompliance, (3) issue a logical consequence for the noncompliance, and (4) give the same task again to check for learning (see Parenting with Love and Logic by Cline and Fay).

37. Instruct the parents to use controlled choices (e.g., homework before or after dinner, ride or walk to school) to shape behavior, promote decision-making abilities, and encourage feelings of empowerment in the depressed child.

19. Implement regularly scheduled family meetings to promote expression of feelings and family cohesion. (38)

38. Instruct the parents to schedule regular family meetings to promote family cohesion and to encourage each child to participate in the plans for family functioning and the resolution of family problems.

20. Increase and record the frequency of verbalizing affirmations to all the children in the family. (39)

39. Teach the parents the therapeutic advantages of giving frequent affirmations to the all children in the family (e.g., enhances self-esteem, expresses encouragement, builds self-confidence) and brainstorm statements of recognition that could be directed toward the child.

21. Teach the children problem-solving skills. (40)

40. Instruct the parents to help the child deal with personal problems using a problem-solving approach that offers support and guidance but leaves the major responsibility for resolution with the child (e.g., listen with empathy, ask for permission to share ideas for resolution, brainstorm possible solutions, allow the child to determine how he/she will handle the situation).

__. ____________________

__. ____________________

__. ____________________

__. ____________________

__. ____________________

__. ____________________

DIAGNOSTIC SUGGESTIONS

ICD-9-CM	*ICD-10-CM*	*DSM-5 Disorder, Condition, or Problem*
309.0	F43.21	Adjustment disorder, With Depressed Mood
300.4	F34.1	Persistent Depressive Disorder
296.xx	F33.x	Major Depressive Disorder, Recurrent Episode
296.xx	F32.x	Major Depressive Disorder, Single Episode
______	______	____________________
______	______	____________________

DIVORCE/SEPARATION

BEHAVIORAL DEFINITIONS

1. Divorce and/or separation are anticipated, in progress, or completed.
2. Various family members experience stress, fatigue, depression, anxiety, and mood swings.
3. Increased workload in the household, disorganization, and feelings of being overwhelmed.
4. Self-absorption and preoccupation with personal problems and reduced focus on the children.
5. Lack of consistent, positive, and compassionate discipline.
6. Drastic drop in income and a change in lifestyle for the mother and the children.
7. Children experience a lack of involvement with, and financial and emotional support from the father.
8. Children are shocked, traumatized, and afraid for their own future.
9. Children express strong opposition to the decision to divorce.
10. Children experience increased anger, anxiety, guilt, depression, low self-esteem, low achievement, and/or negative behavior.

__. ____

____

LONG-TERM GOALS

1. Discuss plans to separate or divorce and the expected effects upon the family unit with the children in a calm, realistic, and truthful manner.
2. Develop an equitable plan for the financial support of all family members.
3. Work together to resolve issues concerning the children.
4. Stabilize living arrangements.

5, Establish consistent, positive child-management techniques and discipline.
6. Share the responsibility for the care, guidance, and emotional support of the children.

—. ____

____

SHORT-TERM OBJECTIVES

1. Describe the status of the current separation or divorce and indicate its effect on the child and family including daily routines, emotional stability, custody, visitation, and possible moves. (1, 2, 3)

2. Reassure the child about personal security express an awareness of and empathy for the child's fears and commit to maintain a close, loving relationship. (4, 5, 6)

THERAPEUTIC INTERVENTIONS

1. Meet with both parents jointly or separately, if necessary, to assess the current family situation and the effects of the separation or divorce on the child.
2. Ask the parents to detail immediate plans for the child including custody, visitation, or possible moves.
3. Assign the parents to read books that describe the effects of divorce on children (e.g., *Helping Children Cope with Divorce* by Teyber).
4. Assist the parents in establishing a time and method of telling the child about the plans to separate or divorce and instruct them to express an awareness of and empathy for the fearful feelings created by this action.
5. Assign the parents to shield the child from their personal arguments and to resist the temptation to use the child as a go-between in their disputes.
6. Instruct the parents that a loving, positive relationship with both parents is in the best interest of the child and

caution them against blaming one another or making derogatory comments about the other parent to the child.

3. List signs and symptoms of the child's emotional distress that will, if they occur, trigger a plan for addressing these problems. (7, 8)

7. Instruct the parents to watch for signs that the child is experiencing excessive sadness, anger, fear, or feelings of helplessness or hopelessness.

8. Advise the parents to schedule individual counseling for the child if the reaction to the divorce is creating serious mental health problems.

4. Express acceptance of the child's feelings and give guidance as to appropriate methods for feelings' expression. (9, 10, 11)

9. Use role play with the parents to teach them to respond to the child's feelings in a nurturing, supportive, non-defensive manner.

10. Discuss and role play with the parents the techniques of using "I" statements and active listening when discussing the divorce and family plans (see *Parent Effectiveness Training* by Gordon).

11. Assign the parents to read *How to Talk so Kids Will Listen and Listen so Kids Will Talk* (Faber and Mazlish) to develop skills for positive communication with the child.

5. List financial needs and resources and develop an equitable plan for meeting the basic requirements of all family members. (12, 13)

12. Assign the parents to create a list of all family assets and a corresponding list of family needs; assist the parents in determining how to allocate the assets to cover the basic needs of all the family members.

13. Solicit a verbal commitment from both parents to work together to provide financial support for their children until they reach adulthood.

6. Seek mediation if financial or other disputed divorce issues become difficult to resolve. (14, 15)

14. Assign the parents to seek information about divorce litigation and family mediation by accessing information from the Internet (e.g., National Mediation: www.nationalmediation.com, Divorce Resolutions: www.coloradodivorcemediation.com).

15. Instruct the parents to seek mediation if they are unable to reach an agreement about financial issues, custody, or visitation.

7. Verbalize a commitment to collaborate to resolve all problems and concerns involving the children. (16, 17)

16. Assist the parents in establishing custody and visitation arrangements that are conducive to the emotional stability of the children involved.

17. Encourage the co-parents to reassure the children about their personal security and to express an awareness of and empathy for their feelings in reaction to the changes occurring in the family structure.

8. Clearly state to the children that divorce is a parental decision not the result of any child-based activity. (18, 19)

18. Instruct the parents to reassure the child that separation and divorce is an adult decision that the child did not cause to happen (or to assign the "Divorce Is Not My Fault" activity from the *Parenting Skills Homework Planner* by Knapp).

19. Assign the parents to read *Divorce Is Not the End of the World* (Stern, Stern, and Stern) with their child to clarify that divorce is an adult decision.

9. Inform the child's school about the change in family status and request the staff's help in resolving school-related issues. (20, 21, 22)

20. Instruct the parents to inform the child's teacher or the school counselor about their plans to separate or divorce and ask to be informed of any signs of the child's distress and emotional reactions in the school setting.

21. Advise the parents to request that supportive services be given to the child at school (e.g., divorce group counseling, individual counseling, academic support, peer mentoring) to help with the adjustment to the family disruption.

22. Assist the parents in developing a post-separation plan for managing school-related issues.

10. Express awareness that divorce can create severe emotional disruption for children of all ages and that limiting volatility and change can help reduce distress. (23, 24)

23. Assign the parents to give appropriate consideration to the effects on the child before making plans for change involving custody, visitation, or possible moves.

24. Assign the parents to read *Children of Divorce: A Developmental Approach to Residence and Visitation* (Baris and Garrity) to gain an understanding of the challenges their children will face in adjusting to the new custody and visitation arrangements.

11. Establish safe and stable housing for the family. (25, 26)

25. Encourage the parents to limit change and volatility by allowing the children and the custodial parent to remain in the current housing arrangement, if it is financially feasible and suitable.

26. Assign the parents to assess their post-separation or divorce arrangements for housing and the neighborhood environment in terms of safety, stability, and suitability and determine if poor and unsafe living conditions are contributing to increased family volatility.

12. Seek information or professional guidance in the area of child management within the context of separation and/or divorce. (27)

27. Refer the parents to a child management class (e.g., *Becoming a Love and Logic Parent* by Fay, Cline, and Fay or *The Parent Talk System* by Moorman and Knapp); discuss the application of the techniques learned to their family situation.

13. Negotiate and agree upon strategies that each parent can utilize when disciplining the children. (28, 29)

28. Instruct the parents to continue to have reasonable expectations for their child's behavior and to discipline in a loving, compassionate, yet firm, manner, which holds the child accountable.

29. Instruct the parents to use a collaborative approach to the larger discipline issues by discussing the problem privately, sharing individual perspectives, brainstorming solutions, and determining an

approach that is acceptable to both parties.

14. Utilize techniques of positive discipline to address all child-behavior concerns. (30, 31, 32)

30. Teach the parents to offer frequent encouragement and descriptive praise when recognizing positive behavior and to use constructive feedback and guidance when behavior requires redirection.
31. Encourage the parents to prioritize the discipline issues of concern to the family and to address them one by one rather than trying resolve all the behavior problems at once.
32. Advise parents to remain intimately involved in the lives and activities of all of their children; explain that careful monitoring of the children's behavior, although not always appreciated, is an essential responsibility of both the custodial and the noncustodial parent.

15. Support each other in child-management issues and eliminate resistance, manipulation, and competition among children and between spouses. (33, 34, 35)

33. Advise the parents to avoid power struggles with the child by setting limits with controlled choices (e.g., "Would you rather clean your room on Saturday or Sunday?") and using contingency management strategies that make privileges dependent on responsible behavior (e.g., "You may watch television as soon as you homework is completed.")
34. Teach the parents the importance of reinforcing positive behavior from the child,

administering discipline in an even-handed and logical manner, and defusing manipulation and triangulation involving the child and the separated parents.

35. Encourage the parents to avoid "over-parenting" and to encourage independent functioning by determining who owns a problem and allowing the child to solve problems alone or with help and guidance, if necessary.

16. List and assign parenting roles and responsibilities for the post-divorce family. (36, 37)

36. Assist the parents in assigning parental roles so that all of the child's physical, financial, and emotional needs are covered (or have the parents complete the "Assuming Our Parental Responsibilities" activity from the *Parenting Skills Homework Planner* by Knapp).

37. Assign the parents to predict emerging needs of the child in the future and to commit to an ongoing relationship and personal involvement with the child that includes nurturing, guidance, discipline, and emotional and financial support.

DIAGNOSTIC SUGGESTIONS:

ICD-9-CM	*ICD-10-CM*	*DSM-5* Disorder, Condition, or Problem
309.24	F43.22	Adjustment Disorder, With Anxiety
309.0	F43.21	Adjustment Disorder, With Depressed Mood
309.21	F93.0	Separation Anxiety Disorder
______	______	______________________
______	______	______________________

EATING DISORDER

BEHAVIORAL DEFINITIONS

1. Rapid consumption of large quantities of food in a short time followed by self-induced vomiting and/or the use of laxatives due to the fear of weight gain.
2. Extreme weight loss (and amenorrhea in females) with refusal to maintain a minimal healthy weight due to very limited ingestion of food and high frequency of secretive, self-induced vomiting, inappropriate use of laxatives, and/or excessive strenuous exercise.
3. Child is overly influenced by media and cultural perceptions about physical attractiveness, success, and male and female roles.
4. Child places overemphasis on outer physical qualities above inner, personal character and strengths.
5. Child's focus is on excessive dieting and exercise as a means to physical attractiveness, happiness, and success.
6. Child's distorted and unrealistic perceptions about food, body image, weight, and body size contribute to dysfunctional eating habits and exercise regime.
7. Child experiences low self-esteem, feelings of inadequacy, lack of control, depression, anxiety, anger, and/or loneliness.
8. Child's eating habits and the resulting damaging physical, psychological, and social effects become the focus of the family's concern.
9. Fear, anxiety, and family trauma result from an inability to alter the child's self-destructive behavior.
10. Volatile family environment and stressful, highly demanding family relationships.

__. ____

____

LONG-TERM GOALS

1. Seek psychological treatment for the child with an eating disorder.
2. Model positive, healthy attitudes about body image, eating habits, and exercise.
3. Resist detrimental cultural and media emphasis on idealized physical attractiveness and unrealistic male and female roles and relationships.
4. Support the child in long-term efforts to overcome the eating disorder.
5. Open the lines of communication and develop supportive, empathetic family relationships.

__. ____

____

SHORT-TERM OBJECTIVES

1. Review the family history and determine the current status of the child's eating disorder and its effects on the child and the family. (1, 2)
2. Arrange for a complete medical, dental, and psychological exam for the child by licensed health professionals. (3, 4, 5)

THERAPEUTIC INTERVENTIONS

1. Meet with the parents and the child, if appropriate, to review the family history and to determine the social, emotional, and cultural environment in which the eating disorder developed.
2. Define an eating disorder as a real and treatable disease and ask the parents and the child to list the existing symptoms, describe the severity of the disorder, and indicate the effects on the child and family.
3. Instruct the parents to schedule a complete medical and dental examination for the child to determine the physical effects of the eating disorder and to accompany the child to the appointments.
4. Assign the parents to schedule a complete psychological evaluation for the child by a

recommended hospital, clinic, or private therapist specializing in the area of eating disorders.

5. Refer the parents to local resources for treatment or assist them in locating treatment by accessing local treatment centers through a referral helpline (e.g., National Eating Disorders Association Information and Referral Helpline; (800) 931-2237 or the "Referral" area of their Web site, www.NationalEatingDisorders.org).

3. Communicate regularly with the child's treatment team and assist the child to implement all treatment recommendations. (6, 7)

6. Instruct the parents to interview potential treatment providers and ask questions relevant to their treatment approach (e.g., treatment experience, field of expertise, treatment methods, length of treatment).

7. Assign the parents to attend regularly scheduled appointments with the child's treatment team and to record all recommended treatment interventions in a treatment journal.

4. Arrange for the child to receive the recommended treatment and level of care for the eating disorder. (8, 9)

8. Assist the parents in becoming familiar with and accessing the level of care recommended for the child's eating disorder depending on the critical nature of the illness (e.g., inpatient, residential, partial hospital, outpatient).

9. Instruct the parents to evaluate their ability to pay for the child's treatment by

determining insurance coverage, applying for state assistance through Medicaid or Medicare, seeking treatment from local mental health clinics or medical schools, and/or by seeking information from a patient advocacy group (e.g., Patient Advocate Foundation, (800) 532-5274; www.patientadvocate.org).

5. Examine and list the family attitudes, values, and expectations that may be contributing to the child's eating disorder. (10, 11)

10. Assign the parents to list all personal and family attitudes and values that could be contributing to the child's eating disorder (e.g., thin equals attractive or successful, overweight equals lazy and lacking control).

11. Challenge the parents to create a list of values and expectations that promote character and self-esteem based on inner qualities (or assign the "Beautiful on the Inside" activity from the *Parenting Skills Homework Planner* by Knapp).

6. Identify and affirm the many character strengths of the child and other family members. (12, 13)

12. Council the parents to recognize and affirm the child's unique contribution to the family and community (e.g., "Jimmy is dependable and does many chores without being asked; Rose follows through with her commitments.") to help the child value internal character assets.

13. Encourage the parents to celebrate the character accomplishments of each family member with a family

outing or recognition at the weekly family meeting.

7. Help the child change perceptions about body image through affirmations and reinforcement of healthy behaviors and positive self-talk. (14, 15)

14. Assign the parents to brainstorm with their child a list of personal assets unrelated to body image and encourage the child to use the positive assets as self-talk to replace negative self-statements.
15. Instruct the parents to encourage the child's behavior that supports a healthy perception of body image and promotes self-acceptance (e.g., eliminate chronic weighing, less time spent in front of mirrors, wear comfortable clothes).

8. Become educated about eating disorders by reading information from professional organizations, recommended books, and by talking with treatment professionals. (16, 17)

16. Assign the parents to read literature that defines eating disorders and offers treatment options and strategies for children and their families (e.g., *Surviving an Eating Disorder* by Siegel, Brisman, and Weinshel).
17. Assign the parents to participate in local support groups for families of children with eating disorders sponsored by hospitals, clinics, or the community mental health organization.

9. Talk with the child about the dysfunctional eating behavior, perceptions, and expectations of self, and how the disorder is affecting the quality of life. (18, 19)

18. Instruct the parents to discuss the eating disorder with the child privately in a nonjudgmental manner and to use the communication tools suggested in *How to Talk so Kids Will Listen and Listen so Kids Will Talk* (Faber and Mazlish).

19. Instruct the parents to discuss critical areas of concern and conflict with the child's therapist rather than being drawn into an argument or power struggle with the child.

10. Engage in family activities that promote a healthy level of eating, exercise, and socialization. (20, 21)

20. Assign the parents to organize and attend, with the child, activities and outings that promote a healthy level of exercise and encourage nutritious eating habits in a social setting.

21. Instruct the parents to schedule regular family meals when the whole family sits down at the table and eats together in a stress-free environment free of television, video, phone calls, and other media interruption.

11. Assess personal values regarding diet and exercise and verbalize a commitment to modeling a positive, healthy attitude and behavior toward body size and image. (22, 23)

22. Assign the parents to record their personal eating habits and comments about weight and body image in a personal journal (or assign the "Modeling Healthy Attitudes about Nutrition, Exercise, and Body Image" activity from the *Parenting Skills Homework Planner* by Knapp).

23. Instruct the parents to read "No Weigh! A Declaration of Independence from a Weight-Obsessed World" from the National Eating Disorders Association (www.nationaleatingdisorders.org/p.asp or phone (206) 382.3587) with their child and pledge to adhere to the proposals to accept their

body's natural shape and size by signing the declaration.

12. Verbalize appreciation for the individual physical attributes of all family members. (24, 25)

24. Brainstorm with the parents a list of positive physical attributes for each family member (e.g., "Arnold has lots of energy, Carla has a winning smile.") and instruct them to verbalize these assets frequently to express an appreciation of the family's diverse physical characteristics.

25. Instruct the parents to devote weekly time for each family member to count their physical blessings and express appreciation and thanks for their own body and how it supports their activities and lifestyle.

13. Verbalize an objective assessment of how the media and other cultural influences have affected the perceptions of the child and other family members regarding the ideal body. (26, 27)

26. Assign the parents to watch television programs and videos with their child to gain an understanding of how the media is distorting the child's view of what is culturally appropriate, desirable, and acceptable.

27. Instruct the parents to talk with their child about how the media influences their lives by presenting abnormally thin, overly energetic, unusually beautiful and highly sexualized models as culturally normal and to encourage their child to select role models from people in their everyday life.

14. Reduce the level of family exposure to television and videos, movies, the Internet, and magazines and assist the child in

28. Instruct the parents to limit family television and video time to one to two hours per day and to encourage other worthwhile activities as a

becoming a discriminating consumer of all media. (28, 29)

substitute that promote self-acceptance and physical affirmation.

29. Assign the parents to monitor the child's exposure to fashion information and Web sites that promote excessive thinness and instructions for extreme dieting, exercise, and bulimic behavior.

15. Implement positive discipline strategies that share control and empower the child to function responsibly and independently. (30, 31, 32)

30. Teach the parents to avoid taking responsibility for solving the child's eating disorder problems by providing empathetic listening rather than rushing to give advice.

31. Instruct the parents to set reasonable limits for the child by using statements that make the child's desired privileges contingent upon the child's appropriate behavior and responsible decisions (e.g., "Feel free to use the computer as soon as we've all finished dinner; We can go shopping as soon as you've helped me plan the meals for next week.").

32. Assist the parents in developing limited choices to share control and facilitate responsible decision making by their child; advise them that choices should be framed so that either option is acceptable to them (e.g., "Would you like to have meat and potatoes or fish and rice for dinner?"), should be limited to specific stated alternatives (e.g., "Would you

like to eat in the kitchen or at the dining room table tonight?"), and the parent should be prepared to choose if the child refuses to choose.

16. Affirm the child for each step taken toward establishing healthy self-esteem, body image, and lifestyle. (33, 34)

33. Instruct the parents to verbally affirm the child for each positive step taken to control the eating disorder, to establish a healthy lifestyle, and to develop an attitude of self-acceptance.

34. Assist the parents in understanding that treatment of an eating disorder is usually a long-term process that requires the support and cooperation of all family members, however the major responsibility for overcoming the disorder and establishing a healthy lifestyle rests with the child.

—. ____________________
____

—. ____________________
____

DIAGNOSTIC SUGGESTIONS:

ICD-9-CM	*ICD-10-CM*	*DSM-5* Disorder, Condition, or Problem
307.1	F50.02	Anorexia Nervosa, Binge-Eating/Purging Type
307.1	F50.01	Anorexia Nervosa, Restricting Type
307.51	F50.2	Bulimia Nervosa
307.50	F50.9	Unspecified Feeding or Eating Disorder
309.28	F43.23	Adjustment Disorder, With Mixed Anxiety and Depressed Mood
309.21	F93.0	Separation Anxiety Disorder
________	________	____________________
________	________	____________________

GIFTED/TALENTED

BEHAVIORAL DEFINITIONS

1. Child in the family is precocious in one or several areas of learning and displays advanced vocabulary and/or reasoning skills when compared to same-age peers.
2. Child has a strong desire to learn in areas of interest and prefers challenges and complex tasks to basic or mundane work.
3. Child displays uneven cognitive development with high ability and maturity in some areas and delayed ability or lack of maturity in others.
4. Child is granted inappropriate adult status and authority in the family, which is perceived as inappropriate by others.
5. Tendency to overestimate the child's social-emotional maturity and assume a level of sophisticated functioning that robs the child of normal childhood development.
6. Lack of positive discipline strategies to set limits and develop independent functioning in the gifted/talented child.
7. A divided parental approach to the gifted/talented child allows manipulation and triangulation of the parents to diffuse discipline and sabotage the parent/child relationship.
8. Conflict with the child's teachers over the best educational strategies to encourage the child's optimal achievement.
9. Opinions and expectations expressed or modeled about work, achievement, and lifelong learning provide poor examples for the gifted/talented child to emulate.

—. ____

____

—. ____

____

LONG-TERM GOALS

1. Model and express opinions and expectations that give the child a positive message about work, academic excellence, and the value of achievement and lifelong learning.
2. Support and cooperate with the child's other parent to provide a united front when dealing with behaviors, demands, and social, emotional, and academic needs.
3. Implement techniques of positive discipline that set limits, enhance self-esteem, and promote independent functioning in the gifted/talented child.
4. Maintain an adult leadership position in the family and grant the child age-appropriate responsibilities and privileges.
5. Teach the child work and study skills that enhance academic success, and promote behavioral and social responsibility.
6. Cooperate with the school to develop academic strategies that encourage the gifted/talented child to develop full potential.

__. ____

____

__. ____

____

SHORT-TERM OBJECTIVES

1. Demonstrate a positive work ethic by making positive comments to the child regarding employment, training, and education.(1, 2)

THERAPEUTIC INTERVENTIONS

1. Assign the parents to communicate a positive attitude about their personal employment by making positive work-related comments directly to their child and during family discussions.
2. Assign the parents to participate in a "Take Your Child to Work Day" or job-shadowing opportunity and to actively engage their gifted/talented child in the experience by helping to create a product, wear a uniform, or

become involved in an actual work process.

2. Discuss with the child how education, planning, and training have contributed to the personal success of various family members. (3, 4, 5)

3. Instruct the parents to enlist their children's help in creating an educational family history that lists the education and career paths of various nuclear and extended family members (or complete the "Career Family Tree" activity from the *Parenting Skills Homework Planner* by Knapp).

4. Instruct the parents to model positive and enthusiastic work habits for the gifted/talented child (e.g., preparing ahead for the workday, limiting sick days).

5. Encourage the parents to relate personal stories and work experiences that will positively shape their child's attitude toward future educational and career decisions.

3. Back up the co-parent in issues of discipline and behavior management. (6, 7)

6. Advise the parents to form a cooperative alliance when addressing child management issues and instruct them to support each other on all discipline decisions.

7. Instruct the parents to discuss child management differences privately away from the child and come to an agreement that both can support.

4. Support the co-parent by emphasizing the co-parent's strengths and positive characteristics to the child. (8, 9)

8. Advise the parents of the child's need to model positive qualities from both parents and instruct them to speak positively and enthusiastically

about the strengths and abilities of their spouse.

9. Instruct separated or divorced parents to point out the positive qualities of their former spouse and/or to avoid disparaging comments that will interfere with the parent/child relationship.

5. Assign age and ability appropriate tasks and responsibilities to the child. (10, 11)

10. Instruct the parents to assign age and ability appropriate tasks and chores to the child at home and to use these assignments to teach the values of quality effort and timely job completion.

11. Assign the parents to use chores and tasks to teach responsibility to the child using the four-step process described in *Parenting with Love and Logic* (Cline and Fay) (or assign the "Teaching Responsibility" activity from the *Parenting Skills Homework Planner* by Knapp).

6. Use controlled choices to set limits for the gifted/talented child. (12, 13)

12. Instruct the parents to build the child's decision-making skills by offering many controlled choices (e.g., wear the red shirt or the green shirt, complete homework before or after dinner).

13. Advise the parents to control the child's choices according to the child's age and ability (e.g., small choices for younger children: cheese or peanut butter, larger choices for older children; learn Spanish or French, piano or violin).

7. Encourage the gifted/talented child through low-key affirmations and discussions that foster self-awareness. (14, 15)

14. Instruct the parents to watch for behavior that emulates positive character, high standards and diligence and to affirm the child privately or in the presence of other family members.

15. Instruct the parents to help the child to develop self-awareness through discussions of feelings, special interests, and abilities or to participate with the child in an Internet survey that helps assess personal traits and values (e.g., Making Choices for Life, http://library.thinkquest.org/J001709, Dealing with Feelings, http://www.kidshealth.org/kid/feeling/).

8. Attend a parenting class and read literature to learn positive parenting techniques that set limits and encourage healthy independence. (16, 17, 18)

16. Refer the parents to a class that focuses on helping children develop self-confidence and responsible behavior (e.g., *Systematic Training for Effective Parenting (STEP)* by Dinkmeyer and McKay or *The Parent Talk System* by Moorman and Knapp).

17. Assign the parents to read literature describing effective parenting techniques for gifted and talented children (e.g., *How to Parent so Children Will Learn* by Rimm).

18. Refer the parents to a support group addressing under-achievement, academic motivation, or giftedness in children (e.g., *Council for*

Exceptional Children (703) 620-3660) [www.cec.sped.org]).

9. Use logical and natural consequences to promote cooperative behavior. (19, 20)

19. Teach the parents the role that natural and logical consequences play in fostering independence and character development in their gifted/talented child (e.g., the establishment of: cause and effect thinking, responsible decision making, problem ownership, self-reliant behavior).

20. Advise the parents that empathy and compassion when combined with a logical consequence (e.g., "You spilled the milk, that's too bad. Please get a cloth and clean it up.") is significantly more powerful and effective than anger combined with punishment (e.g., "You spilled the milk. What a mess! Go to your room, now!").

10. Allow the child to make decisions and earn privileges based on competence and demonstrated level of maturity. (21, 22)

21. Assign the parents to promote responsible decision making by asking the child to make the decision when an issue is noncritical and age-appropriate and to decide within the limitations and guidance provided by the parents for more important issues.

22. Instruct the parents to grant privileges based on the child's demonstrated level of competence and responsibility (e.g., move from high chair to table after child can sit without

throwing food, child crosses street alone after mastering safety rules).

11. Avoid power struggles by clearly designing expectations and setting enforceable limits. (23, 24)

23. Advise parents to avoid power struggles with the child by expressing clearly defined expectations and using contingency management strategies that make privileges dependent upon compliance (e.g., "You may watch television as soon as you homework is completed.").

24. Assign the parents to brainstorm with their child the personal qualities required to work cooperatively with others (e.g., speaking and listening, problem solving, acceptance) and to list opportunities for developing and practicing these skills at home and in school.

12. Encourage positive adult and peer role models. (25, 26)

25. Instruct the parents to communicate with adult role models selected by the child (e.g., coach music teacher, family friend, or family member), advise them of their influence, and request that they keep their message positive and supportive.

26. Assign the parents to diffuse the negative influence of peer role models by explaining to the child that popularity is overrated during the school years and that true friendship based on shared interest, support, and mutual enjoyment lasts well beyond senior high school.

13. Set up predictable procedures for meals, bedtime, the morning routine, and study time. (27, 28)

27. Instruct the parents to establish family procedures for meals, bedtime, and the morning routine so that the child is held accountable for being prepared (or assign the "Procedures for Meals, Bedtime, and the Morning Routine" activity from the *Parenting Skills Homework Planner* by Knapp).

28. Assign the parents to assist their child in developing study skills procedures that designate the time and place for schoolwork, duration of the study time, methods of checking the work, and parental involvement.

14. Teach the child study skills, test preparation, planning for projects, and creative techniques to promote academic success. (29, 30)

29. Encourage the parents to teach the child study habits that will enhance success in school and college (e.g., record assignments in a planner, break large projects into smaller study segments, allow for additional study time).

30. Assign the parents to monitor their children's school attendance, punctuality, and academic achievement, to recognize progress and achievement in these areas and to offer guidance, encouragement, and discipline where necessary.

15. Utilize family trips, outings, and activities to promote the joy of discovery and learning. (31, 32)

31. Assign the parents to take several actual or virtual (using books or video) parent-child field trips to explore community, national, or

worldwide historical sites and points of interest.

32. Assign the parents to expose their children to multilingual diversity by learning a foreign language as a family project and to utilize this second language during trips to multilingual destinations.

16. Meet with the child's teacher and/or other educational staff to develop a plan for effectively challenging and motivating the gifted/talented child to achieve. (33, 34)

33. Advise the parents to consult the school regarding aptitude and interest tests available to their children at various grade levels.

34. Encourage the parents to emphasize the crucial connection between school performance and future success in their child's career choices by detailing how specific curriculum is used in the workplace (e.g., math facilitates money management, reading facilitates awareness of work-related directives; writing facilitates communication with others).

17. Encourage the child to participate in a well-balanced academic, social, and extracurricular program. (35, 36, 37)

35. Instruct the parents to discuss progress reports, grade cards, conference input, and the results of tests and evaluations with the child immediately to keep the child informed, understand the child's perspective, and to emphasize the family's focus upon quality education.

36. Assign the parents to engage the child in at least one extracurricular activity that supports and promotes the child's special interest or ability.

37. Encourage the parents to focus upon the individual interests and abilities of the child and to emphasize personal best achievement rather than competition to prevent sibling and peer rivalry.

18. Set post-graduate educational, career, and lifestyle expectations for the gifted/talented child. (38, 39)

38. Encourage the parents and the child to begin a journal or portfolio for the child that details important demographic and personal data (e.g., early childhood information, health history, school information).

39. Ask the parents to work with the child to create an ongoing list of future goals and aspirations to be entered in the child's academic and career journal.

__. ____________________

__. ____________________

__. ____________________

__. ____________________

__. ____________________

__. ____________________

DIAGNOSTIC SUGGESTIONS:

ICD-9-CM	*ICD-10-CM*	*DSM-5* Disorder, Condition, or Problem
309.24	F43.22	Adjustment Disorder, With Anxiety
309.0	F43.21	Adjustment disorder, With Depressed Mood
313.81	F91.3	Oppositional Defiant Disorder
V61.20	Z62.820	Parent-Child Relational Problem
______	______	____________________
______	______	____________________

GRANDPARENTING STRATEGIES

BEHAVIORAL DEFINITIONS

1. Grandparents are overly involved, offer unwanted advice, and try to impose opinions and values on the adult children and grandchildren.
2. Grandparents lack involvement with the grandchildren and fail to establish a loving bond.
3. Grandparents live a long distance from adult children and grandchildren and interact irregularly.
4. Grandparents override parental authority and sabotage their adult child's efforts to parent the grandchildren.
5. Grandparents spoil the grandchildren with excessive money, gifts, and favors.
6. Grandparents lack discipline skills and fail to set limits for the grandchildren.
7. Grandparents interfere with the marital relationships of their adult children.
8. Grandparents side with the grandchildren in conflicts with their parents.
9. Grandparents are in conflict with the adult children, which restricts or prevents a loving relationship with the grandchildren.
10. Parents make unreasonable demands of the grandparents for childcare, money, and other resources for the grandchildren.

—. ____

____

LONG-TERM GOALS

1. Develop a close personal and loving relationship with the grandchildren and their parents.

2. Support the adult children's efforts to parent responsibly.
3. Offer reasonable financial support, guidance, and personal assistance when needed by the adult children or grandchildren.
4. Resist impulse to overindulge adult children or grandchildren with gifts.
5. Promote independence and responsible behavior in the grandchildren and their parents.
6. Maintain appropriate personal boundaries and parameters for involvement with the grandchildren and their parents.

__. ____
____

SHORT-TERM OBJECTIVES

1. Provide encouragement and support to the parents when the grandchild is born. (1, 2)
2. Interact with the grandchild on a regular basis. (3, 4)

THERAPEUTIC INTERVENTIONS

1. Advise the grandparents of the importance of providing celebratory support during and after each grandchild's birth, according to the parent's wishes (e.g., hospital visits, respite care, phone calls).
2. Instruct the grandparents to participate in the grandchild's birth celebration according to family and cultural customs (e.g., bringing gifts, preparing food, attending the baptism or other birth ritual).
3. Instruct the grandparents to bond with their grandchildren through interactive activities and projects (e.g., reading, playing with games or toys, outdoor activities).
4. Assign the grandparents to plan a mystery trip (e.g., apple orchard, hay ride, nature walk) for their grandchildren to encourage bonding and to build mutual memories.

3. Show interest in the grandchildren and their achievements through attending their special activities and discussing their interests with them. (5, 6)

5. Encourage the grandparents to attend sports events, school presentations, recitals and special events to support and acknowledge their grandchildren's participation.

6. Instruct the grandparents to demonstrate an interest in their grandchild's achievement by discussing school and activity performance and affirming progress shown.

4. Share family history, personal experiences, and values with the grandchildren. (7, 8)

7. Advise the grandparents to share with the grandchildren their knowledge of personal, family, and cultural history.

8. Instruct the grandparents to model personal values by demonstrating ethical behavior in the presence of the grandchildren and by relating stories and examples of values portrayed by other family members.

5. Implement strategies for establishing and maintaining a loving, long-distance relationship with the grandchildren. (9, 10)

9. Assign the grandparents to build a relationship with grandchildren who live far away by using the mail and technology to keep in touch.

10. Assign the grandparents to arrange for regularly scheduled visits with distant grandchildren in their own home, in the grandchildren's home, and/or by meeting at a halfway location.

6. Discuss and explore parenting concepts and strategies with the grandchild's parents. (11, 12, 13)

11. Instruct the grandparents to attend a parenting class with their adult children (e.g., *Becoming a Love and Logic*

Parent by Fay, Cline, and Fay) and to discuss opportunities for applying the strategies with the grandchildren.

12. Encourage the grandparents to read parenting books and literature endorsed by their adult children (e.g., *Kids are Worth It!* by Coloroso) to encourage development of effective strategies for relating to the grandchildren.

13. Advise the grandparents to seek an understanding of their adult children's parenting philosophy and to implement the parents' child-management strategies that are healthy and productive when caring for the grandchildren.

7. Verbally affirm the adult children's efforts to parent responsibly. (14, 15, 16)

14. Instruct the grandparents to verbally affirm their adult children's efforts to parent responsibly.

15. Assign the grandparents to support their adult children by pointing out their strengths and efforts during conversations with the grandchildren (e.g., "Your mom sure does love you"; "Your dad spends a lot of time supporting your interest in tennis.").

16. Instruct the grandparents to discuss child management differences with their adult children privately, come to an agreement that both can support, and then form a united front when dealing with the grandchildren.

8. Verbally reinforce the adult children for responsibly managing their family's financial, social, and emotional needs. (17, 18)

17. Instruct the grandparents to encourage their adult children to manage their family finances responsibly by showing empathy and concern when there is a problem but refusing to rescue them by solving the problem for them.

18. Assign the grandparents to use a problem solving process with adult children and grandchildren when their assistance is requested (e.g., listen with compassion, brainstorm ideas for solution, examine the pros and cons of each strategy, let them decide how and when to solve the problem).

9. Agree to offer child-care based on available time, energy, and interest. (19, 20)

19. Inform the grandparents that child care provided on a regular bases should be offered based on their ability and willingness to give of their personal time and energy and should be set up by establishing a specific written or verbal agreement with their adult children.

20. Advise the grandparents to enter into extended child-care situations cautiously and assist them to list the potential positive and negative aspects before agreeing to long-term or permanent child-care.

10. Offer assistance to the adult children and grandchildren in times of personal and family trauma. (21, 22, 23)

21. Instruct the grandparents to support their adult children and grandchildren during times of emotional upheaval and trauma (e.g., loss of a job, eviction, divorce) by actively listening to their distress and

offering empathy and a willingness to help.

22. Advise the grandparents against taking sides or speaking critically about the parents to their grandchildren during a divorce or custody battle and to offer assurance that their grandparents' love will always remain constant.

23. Assign the grandparents to prepare for helping the grandchildren deal with personal and family trauma by reading *Parenting with Wit and Wisdom in Times of Chaos and Loss* (Coloroso).

11. Extend financial assistance, housing and other resources according to personal ability to provide and the nature of the adult child and grandchildren's needs. (24, 25)

24. Advise the grandparents to offer specific help when their adult child's family is in crisis (e.g., "I can buy the groceries for six weeks; I can watch the kids every other weekend; you can live with us for six months.").

25. Assign the grandparents to research information about extending their grandparenting roles by contacting relevant organizations (e.g., AARP Grandparent Information Center: (800) 424-3410 or www.aarp.org/confacts/programs/gic.html, The Foundation for Grandparenting: www.grandparenting.org).

12. Prevent the development of entitlement attitudes from the adult children or grandchildren by moderating gift giving and indulgences. (26, 27)

26. Instruct the grandparents to limit excessive gift giving and favors to the grandchildren by giving smaller, lower priced presents,

and giving gifts of time, attention, and love rather than material presents.

27. Advise the grandparents to consult with their adult children regarding appropriate gifts, favors, and contributions to the grandchildren that will be truly appreciated.

13. Set limits and establish household rules for the grandchildren when they visit. (28, 29, 30)

28. Assign the grandparents to establish a set of household rules and procedures and to communicate these to the adult children and the grandchildren before they visit.

29. Advise the grandparents to specifically state their rules in advance to avoid confusion (or assign the "Parents' Rules vs. Grandparents' Rules" activity from the *Parenting Skills Homework Planner* by Knapp).

30. Instruct the grandparents to grant privileges based on the child's demonstrated level of competence and responsibility (e.g., child crosses street alone after mastering safety rules, child allowed to play with fragile doll collection after exhibiting cautious behavior).

14. Implement strategies of positive discipline that encourage independence and responsible behavior from the grandchildren. (31, 32, 33, 34)

31. Assign the grandparents to teach responsible behavior to their grandchildren by implementing the "Four Steps to Responsibility" outlined by Cline and Fay in *Grandparenting with Love and Logic* (e.g., (1) Give the child a chance to act responsibly, (2) wait for a mistake to create a learning opportunity, (3) use a

consequence to teach a more appropriate behavior, (4) allow the child the same opportunity to act responsibly as soon as possible).

32. Advise grandparents to avoid power struggles with their grandchildren by expressing clearly defined expectations and using contingency management strategies that make privileges dependent upon compliance (e.g., "Feel free to use the computer after you've helped me with the dishes.").

33. Advise the grandparents that empathy and compassion when combined with a logical consequence (e.g., "You spilled the milk, that's too bad. Please get a cloth and clean it up.") is significantly more powerful and effective than anger combined with punishment (e.g., "You spilled the milk. Go to your room, now!").

34. Instruct the grandparents to build their grandchildren's decision-making skills and sense of responsibility by offering them many controlled choices whenever they visit (e.g., "Join me for a ball game or a movie.").

15. List personal boundaries and parameters for involvement with the grandchildren and verbally express them to their parents. (35, 36)

35. Assign the grandparents to create a list of personal expectations for their involvement with the grandchildren (or assign the "Personal Boundaries for Interaction with the Grandchildren" activity

from the *Parenting Skills Homework Planner* by Knapp).

36. Instruct the grandparents to use "I" or "we" statements when informing the grandchildren or their parents of a personal boundary (e.g., "I can let you borrow the car for two hours, after that I need to run errand; We can take the kids on Sunday but on Saturday we're working on the house.").

16. Remain assertive, proactive, and compassionate when discussing issues of concern or controversy with the adult children and the grandchildren. (37, 38)

37. Advise the grandparents to discuss controversial issues openly with their adult children and to brainstorm for solutions that are acceptable to both parties.

38. Assign the grandparents to engage in active listening without giving advice or becoming antagonistic when an adult child or grandchild expresses a problem or concern.

__. ____________________________

__. ____________________________

DIAGNOSTIC SUGGESTIONS

ICD-9-CM	*ICD-10-CM*	*DSM-5* Disorder, Condition, or Problem
309.28	F43.23	Adjustment Disorder, With Mixed Anxiety and Depressed Mood
300.02	F41.1	Generalized Anxiety Disorder
V61.20	Z62.820	Parent-Child Relational Problem
________	________	____________________
________	________	____________________

GRIEF/LOSS

BEHAVIORAL DEFINITIONS

1. Experience profound grief resulting from the loss of a significant relationship due to death, physical separation, divorce, or emotional abandonment.
2. Feel shock, deep loss, and vulnerability.
3. Lack emotional energy to assume parental responsibilities, work activities, and daily routine.
4. Exhibit mood swings, weariness, depression, and a tendency to withdraw that interfere with normal family functioning.
5. Overwhelming emotional reactions are triggered by internal memories or external reminders of the lost relationship.
6. Feel an overriding personal grief and loss, which prevents an awareness of and an empathetic response to the child's grief.
7. Report difficulty explaining the loss and communicating deep feelings of grief to the child.
8. Child experiences feelings of isolation, confusion, and fear.
9. Child expresses grief through impulsivity, acting out, self-defeating, regressive, or compulsive behavior.
10. Family members move through the stages of grief from shock, intense pain, deep sorrow, to sadness mixed with acceptance and peace at different paces.

__. ____

____

__. ____

____

__. ____

____

LONG-TERM GOALS

1. Identify own feelings of profound grief and loss and communicate them at the child's level of understanding.
2. Work together as a family to gradually accept the loss of the significant relationship.
3. Resume participation in routine family, work, and social activities.
4. Assist the child in moving through the stages of grief and in gaining a sense of self-control over inappropriate or self-defeating expressions of loss.
5. Reassure the child of continued love, care, and support from the family.
6. Develop feelings of optimism toward the future and begin to invest in new relationships.

—. ____

____

—. ____

____

—. ____

____

SHORT-TERM OBJECTIVES

1. Express personal feelings related to the loss and identify appropriate methods for coping with these feelings and sharing them with the children. (1, 2)

THERAPEUTIC INTERVENTIONS

1. Assign the family members to write a letter to the lost loved one expressing personal feelings, questions, fears and perceptions about the loss.
2. Instruct the parents to encourage the child to draw pictures, write songs or poems, play music, or use sculpting or sand play to describe reactions to the loss and to share these artistic expressions with the parents and the counselor.

2. List and implement behavioral techniques for coping with strong grief feelings. (3, 4)

3. Assist the parents in devising a plan for managing strong grief reactions during the week (e.g.,

talk with a friend or family member, draw a picture, write in a journal, take 10 deep breaths.

4. Assist the parents in developing a personalized working definition of grief and to recognize that typical waves of grief that can overwhelm temporarily, but also diminish over time.

3. Verbally acknowledge the children's feelings of grief and loss and encourage an ongoing interchange of feelings. (5, 6)

5. Assign the parents to assist their children to monitor their reactions to the loss through drawings or journal entries (or assign the "Monitoring our Reactions to Change and Loss" activity from the *Parenting Skills Homework Planner* by Knapp).

6. Assign parents to read *How to Talk so Kids Will Listen and Listen so Kids Will Talk* (Faber and Mazlish) to develop additional active and empathetic communication skills with their children.

4. Verbalize an understanding that grieving and adjusting to a loss takes time and effort for both adults and children. (7, 8)

8. Outline for the parents the stages of working through grief (e.g., shock and denial, anger, accepting the loss, experiencing the pain, adjusting to the change, investing in an altered life pattern) and assign them to work with the child to determine which stage is currently being experienced and plan for stages yet to come.

8. Assign the parents to watch *The Secret Garden* (Playhouse

Video) or the *Lion King* (Walt Disney Home Entertainment) with their children and discuss the stages of grief experienced by the characters after the loss or death of loved ones.

5. Gather information about grieving and/or join a grief support group. (9, 10)

9. Refer the parents to a grief support group offered by local hospitals, hospice, religious groups, or community agencies.

10. Assign the parents to gather information about family and personal grieving by reading literature (e.g., *Parenting with Wit and Wisdom in Times of Chaos and Loss* by Coloroso) or by accessing information from the Internet (e.g., Children's Grief and Loss Issues: www.childrens grief.net).

6. Identify sources of comfort within the extended family, school, work environment, and community. (11, 12)

11. Assign the parents to acknowledge their personal support system by identifying several supportive and caring gestures from family, fellow workers, the child's school, and friends (or assign the "Grief and Loss Circle of Support" activity from the *Parenting Skills Homework Planner* by Knapp).

12. Instruct the parents to meet with the child's teacher or school counselor to discuss the effects of the loss on the family and the ramifications on the child.

7. Meet with clergy to discuss the spiritual perspective of death and/or loss. (13, 14)

13. Instruct the parents to arrange a meeting for the child and/or the entire family with a rabbi,

priest, or youth minister to discuss the loss from a spiritual perspective and to receive guidance and support.

14. Assign the parents to encourage the child to join a grief and loss support group sponsored by the family's place of worship.

8. Verbalize an understanding of the child's grieving and reactions to the loss from a developmental perspective. (15, 16)

15. Assign the parents to read *Explaining Death to Children* (Grollman) and *The Way Children Grieve* (Bissler) to gain insight on the effects of grief on children.

16. Assign the parents to read the *Developmental Considerations Concerning Children's Grief* (Metzgar) and discuss the child's reactions to grief and loss from a developmental perspective.

9. Children and the parents describe their emotional and behavioral grief symptoms. (17, 18)

17. Describe to the parents the common reactions to grief and loss (e.g., shock, anger, guilt, shame, lack of focus, behavioral changes, mood swings, regression, and preoccupation); ask the parents to add any symptoms personally experienced or observed in their children.

18. Assign the parents to play "The Talking, Feeling and Doing Game" (Gardner, Western Psychological Services) or "The Ungame" (Taicor Inc.) with their children to help each family member identify and express feelings related to the death or loss.

10. Plan and implement coping strategies for anniversaries, holidays, or other periods of heightened grief. (19, 20)

19. Brainstorm with the parents ideas for facing holidays, birthdays, and the anniversary of the loss (e.g., plan an activity with the family, share fond memories with one another, visit the cemetery, and talk to the lost loved one).

20. Assign the parents to involve the child in planning a memorial devoted to special memories, stories, and experiences involving the lost loved one on the anniversary of the loss, birthday, or holiday.

11. Implement strategies focused on offering comfort and support to the grieving child. (21, 22)

21. Instruct the parents to implement strategies to assist the child in dealing with grief (e.g., be open and tell the truth, don't hesitate to express own grief, reassure that the death or loss was not the child's fault).

22. Encourage parents to read books or watch video's with the child about grief and loss (e.g., *The Fall of Freddie the Leaf* by Buscaglia, *Don't Despair on Thursdays* by Moser) and to discuss the thoughts and emotions triggered by the stories.

12. Facilitate the child's entry into individual counseling if the grief reaction is severe or prolonged. (23, 24)

23. Assign the parents to keep a daily journal of the child's grief reactions; discuss them during subsequent counseling sessions, being alert for signs of a severe or prolonged grief process.

24. Instruct the parents to watch for prolonged or severe grief

reactions from the child (e.g., sustained disinterest in daily activities, loss of appetite, difficulty sleeping, extended regression, withdrawal from relationships) and refer the child for individual therapy if appropriate.

13. Maintain consistent and supportive discipline strategies. (25, 26)

25. Instruct the parents to continue to have reasonable expectations for their child's behavior and to discipline in a loving, compassionate, consistent manner that holds the child accountable.

26. Advise the parents to remain intimately involved in the lives and activities of all of their children; explain that careful monitoring of the children's behavior, although not always appreciated, is an essential responsibility of both the parents especially during times of family trauma.

14. Reassure the child about personal security; express an awareness and empathy for existing fears; and commit to maintaining a close, loving relationship. (27, 28)

27. Assist the parents in planning a time and method of reassuring the child about personal security and expressing awareness and empathy for the child's fears and feelings of grief.

28. Assist the parents in identifying age-appropriate, positive interventions to help the child deal with grief (e.g., active listening, frequent affirmations, answer questions, read books about grief and loss together, and continually express support and encouragement).

15. Verbalize an understanding that losses are an unavoidable part of life. (29, 30)

29. Assign the parents to collaborate with their children to create a time line of significant events including births, deaths, marriages, and graduations to gain a visual perspective of the celebrations and losses encompassed within their family history.

30. Instruct the parents to encourage elder family members to share their wisdom and experiences in dealing with grief and loss with them and the child.

16. Describe ways to turn despair into positive, productive effort. (31, 32)

31. Encourage the parents to assist the child in writing an article about the family's grief experience and share it with members of their grief support group or submit it to a grief newsletter or Web site.

32. Assign the parents to brainstorm with their child methods of turning reactions to a traumatic event into a positive effort (e.g., volunteer to help others who are grieving, work for a significant charity, start a project for change, promote the seatbelt law) and choose one project for family participation.

17. List personal and family goals and express optimism for family and personal relationships in the future. (33, 34)

33. Assign the parents to construct with their children a collage picture representing their family five years in the future focusing on achievements, activities, career paths, personal and family relationships.

34. Assign the parents to read *Lessons from Geese* (Clayton) with their child and follow with a discussion of how people, like geese, can help one another cope in times of grief and loss.

__. ______________________ __. ______________________

______________________ ______________________

__. ______________________ __. ______________________

______________________ ______________________

__. ______________________ __. ______________________

______________________ ______________________

DIAGNOSTIC SUGGESTIONS

ICD-9-CM	*ICD-10-CM*	*DSM-5* Disorder, Condition, or Problem
296.xx	F32.x	Major Depressive Disorder, Single Episode
296.xx	F33.x	Major Depressive Disorder, Recurrent Episode
V62.82	Z63.4	Uncomplicated Bereavement
309.0	F43.21	Adjustment Disorder, With Depressed Mood
300.4	F34.1	Persistent Depressive Disorder
________	________	______________________
________	________	______________________

OPPOSITIONAL DEFIANT DISORDER (ODD)

BEHAVIORAL DEFINITIONS

1. Lack strength, patience, and endurance required for daily management of the oppositional child.
2. Report fatigue, frustration, and confusion caused by the child's angry and resentful behavior.
3. Lack effective and unified behavior management strategies, resulting in the child's manipulation, triangulation, and feelings of inadequacy.
4. Lack a support system and respite resources to help cope with the demanding child.
5. Child engages in frequent confrontation and arguments with parents and other family members.
6. Child deliberately tries to upset or annoy people and projects blame for misbehavior or mistakes onto others.
7. Child has significant difficulty in family, social, or academic functioning due to a negativistic, oppositional attitude.
8. Extended family members and friends criticize the child's behavior and the parents' lack of control.
9. Siblings are resentful of and embarrassed by the oppositional child's behavior and try to distance themselves from their sibling.

__. ____

____

LONG-TERM GOALS

1. Implement a firm, structured, consistent system of discipline for the oppositional/defiant child.

2. Relate to the child with love, support, and empathy even in the face of the oppositional/defiant behavior.
3. Maintain physical, mental, and emotional health and balance in order to cope with the daily challenges of parenting an oppositional/defiant child.
4. Enlist the assistance and understanding of friends and extended family members in offering respite and support for managing the oppositional/defiant behavior of the child.
5. Offer support and guidance to the siblings for dealing appropriately with the child's oppositional/defiant behavior.
6. Seek medical, educational, behavioral, and psychological help for the child with oppositional/defiant behavior.

—. ____

____

SHORT-TERM OBJECTIVES

1. Provide developmental history and a description of current problems presented by the oppositional child. (1)
2. Seek information from professionals and mental health organizations and by reading literature describing the diagnosis and treatment of oppositional/defiant behavior in children. (2, 3, 4)

THERAPEUTIC INTERVENTIONS

1. Gather a developmental history and review the parents' concerns about behavior, academic, and social-emotional problems presented by the child with ODD and the effects on the family.
2. Assist the parents in arranging for a comprehensive psychosocial, medical, and educational evaluation of their child completed by a mental health practitioner in cooperation with the child's school.
3. Assign the parents to read literature that describes ODD in children (e.g., *The Explosive Child* by Greene, *Parenting the Strong-Willed Child* by Forehand and Long).
4. Instruct the parents how to access ODD diagnosis, treatment, and behavior

management information (e.g., American Academy of Child and Adolescent Psychiatry (202) 966-7300 or www.aacap.org, Family Self-Help Group for Parents of Children and Adolescents (800) 950-6264 or www.nami.org).

3. Investigate the possibility of comorbid conditions that may be affecting the defiant child. (5, 6)

5. Advise the parents that ODD often exists with other neuropsychiatric conditions and review the child's psychiatric and psychological evaluations with the parents to identify any other co-existing conditions (e.g., ADHD, depression, anxiety, learning disabilities).

6. Assign the parents to consult with the child's medical doctor to explore the possibility of medication to treat the symptoms of ODD and other existing co-morbid conditions.

4. Child and parents participate in ongoing counseling sessions focusing on the multifaceted problems of parenting an oppositional child. (7, 8)

7. Discuss with the parents the emotionally draining nature of parenting a defiant child and encourage them to participate in regularly scheduled family counseling sessions to help them deal with the critical issues they may face.

8. Advise the parents to arrange for ongoing individual counseling for the oppositional child at school or with a private therapist.

5. Cooperate with the school to insure that the child's oppositional/defiant behavior is not interfering

9. Advise the parents to consult the school regarding special education or Section 504 accommodations to help the

with school achievement and socialization. (9, 10)

child participate successfully in the academic environment (e.g., smaller classroom, assistance from an instructional or behavioral paraprofessional, special classes).

10. Advise the parents to recommend that the school establish a time out area or Student Responsibility Center for students who are disruptive or a Learning Center area in the classroom for students to catch up on academic work.

6. Meet with the child's teacher and other involved educational staff regularly to coordinate strategies for responding to the child's academic and behavior problems. (11, 12)

11. Assign the parents to meet with teachers to evaluate the child's academic potential and determine a mutually agreed upon level of academic performance that must be maintained to earn privileges at home or school.

12. Facilitate a meeting between the parents and the educational staff to determine appropriate academic accommodations for the child that encourage successful academic performance (e.g., close supervision during times of transition; seat near teacher's desk, in an area of low distractions or near a good role model; involve the child in lesson discussions; give simple, clear instructions; arrange for remedial tutoring).

7. Enroll the oppositional child in anger management and social skills classes provided by the school or a community mental health agency. (13, 14)

13. Instruct the parents to consult with the school counselor or school social worker regarding programs that may assist the oppositional child in developing responsible behavior.

14. Assist the parents in locating and enrolling the defiant child in an anger management or a social skills program offered by the school or a local community mental health agency.

8. Implement strategies to enhance communication, reduce stress, and support one another's parenting efforts. (15, 16)

15. Instruct the parents to plan a social evening every week to escape from the pressures of parenting and the demands of their children.

16. Advise the parents to be aware of attempts at triangulation and manipulation by the oppositional child and to stand together and support one another with all of their parenting strategies.

9. Participate in programs designed to promote a healthy lifestyle and enhance physical and mental fitness. (17, 18)

17. Urge the parents to adopt daily habits that will prepare them for the immensely challenging job of parenting a defiant child (e.g., get enough sleep, exercise regularly).

18. Encourage the parents to participate in programs designed to reduce stress and enhance emotional balance (e.g., reduce workload, keep a journal, build a support network).

10. Attend parenting classes and initiate a system of positive discipline in the family. (19, 20)

19. Refer the parents to a parenting class (e.g., *Becoming a Love and Logic Parent* by Fay, Cline, and Fay, or *The Parent Talk System* by Moorman and Knapp) to acquire techniques of positive discipline.

20. Encourage the parents to initiate weekly family meetings to discuss concerns, reflect

upon positive events, coordinate activities, review values, answer questions, and plan for positive interaction.

11. Adopt a parenting approach that is compassionate, yet very firm and highly structured, and takes emotion out of the discipline. (21, 22)

21. Emphasize to the parents the crucial difference between firmness (holding to a disciplinary intervention and focusing on the child's inappropriate behavior) and harshness (attacking the child's personality and demeaning the self-esteem) and instruct them to use empathy and compassion instead of anger and disgust when disciplining their children.

22. Instruct the parents to create a plan for using the time-out technique with the oppositional child when the behavior becomes defiant; explain this process as an opportunity for the child to calm down, regroup, and regain appropriate behavior.

12. Create a behavior management plan that targets the problem behaviors, and provides structured and straightforward parental actions and consequences. (23, 24)

23. Assist the parents in prioritizing a few critical inappropriate behaviors for modification (e.g., hitting, swearing) and defining an alternate expected, appropriate behavior for the child (e.g., use words to describe your feelings, use only "family friendly" vocabulary).

24. Instruct the parents to plan ahead and prepare their responses to the chronic negative behavior and to remain calm and extremely firm when implementing a predetermined intervention (or assign the

"Planning for Disruptive Behavior" activity from the *Parenting Skills Homework Planner* by Knapp).

13. Use privileges to shape cooperation, compliance, and positive behavior. (25, 26)

25. Assist the parents in creating a list of privileges (e.g., use of family computer, listening to music, limited use of television) that can be used as contingent rewards when the child behaves appropriately or denied access when the child does not adhere to the behavior plan.

26. Assign the parents to complete the "Using Privileges as Contingencies and Consequences" activity from the *Parenting Skills Homework Planner* (Knapp) to encourage the defiant child to engage in more appropriate and compliant behavior.

14. Limit and monitor the child's exposure to television, movies, computer, and video games. (27)

27. Assign the parents to monitor their child's use of media including the computer and Internet, and to watch television and videos with their children (or assign the "Family Approved Media List" activity from the *Parenting Skills Homework Planner* by Knapp).

15. Arrange counseling and/or other support services for the siblings. (28, 29)

28. Advise the parents to enroll the siblings in counseling sessions at school or with a private therapist or agency to deal with the emotional stresses of living with a brother or sister with oppositional behavior.

29. Assign the parents to actively listen to the feelings and

16. Educate friends, day-care providers, and family members about ODD by having them attend informational sessions or read literature describing the condition. (30, 31)

—. ______________________

____

concerns of the siblings and schedule quality time with them on a regular basis to help them feel valued and affirmed.

30. Advise the parents to meet regularly with all caregivers of the defiant child to coordinate behavior plans, address problem situations, and clarify the current level of adjustment.

31. Assign the parents to invite family members and day-care providers to attend counseling sessions, parenting classes or informational meetings to become more familiar with the recommended strategies for managing an oppositional child.

—. ______________________

____

DIAGNOSTIC SUGGESTIONS:

ICD-9-CM	*ICD-10-CM*	*DSM-5* Disorder, Condition, or Problem
313.81	F91.3	Oppositional Defiant Disorder
312.9	F91.9	Unspecified Disruptive, Impulse Control, and Conduct Disorder
312.89	F91.8	Other Specified Disruptive, Impulse Control, and Conduct Disorder
314.01	F90.1	Attention-Deficit/Hyperactivity Disorder, Predominately Hyperactive /Impulsive Presentation
314.01	F90.9	Unspecified Attention-Deficit/ Hyperactivity Disorder
314.01	F90.8	Other Specified Attention-Deficit/Hyperactivity Disorder
V61.20	Z62.820	Parent-Child Relational Problem
________	________	______________________
________	________	______________________

PEER RELATIONSHIPS/INFLUENCES

BEHAVIORAL DEFINITIONS

1. Demonstrate a pattern of being unaware, uninvolved, and/or uninterested in the child's friends, social activities, and peer group influences and expectations.
2. Lack awareness of and empathy for the peer problems experienced by the child at school and in the neighborhood and community.
3. Model inappropriate, antisocial, dishonest, or disrespectful social interactions for the child.
4. Use harsh, aggressive, and intimidating forms of discipline.
5. Spend limited time enjoying and socializing with the child due to excessive work, personal activities, or lack of interest.
6. Exhibit an emotional distance and withdrawal from the child due to a chronic physical or psychological disorder.
7. Put excessive pressure on the child to excel socially, academically, athletically, or artistically.
8. Child lacks self-esteem and confidence in own ability to fit in or be socially successful.
9. Child exhibits immature social skills and a lack of polite, expected social behavior.
10. Child demonstrates an inability to form close, positive relationships with peers in the school or community.

__. ____

____

__. ____

____

__. ____

____

LONG-TERM GOALS

1. Develop a current working knowledge of the child's close friends, peer group, and social experiences.
2. Model positive, appropriate social interactions at home and in the community.
3. Create numerous opportunities for positive parent/child interaction at home and in the community.
4. Become familiar with the values, expectations, and influences of the child's peer group.
5. Offer guidance, support, and encouragement for the child to become actively engaged in positive social activities.
6. The child demonstrates appropriate social skills, empathy, assertiveness, self-confidence, and responsible peer group relationships.

—. ____

____

—. ____

____

—. ____

____

SHORT-TERM OBJECTIVES

1. Assess the child's social-emotional adjustment and relationships with friends and peers. (1, 2)
2. Identify existing friendships, peer relationships, and significant others who offer acceptance and a feeling of

THERAPEUTIC INTERVENTIONS

1. Ask the parents to informally assess their child's social-emotional adjustment and ability to form positive relationships with peers by listing areas of strengths and weaknesses.
2. Instruct the parents to obtain social-emotional assessments and informal data from the child's school and other social experiences.
3. Assign the parents to engage the child in creating a list of significant relationships (or assign the "Social Influences in

belonging to the child. (3, 4)

My Child's Life" activity from the *Parenting Skills Homework Planner* by Knapp).

4. Council the parents to rate the child's social acceptance in various areas (e.g., family, peer group, neighborhood) on a scale of one to five in each area and compare their ratings to the child's personal assessment.

3. Arrange for and encourage the child to engage in positive social interactions with peers. (5, 6, 7)

5. Instruct the parents to arrange opportunities for positive social interaction for the child (e.g., play groups, church activities, Boy/Girl Scouts).

6. Assign the parents to brainstorm and role play with the child strategies for establishing friendships (e.g., smiling, conversing, taking turns).

7. Council the parents to define empathy for the child (e.g., understanding another's feelings and perceptions versus focusing only on one's own thoughts and feelings) and discuss the role of empathy in maintaining friendships and positive relationships.

4. Utilize effective communication strategies with the child. (8, 9)

8. Role play with the parents the use of "I" messages (see *Teaching Children Self-Discipline at Home and at School* by Gordon) and the Bug-Wish Technique (e.g., "It bugs me when you . . . I wish you would . . ."); assign them to teach the child to use these strategies in response to negative behavior from others.

9. Define active listening (see *Teaching Children Self-Discipline at Home and at School* by Gordon) for the parents (e.g., listening without interruption, decoding the other person's message, and reflecting back the perceived message); assign them to practice this technique during conversations with the child.

5. Teach appropriate social skills to the child at home through discussion and example. (10, 11)

10. Encourage the parents to help the child develop strategies for resolving peer problems using a mutual storytelling process with the child that describes the problem and develops a possible solution.

11. Assign the parents to teach loving and respectful sibling interaction in the home by stressing the concept of *unique* rather than *equal* to govern the distribution of love and other family resources to encourage all family members to treat one another with respect and dignity.

6. Teach the child to be tolerant, empathetic, and respectful of others. (12, 13)

12. Instruct the parents to list intolerant family perceptions (e.g., racial slurs, ethnic stereotypes) that negatively influence the child's ability to accept differences in others.

13. Assign the parents to brainstorm with the child roadblocks to positive peer interaction and list strategies for building bridges between diverse groups (e.g., eat lunch with an unfamiliar student,

welcome new students to the school).

7. Model positive interpersonal strategies by engaging the child in numerous interactive parent/child and family-based activities. (14, 15)

14. Assign the parents to brainstorm with the child a list of entertaining parent/child activities (e.g., board games, collaborative cooking, reading together) and select one or two per week for family participation.

15. Familiarize the child with community and cultural social norms and expectations through participation in family gatherings, faith-based events, and outings with family friends.

8. Enroll the child in school activities and programs designed to promote healthy peer interaction. (16, 17)

16. Assign the parents to enroll the child in a school-sponsored social skills group for students having difficulty with interpersonal relationships.

17. Encourage the parents to endorse the child's participation in life skills classes offered by the school and to discuss the strategies and values taught.

9. Become active in parent meetings within the child's school. (18, 19)

18. Instruct the parents to become active in parent/school activities to offer encouragement for the child's participation and to become familiar with the school's atmosphere and culture.

19. Council the parents to maintain regular contact with the child's teacher, counselor, and other parents of the child's friends and peer group members.

10. Monitor and communicate with the child about peer group values, expectations, and activities. (20, 21)

20. Assign the parents to list their perceptions of the child's current peer group influences and compare their perceptions with the child's view-point (or assign the "Peer Pressures, Values, and Influences" activity from the *Parenting Skills Homework Planner* by Knapp).

21. Identify for the parents the power of using referential speaking (explaining while doing) to emphasize to the child the importance of adhering to personal and/or family values when faced with opposing peer values (e.g., "I follow through with my commitments, I call home when my plans have changed.").

11. Encourage the child to participate in positive social and extracurricular activities of interest. (22, 23)

22. Assign the parents to collaborate with their child to list the various extracurricular activities offered by the school or community and to support the child in selecting one group or activity for involvement.

23. Instruct the parents to contract with the child to balance employment, social activities, academics, healthy lifestyle, and other commitments and to intervene and limit activities when the balance becomes inappropriate.

12. Set reasonable limits for the child's involvement with friends and in peer group activities. (24, 25)

24. Advise the parents to set limits for the child's interaction with peers (e.g., age-appropriate curfew, advising of where-

abouts) that can be modified depending on the level of responsibility demonstrated by the child.

25. Council the parents that granting permission for the child to participate in nonschool sponsored activities should require that the child present a plan detailing reasonable strategies for parent-approved behavior.

13. Teach the child strategies for dealing with negative peer pressure and solving peer relationship problems. (26, 27)

26. Assign the parents to read *Mop, Moondance, and the Nagasaki Knights* (Meyers) with their child to illustrate how positive peer problem solving (win/win) helps to strengthen friendships.

27. Instruct the parents to work with the school to develop effective anti-bullying programs and policies (e.g., an awareness campaign, classroom discussions and rules, conflict-resolution).

14. Assist the child in developing conflict resolution strategies to deal with social conflict. (28, 29)

28. Council the parents to brainstorm with the child appropriate, socially acceptable methods of dealing with the triggers and targets of aggressive or inappropriate social interactions (e.g., use an "I" statement, walk away, use humor, take a personal time out, get help from an adult).

29. Assign the parents to assist the child in creating a conflict resolution chart that lists various ways to solve a dispute (e.g., share, take turns, listen,

talk it over) for use when trying to solve peer conflicts.

15. Encourage the child to demonstrate responsibility for personal behavior and to develop positive alternatives to socially inappropriate behavior. (30, 31)

30. Instruct the parents to require that the child make amends for disrespectful, negative behavior in the home by: (1) Identifying the damage done by inappropriate personal actions and (2) apologizing and pledging to correct the hurtful behavior.

31. Assign the parents to read *Everything I Do You Blame on Me* (Abern) with the child to stress the importance of taking responsibility for personal actions both at home and in social settings.

16. Support programs that promote a sense of belonging in the classroom and community. (32, 33)

32. Advise the parents to encourage the teacher and other school personnel to involve the child in reciprocal activities that enhance a feeling of belonging and self-worth (e.g., one-to-one chats, daily greetings, reciprocal smiles).

33. Instruct the parents to encourage the child to participate in a volunteer effort designed to help others that requires cooperation and team playing (e.g., school food drive, becoming a conflict manager, working with Habitat for Humanity).

17. Promote responsible social interaction with peers at school and in the community. (34, 35)

34. Council the parents to provide the child with many home-based opportunities to develop leadership qualities and responsibility (e.g., babysitting, teaching a skill to a sibling, completing weekly chores) to

enhance self-confidence and independent social functioning.

35. Instruct the parents to encourage the child to initiate one new social interaction each week and chart the progress at a subsequent counseling session.

__. ____________________________ __. ____________________________

__. ____________________________ __. ____________________________

__. ____________________________ __. ____________________________

DIAGNOSTIC SUGGESTIONS:

ICD-9-CM	*ICD-10-CM*	*DSM-5* Disorder, Condition, or Problem
300.23	F40.10	Social Anxiety Disorder (Social Phobia)
312.9	F91.9	Unspecified Disruptive, Impulse Control, and Conduct Disorder
312.89	F91.8	Other Specified Disruptive, Impulse Control, and Conduct Disorder
V71.02	Z72.810	Child Antisocial Behavior
________	________	________________________
________	________	________________________

POSTTRAUMATIC STRESS DISORDER (PTSD)

BEHAVIORAL DEFINITIONS

1. Unable to give support, nurturing, and comfort to the traumatized child due to a high level of personal anxiety.
2. Lack the knowledge and skills necessary to help the traumatized child deal with overwhelming fear and anxiety.
3. Lack the resources necessary to protect the child from exposure to future traumatic events.
4. Unable or unwilling to acknowledge the profound effect of the trauma on the child's overall functioning.
5. The child has experienced physical and emotional trauma resulting from exposure to a catastrophic event (e.g., natural disaster, death, serious injury, terrorism, violence, war).
6. The child has been chronically exposed to highly disturbing life experiences (e.g., physical abuse, emotional abuse, sexual molestation, neglect, intense poverty, abandonment).
7. The child exhibits repression, denial, and failure to acknowledge, discuss, and deal with the traumatizing event.
8. The child demonstrates long-term obsession with the traumatizing event and the inability to adjust and normalize the life pattern.
9. The child re-experiences the event through flashbacks, nightmares, and/or constant thought pattern interruptions focusing on the traumatic experience.
10. The child experiences ongoing symptoms of increased arousal due to the traumatic experience including sleep difficulties, irritability, concentration difficulties, and hypervigilance.

—. ____

____

LONG-TERM GOALS

1. Stabilize the family environment and offer physical and emotional protection, comfort, support, and nurturing to the child.
2. Recognize the symptoms of intense stress and anxiety in self and the child.
3. Learn strategies to help family members cope with and adjust to the traumatizing experience.
4. Acquire skills to prepare self and child to survive a future catastrophic event.
5. Reduce the overall level of worry and fear.

—. ____

____

SHORT-TERM OBJECTIVES

1. Describe the traumatic event and identify reactions of elevated anxiety. (1, 2)
2. Debrief the child regarding the traumatic incident. (3, 4, 5)

THERAPEUTIC INTERVENTIONS

1. Gather information from the parents regarding the traumatic incident and the effects on themselves, the child, and other family members.
2. Assess the child's current level of anxiety by administering an anxiety scale designed for children (e.g., the Revised Children's Manifest Anxiety Scale [RCMAS], the Trauma Symptom Checklist for Children by Briere) or obtain an evaluation from the child's counselor or therapist.
3. Teach the parents to debrief their child regarding the anxiety-producing trauma using an open-ended, nonjudgmental, and supportive conversational style that is accepting of all expressed feeling and opinions.

4. Instruct the parents to encourage the child to express anxieties, feelings and reactions to the trauma through drawings, unstructured play, and mutual storytelling.

5. Assign the parents to play therapeutic games with their child (e.g., *Talking, Feeling and Doing Game* from Creative Therapeutics, or the *Ungame* from the Ungame Company) to discover unexpressed thoughts and feelings that may be contributing to the elevated anxiety.

3. Reassure the child about personal and family well-being. (6, 7, 8)

6. Advise the parents to reassure the child of their ongoing unconditional love and support throughout and beyond the posttraumatic adjustment period.

7. Instruct the parents to work together to provide for the emotional and physical needs of all family members despite the unsettling effect of the traumatic experience.

8. Refer the parents to private and community organizations that offer relief for families experiencing trauma (e.g., Red Cross, church relief groups, hospitals, mental health organizations).

4. Encourage open communication of fears, feelings, and trauma-related thoughts. (9, 10, 11)

9. Role play with the parents to prepare them for responding to the child's ongoing feelings of stress and anxiety in a nurturing, supportive, nondefensive manner.

10. Discuss and role play with the parents the techniques of using "I" statements and active listening to use when discussing the anxiety-producing situation. (See *Parent Effectiveness Training* by Gordon.)

11. Assign parents to read material that will help them develop skills for positive communication with the child (e.g., *How to Talk so Kids Will Listen and Listen so Kids Will Talk* by Faber and Mazlish).

5. List the effects of trauma-induced stress on the daily functioning of self and the child. (12, 13)

12. Brainstorm with the parents an extensive list of posttrauma reactions and prioritize them from greatest to least troubling, eliminating duplications, and consolidating overlapping items.

13. Assign the parents to draw therapeutic pictures with their child entitled "What stress looks like to me," and "What serenity looks like to me," and place the drawings in their parent/child therapeutic portfolio.

6. Teach the child problem-solving and decision-making skills to manage stress and anxiety. (14, 15)

14. Assign the parents to assist the child in coping with a traumatic experience (e.g., a fire) by taking proactive measures to prevent a future fire (e.g., buy smoke alarms, create an escape plan, arrange for a fire safety inspection).

15. Ask the parents to brainstorm with the child possible remedies to an anxiety

producing situation, choose an option most likely to reduce the level of concern, agree to implement the strategy and follow up with an evaluation of the effectiveness of the plan.

7. Teach skills for managing an emergency situation. (16, 17)

16. Instruct the parents and school personnel to establish procedures for dealing with emergency situations (e.g., dial 911, fire drills, tornado plans, school lockdown process) that are explained in detail and practiced frequently.

17. Assign the parents to discuss, define, and role-play with the child strategies for mitigating inappropriate adult/child interactions (e.g., how to say "no" to inappropriate touch, never go with strangers, how to get immediate help).

8. Assist child in differentiating threatening and nonthreatening circumstances. (18)

18. Council the parents to brainstorm with the child a list of situations that create anxiety and to differentiate those that pose a danger from those that are harmless (e.g., stranger offering candy versus classmate passing out a birthday treat).

9. Implement strategies that reduce the child's anxiety when interacting with others. (19, 20)

19. Instruct the parents to enroll the child in a social skills or anxiety-reduction therapeutic group offered by the school or a counseling agency.

20. Assign the parents to use activities from *Peacemaking Skills for Little Kids* (Schmidt, Friedman, Brunt, and Solotoff) to encourage the

child to develop social assertiveness and conflict management skills.

10. Reframe trauma-related feelings of guilt that affect the child and other family members. (21, 22)

21. Council the parents to help the child reframe feelings of guilt related to the trauma by discussing events rationally and logically and pointing out that the child's reaction and behavior was normal and appropriate given the circumstances.

22. Teach the parents to use rational emotive techniques to help the child deal with chronic worry and anxiety (or assign the "Reframing My Worries" activity from the *Parenting Skills Homework Planner* by Knapp).

11. Identify anxiety-induced physical symptoms evidenced by the child. (23, 24)

23. Assign the parents to note in a personal journal all incidents of elevated stress and related physical symptoms evidenced by themselves and the child, (e.g., rapid heart beat, headache, stomach or bowel distress) and refer to a physician for possible anti-anxiety medication if the symptoms appear excessive.

24. Instruct the parents to compare their own physical receptors of stress to those of the child (or assign the "Physical Receptors of Stress" activity from the *Parenting Skills Homework Planner* by Knapp).

12. Teach the child relaxation techniques to use during periods of posttraumatic stress. (25, 26)

25 Assign the parents to practice deep and even breathing with the child during periods of stress and elevated anxiety.

26 Encourage the parents to engage the child in an aerobic exercise for one half-hour, three to four times per week to release the accumulated physical effects of stress.

13. Increase the frequency of the child reporting a sense of safety, calm, and well being. (27, 28)

27. Advise the parents to adopt a "one day at a time" philosophy for overcoming the effects of trauma on the family and to expect small steps toward reclaiming a feeling of calm and well being rather than sweeping changes.

28. Assign the parents to engage in family nurturing and bonding activities (e.g., family prayer, reading together, singing, storytelling) on a daily basis to restore a sense of well being for themselves and the child.

14. Reestablish a consistent, positive, and loving system of discipline. (29, 30)

29. Instruct the parents to help the child regain a sense of personal control by using choices to encourage responsible behavior (e.g., "Will you do your homework before or after dinner?").

30. Assign the parents to reestablish positive discipline with the child by using consequences with empathy to modify inappropriate behavior ("I'm so sorry that you're not finished with the video but it's bedtime now.").

15. Teach the child techniques for reducing nighttime terrors. (31, 32)

31. Council parents to provide the child with an environment conducive to peaceful nighttime sleep and to develop and enforce a bedtime routine.

32. Assist the parents and child in developing a plan to deal with distressing dreams and periods of wakefulness during the night (e.g., stay in bed, play soft music, read a calming book, draw a picture).

16. Acknowledge and affirm the child's development of confidence and ability to deal with personal stress and anxiety. (33)

33. Council the parents to affirm the child for any progress demonstrated in reducing the influence of stress and anxiety on daily behavior and participation in routine activities.

17. Verbalize to the child a personal optimism toward the present and future. (34)

34. Advise the parents to hold family discussions focusing upon positive plans for the future (e.g., vacation plans, college and career decisions, holiday arrangements, social gatherings, community projects) to emphasize the reestablishment of optimism and normalcy in the family life.

—. ____________________

—. ____________________

—. ____________________

—. ____________________

DIAGNOSTIC SUGGESTIONS

ICD-9-CM	*ICD-10-CM*	*DSM-5* Disorder, Condition, or Problem
309.24	F43.22	Adjustment Disorder, With Anxiety
309.81	F43.10	Posttraumatic Stress Disorder
309.21	F93.0	Separation Anxiety Disorder
______	______	____________________
______	______	____________________

POVERTY-RELATED ISSUES

BEHAVIORAL DEFINITIONS

1. Receive welfare payments, food stamps, Medicaid, and/or qualify for free or reduced school meal programs.
2. Reside in substandard housing.
3. Unemployed or earn income below poverty level.
4. Lack of transportation, phone, medical assistance, utilities, and other essential resources.
5. Impoverished due to recent economic downturn.
6. Extended family has been in poverty for more than one generation.
7. High incidence of teen pregnancies in extended family leading to lowered socioeconomic status.
8. Single-parent family with a matriarchal structure and inconsistent financial and emotional support from the child's father.
9. Financial resources are spent to meet immediate personal needs and extra money is shared with family and friends rather than saved.
10. Education is viewed with skepticism and suspicion rather than a means to overcome poverty.

—. ____

____

—. ____

____

—. ____

____

LONG-TERM GOALS

1. Access community and social services that provide social, economic, and medical resources.
2. Prioritize education as a means of overcoming economic challenges.
3. Prepare for the transition from unemployment and welfare to work.
4. Acquire skills and resources necessary to move toward economic independence and financial self-reliance.
5. Abstain from substance abuse and other self-defeating behaviors.
6. Implement discipline strategies that teach responsibility and encourage independent functioning in the child.

—. ____

____

—. ____

____

—. ____

____

SHORT-TERM OBJECTIVES

1. Identify long- and short-term personal and family goals and create a plan for their attainment. (1, 2)
2. Access community agencies that provide social, financial, and medical assistance. (3, 4)

THERAPEUTIC INTERVENTIONS

1. Meet with the parents to take a family history, clarify family issues and concerns and identify immediate financial, social, and emotional needs.
2. Assist the parents in planning for long- and short-term goal attainment (or assign the "Achieving Family Goals" activity from the *Parenting Skills Homework Planner* by Knapp).
3. Assist the parents in developing a plan for obtaining needed assistance and services by asking them to describe any problems that

may interfere (e.g., transportation, day-care, appropriate clothing) and assist in planning to overcome these hurdles.

4. Refer the parents to agencies that provide social, financial, and medical services (e.g., public assistance, food stamps, Medicaid, head start) and help them access these resources.

3. Attend a class focused on teaching effective parenting skills. (5)

5. Refer the parents to a school or community-sponsored parenting class (e.g., *Becoming a Love and Logic Parent* by Fay, Cline, and Fay) to acquire techniques of positive discipline to use with the child.

4. Attend a class focused on teaching reading skills. (6)

6. Instruct the parents to attend a school- or community-sponsored literacy class.

5. Increase involvement in community-based groups. (7)

7. Assign the parents to attend community or school sponsored forums for discussion of school and community issues (e.g., neighborhood political action groups, church-sponsored social groups).

6. Attend school conferences and participate in other programs sponsored by the child's school. (8, 9)

8. Assign the parents to attend all regularly scheduled school conferences for their child.

9. Instruct the parents to express their willingness to participate in school events (e.g., Parent Teacher Association meetings) to establish a familiar and positive relationship with the child's teachers and other educational staff.

7. Insist that the child attend school on a regular basis and cooperate with the school rules and discipline structure. (10, 11)

10. Instruct the parents to demonstrate an emphasis on the importance of education insisting that the child attend school on a regular basis and requiring a personal best level of performance.

11. Assign the parents to brainstorm with the child how school rules differ from family or "street" rules and discuss the necessity of adhering to different rules in different situations (or assign the "Different Rules for Home and School" activity from the *Parenting Skills Homework Planner* by Knapp).

8. Establish a cooperative relationship with staff members at the child's school. (12, 13)

12. Instruct the parents to support the school staff in implementing a positive system of discipline that incorporates logical consequences that are individually designed to teach appropriate and responsible behavior.

13. Monitor relationships between the parent, child and the educational staff at the child's school to encourage connectedness and trust.

9. Establish career goals, mentors, and role models to assist in the transition from welfare to work. (14, 15)

14. Brainstorm with the parents a list of role models, mentors, and extended family or community members available to support the achievement of personal and career goals.

15. Teach the parents to set personal goals by recording daily, weekly, and monthly

objectives in a personal journal and listing steps necessary to achieve each objective.

10. Enroll in educational classes or training programs to enhance marketable skills and increase opportunities for employment. (16, 17)

16. Assist the parents in assessing career goals and planning a job search strategy or training curriculum consistent with these goals.

17. Instruct the parents to encourage their child to enroll in school-sponsored community-based instruction or school to career programs designed to provide employment skills and work experience for students.

11. Participate in substance abuse prevention and wellness programs at school or in the community. (18, 19)

18. Refer the parents to a support group (e.g., *FAST, Families and Schools Together* [The Alliance for Children and Families]) to strengthen the parent-child relationship, build a partnership between parents and the school and community, and to provide ongoing encouragement for the parents and the child.

19. Instruct the parents to support the child's participation in substance abuse prevention programs presented at school as part of the K-12 curriculum.

12. Participate in substance abuse or psychological assessment and treatment services for self and/or the child. (20, 21)

20. Refer the parents and the child if necessary to community programs or services addressing substance abuse (e.g., Alcoholics Anonymous, Alanon, psychiatric hospitals).

21. Discuss lifestyle choices with the parents during counseling

sessions and support and encourage healthy choices.

13. Identify future family-planning goals and create a plan for their attainment. (22, 23)

22. Assist the parents in determining future parental and family goals and to develop a plan for preventing unplanned pregnancies.

23. Brainstorm with the parents the negative economic impact of another pregnancy and the positive effects of postponing additional pregnancies until the family becomes self-supporting.

14. Participate in family-planning and child development classes provided by local medical facilities or community clinics. (24)

24. Refer the parents to community clinics, church programs, or medial workshops that focus on family planning, prenatal self-care, birthing classes, and infant child care to acquire the skills necessary for family planning and mastering their role as parents.

15. Implement strategies of positive discipline that help the child develop responsible behavior. (25, 26)

25. Assign the parents to remain respectful when disciplining by focusing on the behavior and not the child and by letting the child know that, although the deed is not acceptable, the doer remains loved unconditionally.

26. Instruct the parents to implement the "Four Steps to Responsibility": (1) Assign chores and tasks to the child; (2) Expect some noncompliance; (3) Issue a logical consequence for the noncompliance; (4) Give the same task again to check for learning (see *Parenting with Love and Logic* by Cline and Fay).

16. Implement discipline strategies that encourage independence and self-reliance in the child. (27, 28)

27. Instruct the parents to teach the child the skill of completing a large task by dividing it into smaller more manageable tasks (e.g., making a bed: smooth the sheets, pull up the covers, place the pillow, put on the spread) and then engage the child in completing the step-by-step process.

28. Ask parents to use the Statement, "Check Yourself" (e.g., "This is sharing day at school, check yourself to make sure you have what you need when it's your turn to share.") to help the child develop the ability to prepare successfully for upcoming events (see *Parent Talk* by Moorman).

17. Use conflict-resolution and problem-solving skills to address economic, family, and social issues. (29, 30)

29. Teach parents to use a simple problem-solving process to deal with issues of concern that involves: stating the problem, listing potential solutions, listing the pros and cons of each solution, choosing an action to deal with the situation, and evaluating the result.

30. Teach a conflict resolution process for parents to use in resolving personal disputes and in mediating disputes involving their child (e.g., (1) Find a private place to talk, (2) discuss the problem with out judging, (3) brainstorm possible solutions, (4) agree on a solution that works for both, and (5) try the solution and

agree to renegotiate if it is not effective).

18. Reframe negative self-talk into positive realistic messages. (31, 32)

31. Assist the parents in identifying their propensity for negative self-talk by reviewing situations in which the they have felt anxious, inferior, or rejected; reframe their thinking into more positive, realistic self-talk.

32. Brainstorm positive statements of and encouragement that could be used by the parents to affirm the child; assign the parents to use these statements to positively reinforce the child at least five to ten times daily.

__. ____________________ __. ____________________

__. ____________________ __. ____________________

__. ____________________ __. ____________________

DIAGNOSTIC SUGGESTIONS

ICD-9-CM	*ICD-10-CM*	*DSM-5* Disorder, Condition, or Problem
309.28	F43.23	Adjustment Disorder, With Mixed Anxiety and Depressed Mood
300.02	F41.1	Generalized Anxiety Disorder
______	______	____________________
______	______	____________________

PRENATAL PARENTING PREPARATION

BEHAVIORAL DEFINITIONS

1. Demonstrate a lack of knowledge of prenatal medical care, pregnancy, and the birthing process.
2. Exhibit a lack of emotional preparation for the pregnancy and the subsequent responsibility of child-rearing.
3. Lack insurance and financial resources to cover the cost of the pregnancy, delivery, and needs of the infant.
4. Evidence of poor nutrition and health habits that endanger the pregnancy and the normal development of the fetus.
5. Verbalize high levels of anxiety and worries about the pregnancy and birth.
6. The pregnancy is unwanted due to the parent's marital status, age, number of existing children and/or lifestyle preferences.
7. Lack communication and a unified supportive approach to the pregnancy.
8. Exhibit a reluctance to make the lifestyle changes necessary to ensure a healthy pregnancy, delivery, and responsible parenting of a newborn.
9. Emotionally and physically drained of the energy to adequately bond with and parent the newborn after a difficult pregnancy and/or delivery.
10. Lack positive support and/or suffer interference from the extended family, creating feelings of confusion, self-doubt, and resentment in the expectant couple.

__. ____

____

__. ____

____

LONG-TERM GOALS

1. Commit to a lifestyle that contributes to a healthy pregnancy and normal fetal development.
2. Obtain early and regular prenatal counseling, education, and health care from a prenatal health care provider.
3. Strengthen the spousal relationship and develop a unified and loving approach to resolving prenatal and family issues.
4. Create a network of supportive friends and family.
5. Collaborate to prepare for the physical and emotional demands of the delivery and parenting of an infant.
6. Plan to meet the financial needs of the child and family.

__. ____

____

__. ____

____

SHORT-TERM OBJECTIVES

1. Develop healthy eating and lifestyle habits prior to conception. (1, 2)

2. Confirm pregnancy during the early stages. (3, 4)

THERAPEUTIC INTERVENTIONS

1. Advise the parents to see a prenatal heath care provider for a preconception health evaluation and to learn about recommended guidelines for initiating a healthy pregnancy (e.g., eat healthy foods, exercise daily, get adequate sleep, take a multivitamin containing folic acid).
2. Caution the parents to eliminate exposure to harmful substances (e.g., cigarettes and second-hand smoke, alcohol, illegal drugs, unauthorized medications, cat litter).
3. Instruct the parents to take an at-home or medically administered pregnancy test at the first sign of pregnancy).

4. Encourage the mother to make and keep appointments with a medical practitioner according to the recommended prenatal schedule (e.g., first 20 weeks one visit every four weeks, 20–36 weeks one visit every two weeks, 36 weeks to birth one visit per week).

3. Read literature or view videos to prepare for the pregnancy, delivery and care of the infant. (5, 6)

5. View *The Baby System* video with the prospective parents to help them understand the process of pregnancy and birth including fetal development, physical changes of the mother and ways the father can be involved and supportive.

6. Review the weekly changes in the pregnancy with the parents by referring to literature describing the stages of pregnancy (e.g., *Your Pregnancy Week by Week* by Curtis and Schuler).

4. Take childbirth education and parenting classes. (7, 8)

7. Assist the prospective parents in choosing a prenatal and birthing class consistent with their preferred type of delivery (e.g., natural, at home, Lamaze, with or without anesthetic and/or pharmaceutical intervention) and encourage them to attend as a couple.

8. Refer the parents to a parenting class (e.g., *The Parent Talk System* by Moorman and Knapp) to acquire appropriate child management techniques to use with their developing child.

5. Develop a family routine, work program, and social

9. Council the parents to adjust their work and social schedules

activities supportive of a safe and healthy pregnancy. (9, 10)

to a healthier, more family friendly pace or assign the "Creating a Family Friendly Lifestyle" activity from the *Parenting Skills Homework Planner* (Knapp).

10. Assign the parents to list any of their current habits that may negatively affect the pregnancy, delivery or future health of the child (e.g., an unhealthy diet, use of hot tubs or saunas, taking over the counter medications) and brainstorm methods of replacing the negative habits with healthy behaviors.

6. Follow medical guidelines recommended by the prenatal health care provider. (11, 12)

11. Review with the parents the nutritional guidelines to follow during the pregnancy and help them plan well-balanced meals and snacks that promote a healthy pregnancy; discuss cravings and normal weight gain.

12. Council the parents to keep regularly scheduled appointments with their health care provider and to submit to any medically recommended tests that are necessary to monitor the status of the pregnancy.

7. Create a plan for developing a loving bond with the new baby. (13, 14)

13. Instruct the parents to begin communicating with their unborn infant using loving interactions (or assign the "Bonding with Our Prenatal Baby" activity from the *Parenting Skills Homework Planner* by Knapp).

14. Council the parents to guard against "gatekeeping"

tendencies (e.g., competition for the baby's time, attention, attachment, and affection) by encouraging one another to develop a positive and loving relationship with the infant. (See *Touchpoints* by Brazelton.)

8. Accept the role assignments that allow for sharing responsibility for the care of the needs of the child, the home, and the family. (15, 16)

15. Brainstorm with the parents a list of their parental responsibilities and assist them in assigning these obligations so that both parents engage equitably in providing for the infant's physical, financial, and emotional needs.

16. Encourage the couple to predict how their spousal roles will change as the marriage and family evolves (or assign the "Our Evolving Marriage and Spousal Roles" activity from the *Parenting Skills Homework Planner* by Knapp).

9. Commit to a cooperative co-parent strategy for resolving all child- and family-related issues. (17, 18)

17. Advise the parents of the importance of forming a cooperative alliance when addressing all child management issues and instruct them to consult one another on all child- and family-related decisions.

18. Instruct the parents to keep conflict away from the infant by discussing their differences privately, coming to an agreement that both can support, and then forming a loving, united front when interacting with the infant.

10. Create a family budget that allows for the needs and

19. Review the importance of pre-natal health care with the

accommodations required by the new baby. (19, 20)

parents and ask if there are personal or family resources or insurance to cover the recommended medical care.

20. Assign the parents to create a family budget that lists available income and additional expenses incurred by the pregnancy (e.g., loss of mother's income, medical expenses, child care) and brainstorm methods of reducing costs while adequately providing for the needs of the child.

11. Seek assistance for unmet financial needs from extended family, church, community organizations or social service agencies. (21, 22)

21. Instruct the expectant parents to list the resources and financial support available from their extended family and brainstorm additional solutions for housing, medical care, living expenses, education, and employment.

22. Assist the expectant parents to obtain needed financial support by applying for community assistance (e.g., child and family services, Medicaid, food stamps, State Department of Social Services).

12. Plan for the pediatric care of the infant. (23, 24)

23. Advise the couple to select a pediatric health care provider for the infant and schedule an appointment for both parents during the seventh month of pregnancy.

24. Instruct the couple to create a list of questions to discuss with the pediatrician during the first predelivery appointment (e.g., whether to circumcise, nurse or bottle feed, eating and sleeping schedule).

13. List and arrange to provide for the initial needs of the newborn. (25, 26)

25. Council the parents to work together to plan and prepare a safe and comfortable environment for the baby in their home (e.g., quiet sleeping area, diaper changing table, comfortable nursing chair).

26. Brainstorm with the parents the steps necessary to prepare for the baby's birth (e.g., plan ahead for the trip to the hospital, select a pediatrician, acquire an approved infant car seat).

14. Involve the siblings in the prenatal process through age appropriate discussions and involvement. (27, 28, 29)

27. Instruct the parents to lovingly introduce the expected birth of the baby to their other children by providing basic details and answering questions by giving positive, truthful, and age-appropriate information.

28. Council the parents to include the siblings in planning for the baby by actively listening to their ideas and inviting them to assist with preparing the new baby's area in the home.

29. Assign the parents to use verbal affirmations, hugs, smiles, and quality time to reassure the siblings that they are loved unconditionally and hold an irreplaceable place in the family.

15. Involve close friends and extended family in prenatal plans and expectations. (30)

30. Instruct the parents to encourage the participation of family and friends in the birth celebration according to family and cultural customs (e.g., taking pictures of the newborn, bringing gifts, preparing food, attending the baptism or other birth ritual).

16. Complete a personalized birth plan. (31, 32)

31. Assign the parents to talk with their prenatal health care provider about their specific treatment wishes during the delivery and immediate afterbirth care of the mother and baby (e.g., place of delivery, use of anesthetic, people in delivery room).

32. Instruct the parents to complete a personalized birth plan (available from their hospital, health care provider or iVillage the Internet for Women: www.parents place.com/pregnancy /birthplan) that outlines their specific directions for medical care and interventions during the delivery and immediate aftercare.

17. Gather information about parenting an infant from video, books, and Internet resources. (33, 34)

33. View the video *Expect More Than a Baby!* with the expectant couple to develop an awareness of issues that concern new parents of infants (e.g., sleep deprivation, shift in family dynamics, volatile emotions, postpartum depression, time management).

34. Assign the parents to access web sites that give helpful information to young parents about their infants (e.g., the Gerber Web site: www.geber.com, the Similac Formula Web site, www.welcomeaddition.com, or the Enfamil Formula Web site www.herhealthcare.com).

__. ____________________ __. ____________________

__. ____________________ __. ____________________

__. ____________________ __. ____________________

DIAGNOSTIC SUGGESTIONS:

ICD-9-CM	*ICD-10-CM*	*DSM-5* Disorder, Condition, or Problem
309.28	F43.23	Adjustment Disorder, With Mixed Anxiety and Depressed Mood
300.02	F41.1	Generalized Anxiety Disorder
V61.20	Z62.820	Parent-Child Relational Problem

SCHOOL ADJUSTMENT DIFFICULTIES

BEHAVIORAL DEFINITIONS

1. Exhibit a high level of anxiety over separation from the child during the school day.
2. Verbalize a fear of school attendance as a threat to the close parent/child relationship.
3. Have failed to adequately prepare the child for a successful adjustment to school.
4. Express negative opinions about school and the overall benefits of an education.
5. Demonstrate over-involvement in the child's school experience.
6. Demonstrate a lack of interest in the child's adjustment to school.
7. Verbalize unrealistic expectations for high achievement which create anxiety and a lack of self-confidence in the child.
8. Engage in conflict with the child's teachers over educational strategies.
9. Provide poor examples of effort, achievement, and lifelong learning for the child to emulate.
10. The child verbalizes feelings of inadequacy in areas of academic, social, and independent functioning.

__. ____

____

__. ____

____

__. ____

____

LONG-TERM GOALS

1. Reduce anxiety caused by separation from the child.
2. Teach the child basic school-readiness skills.
3. Implement strategies that promote feelings of capability, adequacy, and academic confidence in the child.
4. Verbalize a sustained interest in the child's academic and social/ emotional adjustment in school.
5. Support the school and the child's teacher in their efforts to effectively educate the child.
6. Verbalize and model personal and family values that prioritize effort, academic achievement, and lifelong learning.

__. ____
____

__. ____
____

__. ____
____

SHORT-TERM OBJECTIVES

1. Schedule extra time to prepare self and the child for the transition from home to school. (1, 2)
2. Verbalize confidence in the child's ability to adjust to school. (3, 4)

THERAPEUTIC INTERVENTIONS

1. Council the parents to visit the school several times if necessary, meeting the teacher and becoming familiar with the facilities.
2. Instruct the parents to involve the child in the school preparation process (e.g., listing necessary school supplies, picking out a backpack).
3. Assign the parents to use I-statements to verbalize confidence in the child's ability to adjust to school (e.g., "I think you will like your teacher; I believe you will learn many new things.").

4. Teach the parents to use low-key descriptive praise to affirm the child's progress in school (e.g., "You've learned five new words this week.") rather than global, evaluative praise (e.g., "You're such a smart girl.").

3. Verbalize reduction in feelings of guilt, anxiety, fear, or jealousy that may be contributing to the parent/child separation anxiety. (5, 6)

5. Assist the parents in reframing their separation anxiety by suggesting alternative methods of interpreting their concerns (e.g., "My child will miss me all day," reframed to, "Maria will miss me at first and then begin to enjoy the activities at school.").

6. Assist the parents in identifying their child's anxieties that may be unintentionally supported by their reactions; council them to reframe the child's feelings of fear by discussing events rationally and logically.

4. Establish a morning routine designed to help organize and prepare for the school day. (7, 8, 9)

7. Assist the parents in developing a plan for the morning routine that outlines steps necessary for the child's organized departure for school.

8. Assign the parents and their child to complete the "Organizing for the School Day" activity from the *Parenting Skills Homework Planner* (Knapp) to aid in planning for the school day.

9. Advise the parents that no television or play time should be allowed until the child is completely organized for departure for school.

5. Verbalize a belief that the child can successfully participate in the school day. (10, 11)

10. Assign the parents to imagine with their child what a perfect day in school would be like, compare this description with the child's actual experiences and brainstorm ways improve each school day (or assign the "My Ideal School Day" activity from the *Parenting Skills Homework Planner* by Knapp).

11. Assist the parents in creating a written list of the child's positive personal attributes, skills, and abilities.

6. Assist the child in developing the readiness skills necessary for success at each academic level. (12, 13)

12. Assign the parents to obtain a list of grade-level skills and requirements from the child's school (e.g., knowledge of numbers and letters, reading and calculation skills, knowledge of history); assist the child in meeting these readiness requirements.

13. Council the parents to involve the child in enriching activities which will contribute to a successful school experience (e.g., arrange for social interaction with peers; read with the child daily, visit the community library or museum).

7. Assign age- and ability-appropriate tasks and responsibilities to the child. (14, 15)

14. Emphasize the connection between responsible behavior at home and success at school by instructing the parents to assign age- and ability-appropriate tasks and chores to the child at home.

15. Assign the parents to use chores and tasks to teach responsibility to the child using the four-step process described in *Parenting with Love and Logic* by Cline and Fay: (1) Give the child an age-appropriate task, (2) hope that the child "blows it," (3) let the resulting consequences and empathy do the teaching, and (4) give the same task again.

8. Agree to ensure school attendance on a daily basis. (16, 17)

16. Contract with the parents to ensure daily school attendance by the child.
17. Suggest methods of coping with attendance resistance from a timid child (e.g., speak calmly but firmly and keep repeating, "I'm sorry you feel that way, but you must go to school."); urge them not to argue with any of the child's complaints.

9. Help the child establish procedures for effective study habits. (18, 19)

18. Encourage the parents to teach the child study habits which will enhance success in school (e.g., record assignments in a planner, break large projects into smaller study segments).
19. Assign the parents to monitor and reinforce their child's school attendance, punctuality, and academic achievement.

10. Set up routine procedures for meals, bedtime, the morning preparation for school, and study time. (20, 21)

20. Instruct the parents to establish family procedures for meals, bedtime, and the morning routine so that the child is held accountable for being prepared (or assign the "Procedures for Meals, Bedtime and the Morning

Routine" activity from the *Parenting Skills Homework Planner* by Knapp).

21. Assign the parents to assist their child in establishing procedures that designate the time and place for schoolwork, duration of the study time, methods of checking the work, and limits for parental involvement.

11. Verbalize and implement strategies designed to promote independence and responsible behavior. (22, 23)

22. Assign the parents to substitute the phrase "Next Time" (see *Parent Talk* by Moorman) for "don't" to shape positive future efforts from the child (e.g., "Next time you have a spelling test, I'll be happy to help you if you ask me in advance." versus "Don't ask me to help you with your spelling test at the last minute.").

23. Counsel the parents to use "Act as if" (see *Parent Talk* by Moorman) to encourage the child to make an effort despite fear of failure, (e.g., "Act as if you felt great about going to school.").

12. Attend a class or didactic series focusing on positive parenting. (24, 25)

24. Refer the parents to a positive parenting class (e.g., *Systematic Training for Effective Parenting (STEP)* by Dinkmeyer and Mckay), *Discipline with Love and Logic* by Fay, Cline, and Fay, or *The Parent Talk System* by Moorman and Knapp).

25. Assign parents to listen to the audio tape, *Helicopters, Drill Sergeants, and Consultants* by Fay to recognize the advantage

of allowing their child to resolve their own problems.

13. Avoid power struggles by clearly defining expectations and setting enforceable limits. (26, 27)

26. Advise parents to avoid power struggles with the child by expressing clearly defined expectations and using contingency management strategies that make privileges dependent upon compliance (e.g., "Feel free to play the computer game after you've organized your backpack.").

27. Assign the parents to brainstorm with their child the personal qualities required to work cooperatively with others (e.g., active listening, eye contact, promptness, following directions).

14. Promote the child's appropriate social interaction with classmates and friends. (28, 29)

28. Instruct the parents to assist their child in planning for an after school or weekend activity with a friend; record the event with a photo, paragraph, and/or drawing entry from the child.

29. Council the parents to encourage the child to join a social group or club by listing options available at school.

15. Encourage the child to participate in a well-balanced academic, social, and extracurricular program. (30, 31, 32)

30. Instruct the parents to discuss progress reports, grade cards, conference input, and the results of tests and evaluations with the child immediately to emphasize the family's focus on quality education.

31. Assign the parents to engage the child in at least one extra-curricular activity that promotes the child's special

interest or ability (e.g., music or art lessons).

32. Encourage the parents to focus on the individual interests and abilities of the child and to emphasize personal best achievement rather than competition.

16. Meet with the child's teacher and/or other educational staff to develop a plan for effectively challenging and motivating the child to achieve. (33, 34, 35)

33. Instruct the parents to establish a communication schedule that provides for regular interchange between the child's teacher and home.

34. Advise the parents to consult the school regarding aptitude and interest tests available to their child at various grade levels; ask them to discuss how the test results may relate to future educational decisions.

35. Encourage the parents to emphasize to their child the crucial connection between school performance and future career choices by detailing how specific curriculum is used in the workplace (e.g., math facilitates money management, reading facilitates following directions, writing facilitates communication with others).

17. Discuss with the child how education, planning, and training have contributed to the personal success of various family members. (36, 37, 38)

36. Instruct the parents to enlist their child's help in creating a list of the education and career paths of various family members.

37. Instruct the parents to model positive and enthusiastic work habits for the child (e.g., leaving for work on time, limiting sick days).

38. Advise the parents of their position as career role model; encourage them to relate personal work experiences that will positively shape their child's attitudes toward future educational and career decisions.

18. Increase recognition and encouragement to reinforce the child's active attempts to attend school and build positive academic and social habits. (39)

39. Teach the parents the one-sentence intervention (e.g., "I noticed that you get up on time each morning"; "I noticed that you enjoy reading.") to affirm the child's daily attempts to successfully adjust to school. (See *Parenting with Love and Logic* by Cline and Fay.)

__. ____________________

__. ____________________

__. ____________________

__. ____________________

__. ____________________

__. ____________________

DIAGNOSTIC SUGGESTIONS

ICD-9-CM	*ICD-10-CM*	*DSM-5 Disorder, Condition, or Problem*
308.3	F43.0	Acute Stress Disorder
309.21	F93.0	Separation Anxiety Disorder
300.02	F41.1	Generalized Anxiety Disorder
300.81	F45.1	Somatic Symptom Disorder
309.24	F43.22	Adjustment Disorder, With Anxiety
_____	_____	____________________
_____	_____	____________________

SEXUAL RESPONSIBILITY

BEHAVIORAL DEFINITIONS

1. Fail to set reasonable limits and expectations for their child's dating and social activities.
2. Lack strategies to educate the child about protection from sexually transmitted diseases, AIDS, sex abuse, date rape, and the negative emotional consequences of irresponsible sexual activity.
3. Acknowledge discomfort with discussing the various aspects of sexual activity with the child.
4. Display an ignorance of and an unwillingness to learn about the current trends and patterns of sexual activity in today's youth.
5. Model poor personal choices and sexually irresponsible behavior.
6. Verbalize a deep concern about unplanned adolescent pregnancy and out-of-wedlock childbearing.
7. Verbalize strong belief in an abstinence only approach to adolescent sexuality.
8. Express rigid and judgmental reactions to the child's questions and concerns about sexual responsibility.
9. Child demonstrates excessive interest in sex and sexuality at a pre-puberty level of maturity.
10. Child engages in promiscuous sexual activity.
11. Child's sexual activity without the use of protection has resulted in an unplanned pregnancy.
12. Child's sexual activity without the use of protection has resulted in contraction of a sexually transmitted disease.

__. ____

____

__. ____

____

LONG-TERM GOALS

1. Set clear and reasonable limits for the child's dating and social activities.
2. Become the child's primary educator about sexual development and responsible sexual activity.
3. Learn the facts about current trends and patterns of sexual development and adolescent sexual activity.
4. Model responsibility and sexually healthy attitudes in personal relationships.
5. Discuss personal and family sexual ethics and values with the child openly and nonjudgmentally.
6. Support school, faith-based, and community programs that educate youth about sexual development and responsibility.

__. ____

____

__. ____

____

SHORT-TERM OBJECTIVES

1. Identify personal attitudes and sexual behaviors that positively and negatively shape the child's attitude about sexuality. (1, 2)

THERAPEUTIC INTERVENTIONS

1. Advise the parents that their sexual attitudes and behavior shape the child's perceptions about sexuality; ask them to define the values they are attempting to promote.
2. Brainstorm with the parents the positive and negative behaviors and opinions they are modeling for the child; ask them to choose several examples they would like to eliminate (e.g., statements condoning sexual irresponsibility, excessive sexualized behavior in the child's presence, viewing highly sexualized material).

2. Discuss sexual ethics and values with the child on an ongoing basis while fostering an atmosphere of intimacy and trust. (3, 4, 5)

3. Stress the importance of maintaining open lines of communication with the child about sexual responsibility; prepare for questions that might arise (e.g., "What is happening to my body? What causes STDs and AIDS?").

4. Teach the parents effective communication techniques by role playing conversations using "I" statements, active listening, and not interrupting.

5. Emphasize the importance of practicing honesty and sincerity while discussing sexuality; assign the parents to initiate a dialogue with their child using a television show, video, book, or life experience as a conversation starter.

3. Verbalize the connection between the child's self-respect, defined goals for the future, and the ability to refuse or delay sexual activity. (6, 7)

6. Instruct the parents to use the "Sexual Responsibility and Healthy Self-esteem" activity from the *Parenting Skills Homework Planner* (Knapp) to help their child identify the connection between sexual responsibility and healthy self-esteem.

7. Assign the parents to brainstorm with the child ways they can demonstrate sexual responsibility (e.g., confronting harassment, choosing abstinence, or adequate protection).

4. Verbalize the understanding that sex and sexuality are two separate issues and define each in terms of

8. Instruct the parents to assist the child in listing a full range of actions and feelings that influence sexual attitudes

adolescent maturation. (8, 9, 10)

including physical attraction to another person, dating, holding hands, kissing, intimate touching; differentiate from sexual intercourse.

9. Assign the parents to encourage their preteen child to read a book (e.g., *Changing Bodies, Changing Lives* by Bell) or view a video (e.g., *Dear Diary*) about puberty and intimate relationships.

10. Teach the parents how to help their child differentiate between love (e.g., caring, empathy, respect) and sexual desire by listing examples and the long-term effects of each.

5. Identify sexual myths and learn facts about sex and sexuality. (11, 12, 13)

11. Ask the parents to review some common statements about sexuality with their child and identify whether the statement is fact or myth (e.g., "All teens are having sex these days" [myth]; "HIV can be contracted by both heterosexuals and homosexuals." [fact]).

12. Assign the parents to view with the child the video *Sex Myths and Facts* and follow up with a discussion of typical myths that create confusion for adolescents.

13. Direct the parents to seek information about sexuality education for youth by contacting local agencies, school, or Web sites (e.g., Sexuality Information and Education Council of the United States, [SIECUS]

www.siecus.org; Whole Family.com, www.whole family.com/aboutteensnow).

6. Participate in and/or support ongoing sexuality education classes or an information series for youth offered by the school, a faith-based organization, or a community agency. (14, 15)

14. Assign the parents to contact their child's school to learn about sexuality education being offered for students.

15. Encourage the parents to advocate for effective sexuality education in the school, faith-based organization, and local youth agencies that meet research-based criteria for effectiveness (see *Effective Curricula and Their Common Characteristics* by Kirby at www.etr.org/recapp/programs /effectiveprograms.

7. Set clear expectations for adolescents in areas of curfew deadline, dress code, dating guidelines, substance abuse, and sexual activity. (16, 17, 18)

16. Instruct the parents to view the video *Everyone Is Not Doing It: Parts I, II and III* with their child and discuss reasonable limits in the areas of substance abuse, curfew, and abstaining from sexual activity.

17. Teach the parents that close parental supervision of their child decreases sexual activity in younger adolescents and is a major deterrent to teen pregnancies.

18. Instruct the parents to remain firm yet compassionate when resistance from the child occurs by combining empathy with the rule or limit.

8. Verbalize abstinence as a viable option for avoiding the physical and emotional dangers of adolescent sex. (19, 20, 21)

19. Assign the parents to brainstorm with the child the reasons for choosing abstinence as the preferred method of avoiding the pitfalls

of adolescent sexual intercourse (e.g., avoiding STDs, avoiding the emotional trauma of adolescent sex and pregnancy, remaining faithful to religious values).

20. Council the parents to brainstorm with the child the primary indicators of not being ready for a sexual relationship (e.g., not ready for the responsibilities of parenthood, not sure about the relationship with partner, fear of the emotional reaction to having had sex, desire to postpone sex until marriage).

21. Assign the parents to rehearse with the child strategies for maintaining abstinence (e.g., avoid alcohol and drugs; say, "No, I've made a commitment to wait.").

9. Assist the child in writing a personal sexuality responsibility code and a behavior plan for its implementation. (22, 23)

22. Instruct the parents to complete the "My Personal Sexual Responsibility Code" activity from the *Parenting Skills Homework Planner* (Knapp) with the child to encourage the development of positive intentions in the areas of sexuality.

23. Assign the parents to brainstorm with the child loving ways to relate to dating partners without breaking the commitment to abstinence (e.g., hugging, sending flowers, taking walks) (see *Sexual Integrity for Teens* by Hansen).

10. Encourage the child to communicate personal views

24. Assign the parents to role play with the child several strategies

about sexual responsibility and appropriate sexual behaviors to dating partners and peers. (24, 25)

for communicating their ideas about sexual responsibility to their peers.

25. Instruct the parents to encourage the child to communicate personal standards with their dating partner, friends, and peer group, and to share the outcome during a parent/child discussion.

11. Practice refusal skills for undesired sexual behavior with the child. (26, 27)

26. Assign the parents to teach effective refusal skills to the child (e.g., say, "No, I'm committed to abstinence until marriage.") and to seek information about refusal skills from programs offered by the school, faith-based, or community organizations.

27. Assign the parents to brainstorm with the child several anticipated situations that call for sexual refusal skills; develop a role play with the parents that addresses each circumstance.

12. List the life-altering and life-threatening dangers of sexual risk-taking. (28, 29)

28. Assign the parents and their child to watch the video *Teens at Risk: Breaking the Immortality Myth*; discuss the consequences of sexual risk-taking.

29. Instruct the parents to assist the child in listing personal goals for the future in the areas of marriage, family, education, and career; then identify how risky sexual behavior can potentially impact the achievement of these goals.

13. Collaborate with the child to develop a sexual action plan to prevent the negative consequences of engaging in unprotected sexual relations. (30, 31)

30. Assign the parents to help their child identify the several options for preventing the unwanted results of unprotected sexual intercourse (e.g., abstinence, condoms, birth control pills, morning after pill); list the benefits and drawbacks of each method.

31. Council the parents to advice their sexually active child about community resources where information about birth control and protection from STDs can be acquired (e.g., Planned Parenthood, Health Department, physicians, hospital-sponsored clinics).

14. Verbalize the belief that abstinence continues to remain as an option even after the child has been sexually active. (32, 33)

32. Council the parents to teach the child that abstinence is a choice that can be made at any time even after a period of sexual activity.

33. Inform the parents that many adolescents do not have sex again for months or years after their first sexual experience (see *Adolescent Sexuality and Childbearing* by Mercer); encourage them to review with the child reasons why abstinence may be chosen after an initial sexual encounter (e.g., feelings of guilt or fear, reputation concerns, didn't meet expectations).

15. Encourage the child to enroll in a class focusing on adolescent sexuality offered by the school, a community agency, or a place of worship. (34, 35)

34. Refer the parents and the child to a class on adolescent sexuality (e.g., *Sexual Integrity for Teens* by Hansen: www.agnr.umd.edu/nnfr/adolsex/fact/) to clarify sexual

values and gather relevant information on sexual development.

35. Instruct the parents to enroll the child in a class offered by the school, a faith-based organization, or youth center that focus on topics of concern to adolescents (e.g., teen dating, physical maturation, sexuality).

16. Teach the child to confront sexual harassment by naming it and asking the offender to terminate the behavior. (36, 37)

36. Teach the parents to define sexual harassment for the child (i.e., unwanted verbal or physical sexual behavior that interferes with school or work performance or creates an environment that is intimidating); identify examples (e.g., sexual jokes or remarks, unwelcome touching, pressure to engage in sex). (See *Sexual Integrity for Teens* by Hansen.)

37. Assign the parents to review the school policy on sexual harassment with the child and discuss the process of reporting any incidents of concern.

17. Assist the child in terminating a potentially violent dating relationship. (38, 39, 40)

38. Instruct the parents to refer the child to counseling to explore the underlying psychology of abuse and to gain an understanding of the causes, violent tendencies, and prevention of victimization in dating relationships.

39. Assign the parents and the child to view the video *Matter of Choice: A Program Confronting Teenage Sexual Abuse* to gain an understanding of adolescent abuse.

40. Instruct the parents to encourage the child to adopt a personal zero tolerance policy for dating violence by writing a personal pledge and signing it.

—. ______________________ —. ______________________

—. ______________________ —. ______________________

—. ______________________ —. ______________________

DIAGNOSTIC SUGGESTIONS

ICD-9-CM	*ICD-10-CM*	*DSM-5* Disorder, Condition, or Problem
313.81	F91.3	Oppositional Defiant Disorder
300.02	F41.1	Generalized Anxiety Disorder
V71.02	Z72.810	Child Antisocial Behavior
______	______	______________________
______	______	______________________

SIBLING RIVALRY

BEHAVIORAL DEFINITIONS

1. Report feelings of guilt and inadequacy over perceived inability to effectively manage sibling jealousy and conflict.
2. Lack conflict resolution strategies to assist the children in settling disputes and learning to live peacefully with all family members.
3. Attempt to distribute family resources equally rather than based on the individual and unique needs of each child.
4. Foster jealousy and rivalry by favoring one child and/or comparing the talents, actions and attributes of the siblings.
5. Too quickly and too often intervene in sibling disputes and punish the perceived perpetrator.
6. Report feeling frustrated by the hostility and confusion resulting from the sibling conflicts.
7. Ignore serious sibling conflicts that can result in destructive long-term effects.
8. Support a win/lose attitude among the siblings that contributes to intensified conflict.
9. Siblings engage in manipulation and triangulation to become the favored child.

—. ____

____

—. ____

____

—. ____

____

LONG-TERM GOALS

1. Stop hurtful verbal and/or aggressive physical interactions among siblings.
2. View each sibling as unique and focus on the individual strengths and abilities of each child.
3. Learn conflict management techniques and settle disputes among the siblings using peace-making strategies.
4. Channel the sibling's negative feelings into creative or acceptable methods of expression.
5. Refrain from expressing favoritism or comparing siblings with one another.
6. Siblings co-exist peacefully within the family unit and develop a positive relationship.

__. ____

____

__. ____

____

__. ____

____

SHORT-TERM OBJECTIVES

1. Verbalize empathy for the child's feelings of insecurity and fears of loss of attention or affection to a sibling and give reassurance of the continuation of a strong, positive parent/child relationship. (1, 2, 3)

THERAPEUTIC INTERVENTIONS

1. Assist the parents in listing each child's fears and feelings of inadequacy that contribute to sibling jealousy (e.g., reduced time with parents, loss of favored status in family).
2. Define empathy and discuss its critical role in the prevention and resolution of sibling conflicts.
3. Brainstorm with the parents a list of affirmations they can give each child to enhance self-confidence (or assign the "Affirming Each Child's

Uniqueness" activity from the *Parenting Skills Homework Planner* by Knapp).

2. Recognize the warning signals of potential sibling conflict before it begins to escalate. (4, 5, 6)

4. Teach the parents to anticipate the thoughts, feelings, and actions of each child prior to the outbreak of a conflict and to encourage the positive efforts of each sibling to de-escalate the dispute.

5. Assign the parents to read a story to the children involving sibling rivalry (e.g., *Pain and the Great One* by Blume and Trivas or *I'd Rather Have an Iguana* by Mario) and discuss with the siblings how empathy and communication can prevent conflicts.

6. Assist the parents in recognizing and addressing their own personal underlying scripts, behaviors, thought processes, and dysfunctional interactions that are contributing to the sibling rivalry (e.g., comparing the siblings, encouraging sibling competition).

3. Verbalize an awarness of the child's negative feelings toward siblings as a normal part of learning to share family resources and developing empathy. (7, 8)

7. Advise the parents of the importance of providing time for emotional expression; council them to actively listen to each child's feelings concerning sibling conflict without taking sides.

8. Assign the parents and siblings to create a list of family resources (e.g., attention, emotional and financial support); discuss how each family member contributes to and

utilizes the family assets (or assign the "Sharing the Family Resources" activity from the *Parenting Skills Homework Planner* by Knapp).

4. Verbalize the belief that parental love and recognition are abundant resources that can be shared by all of the siblings without any child being deprived. (9, 10, 11)

9. Assist the parents in writing a definition of unconditional love (e.g., constant love given regardless of personal attributes or performance); assign them to list examples in their personal journal.

10. Ask the parents and siblings to list the benefits of developing a close relationship with all family members (e.g., gaining help and support, increased family harmony); then brainstorm methods of improving family interactions among the parents and siblings (e.g., stop put-downs, don't interrupt, share).

11. Assign the parents and the siblings to draw a large heart and paste a picture of each family member in it to illustrate that the heart's capacity to love is great.

5. List methods of resolving sibling conflict fairly and positively. (12, 13, 14)

12. Council the parents that interference in sibling disputes often intensifies the conflict; instruct them to involve themselves as a coach rather than a referee.

13. Teach the parents a basic process to assist the siblings in resolving disputes: (1) State the problem, (2) listen to the other's point of view, (3) share feelings about the problem, (4) brainstorm ideas for

solving the problem, and (5) agree to a solution and implement it.

14. Assign parents to read *Help! The Kids Are at It Again* (Crary and Katayama) for an understanding of how to use sibling disputes to teach problem solving.

6. Diffuse sibling rivalry and strengthen the bonds between siblings through positive recognition, fair treatment, and awareness of personal feelings. (15, 16)

15. Encourage the parents to reinforce positive behavior from all siblings and administer discipline to each in an even-handed and logical manner.

16. Assign the parents to use the criterion of "unique" rather than "equal" in the distribution of love, attention, time and physical needs (e.g., "I love you each uniquely.").

7. Recognize the individual personality, needs, sensitivities, goals, and aspirations of each child and work to reduce competition between the siblings. (17, 18)

17. Instruct the parents to use descriptive rather than comparative words when addressing either a positive or negative behavior (e.g., "I see you're finished with you're homework." versus "You've finished your homework and your brother hasn't even started.").

18. Assign the parents to affirm the efforts of each child based on individual merit and never in comparison to the accomplishment or failure of a sibling.

8. Attend a parenting class or read literature on the topic of sibling rivalry, its causes and cures. (19, 20)

19. Refer the parents to a parenting group that addresses the topic of sibling rivalry (e.g., *Siblings Without Rivalry*

Workshop Kit by Faber and Mazlish).

20. Assign parents to read *How to Talk so Kids Will Listen and Listen so Kids Will Talk* (Faber and Mazlish) and *Siblings Without Rivalry* (Faber and Mazlish) to learn strategies to promote positive sibling relationships.

9. Establish a pro-active system of positive discipline that is balanced with love and designed to promote healthy self-esteem and responsible behavior. (21, 22, 23)

21. Ask parents to read a book on parent/child interaction (e.g., *Parent Talk* by Moorman); discuss how the strategies can help in managing sibling disharmony.

22. Suggest that the parents use disciplinary interventions that promote cooperation between siblings (e.g., require the disputing siblings to work together on a 1,000-piece jigsaw puzzle).

23. Instruct the parents to require that the siblings role play a more positive method of communicating their point of view when they engage in disparaging remarks and put-downs.

10. Divide the family workload and discuss responsibilities and other family issues in a family forum. (24)

24. Council the parents to hold weekly meetings during which family chores are delegated, family problems are resolved, and recognition is given for the efforts of each family member.

11. Encourage the child to use dramatization or drawing to express feelings about siblings and family interactions. (25, 26)

25. Instruct the parents to use role play or mutual story telling with the siblings to help them resolve a conflict using peace-making strategies.

26. Teach the parents to use cartooning (see "Cartooning as a Counseling Approach to a Socially Isolated Child" by Sonntag) to encourage the siblings to illustrate a dispute that has a peaceful outcome.

12. Establish social outlets or hobbies for each child to develop personal interests and diffuse sibling rivalry issues. (27, 28)

27. Council the parents to encourage the children to explore the acquisition of a new hobby or activity that reflects each child's unique interests and talents.

28. Instruct the parents to encourage each child to join a social or interest-related group in school or the community.

13. Allow for feelings of acceptance and attachment to evolve slowly and resist the inclination to force an instantly strong relationship among the siblings. (29, 30)

29. Assign the parents to record the status of the sibling relationships in a journal to gain an accurate perception of the children's growing bond.

30. Assign the parents and siblings to describe in writing or picture format the evolving nature of the sibling relationships in the past, present, and future.

14. Encourage and participate in activities that involve both total family and one-to-one interaction among family members (31, 32)

31. Encourage the parents to plan for a weekly family outing and to enlist the participation of each family member.

32. Assign the parents to engage the each child in a daily activity that strengthens the parent/child bond (e.g., playing games that require interaction, nightly prayers, reciprocal reading).

15. Watch for symptoms that the siblings may need

33. Council the parents to refer the siblings to a group for

professional help to resolve conflict and seek individual therapy if indicated. (33, 34)

children dealing with sibling rivalry.

34. Instruct the parents to support the child in managing feelings of frustration experienced as a result of typical sibling rivalry and to arrange for private therapy if the symptoms appear overwhelming.

16. Family members work together to establish a loving respectful, cooperative family atmosphere. (35, 36)

35. Assign the parents to read *The Seven Habits of Highly Effective Families* (Covey) to learn how to attain a positive family atmosphere by maintaining a respectful, couple-centered marriage.

36. Assist the parents in terminating any sabotaging that is occurring in the family through open discussions and presenting a united parental front.

17. Verbalize the dangers of locking family members into negative or rigid roles and work to value each person for their unique contribution to the family unit. (37, 38)

37. Teach the parents the damage caused by assigning negative family roles (e.g., bully, untrustworthy, loser) or exclusively positive family roles (e.g., most gifted, athletic, beautiful).

38. Encourage the parents to model and affirm the behavior they hope to bring out in each of their children (e.g., persistence, responsibility) rather than identifying negative traits they wish to eliminate (e.g., giving up, shirking duties).

18. Acknowledge progress made toward family peace and harmony. (39)

__. ____________________

__. ____________________

__. ____________________

39. Assign the parents to brainstorm with the family points of pride and unity as well as areas that could be improved to promote positive sibling relationships.

__. ____________________

__. ____________________

__. ____________________

DIAGNOSTIC SUGGESTIONS

ICD-9-CM	*ICD-10-CM*	*DSM-5* Disorder, Condition, or Problem
312.9	F91.9	Unspecified Disruptive, Impulse Control, and Conduct Disorder
312.89	F91.8	Other Specified Disruptive, Impulse Control, and Conduct Disorder
314.01	F90.1	Attention-Deficit/Hyperactivity Disorder, Predominately Hyperactive /Impulsive Presentation
309.3	F43.24	Adjustment Disorder, With Disturbance of Conduct
____	____	________________
____	____	________________

SINGLE PARENTING

BEHAVIORAL DEFINITIONS

1. Raising children alone or in partnership with a co-parent living in a separate residence.
2. Verbalizes feeling overwhelmed with the stress of multiple responsibilities of raising children.
3. Lacks financial resources to support the family on a single income.
4. Lacks consistent, positive, and compassionate discipline.
5. Reports feelings of guilt and inadequacy caused by raising children in a nontraditional family.
6. Reports feelings of grief and loss caused by divorce, death, or absence of the co-parent.
7. Complains of a lack of involvement, and/or financial and emotional support from the other parent.
8. Verbalizes feelings of resentment toward the absent or unhelpful parent.
9. Lacks access to family, friends, or community resources to provide assistance to the family.
10. Lacks education and skills necessary to become self-supporting.
11. Children are traumatized by the breakup of the family and/or feel stigmatized by living in a nontraditional family.
12. Children are unable or unwilling to help with the daily and long-term responsibilities of managing the household.

__. ______________________________

____

__. ______________________________

____

__. ______________________________

____

LONG-TERM GOALS

1. Establish a positive working relationship with the children's co-parent.
2. Obtain the financial resources necessary to support the household.
3. Secure adequate housing, health benefits, and child care.
4. Establish a positive parent/child relationship that includes consistent, positive child-management techniques and discipline.
5. Access family friends and community resources who will assist with the numerous challenges of single parenting.

__. ____

____

__. ____

____

__. ____

____

SHORT-TERM OBJECTIVES

1. Describe the status of the current single-parent family and identify long- and short-term personal and family goals. (1, 2, 3)

THERAPEUTIC INTERVENTIONS

1. Take a complete family history, clarify family issues and concerns, and explore the immediate financial, social, and emotional needs of the household.
2. Ask the parent to detail any imminent changes for the child and family including custody, visitation, and possible moves.
3. Assist the parent in planning for long- and short-term goal attainment by: (1) Listing goals, (2) identifying potential resources and roadblocks, and (3) creating a strategy for success (or assign the "Achieving Family Goals" activity from the *Parenting Skills Homework Planner* by Knapp).

2. Assess financial needs and resources and determine an equitable plan for meeting the basic requirements of all the family members. (4, 5)

3. Negotiate with the co-parent for appropriate child-support. (6, 7)

4. Evaluate the family's financial, food, shelter, medical, and social needs and identify available resources and services. (8, 9)

5. Develop a plan for obtaining viable employment. (10, 11)

4. Assign the parent to create a list of all the family assets and a corresponding list of the family needs; assist in determining how to allocate the assets to cover the basic needs of the family.

5. Solicit a verbal commitment from the parent to collaborate with the co-parent to provide financial support for the children until they reach adulthood.

6. Assign the parent to negotiate and collect appropriate child support from the co-parent through voluntary or court-ordered contributions.

7. Support and encourage the single parent to pursue mediation or legal action if unable to reach an agreement with the co-parent about financial issues, custody, or visitation.

8. Refer the single parent to agencies that provide social, financial, and medical services; facilitate access to these resources.

9. Develop a plan with the parent for obtaining needed assistance by brainstorming solutions to any problems that may interfere (e.g., transportation, day care, appropriate clothing).

10. Assist the parent in planning a job search strategy or training curriculum.

11. Help the parent develop a written resume and prepare for

job interviews by role playing responses to commonly asked questions.

6. Enroll in educational classes or training programs to enhance marketable skills and increase opportunities for employment. (12, 13)

12. Refer the parent to agencies that can help with a job search or training program to become more employable (e.g., Employment Security Commission, State Rehabilitation Services).

13. Assist the parent in identifying adult education, community-based instruction, or welfare-to-career programs designed to provide employment skills and work experience.

7. Establish safe and stable housing for the family. (14, 15)

14. Assist the single parent in evaluating housing and the neighborhood environment in terms of safety, stability, and suitability; determine if unsafe living conditions are contributing to family volatility or the child's feelings of insecurity.

15. Assist the parent in enlisting the help of community agencies (e.g., Habitat for Humanity, www.habitat.org; Department of Housing and Urban Development programs, (800) 569-4287) in finding safe and suitable housing.

8. Arrange for affordable and quality day care through family, friends, or a day care referral service. (16, 17, 18)

16. Assign the parent to select quality day care by obtaining a list of licensed providers and thoroughly evaluating potential facilities.

17. Council the single parent to create a list of family and

friends willing to provide emergency or back-up child care necessary for a working parent.

18. Instruct the parent to investigate after school programs for school-age children offered by school districts and community recreation departments.

9. Secure an affordable family health care plan. (19, 20)

19. Facilitate the parent in seeking employment that includes family health care benefits as part of the salary package.

20. Assign the uninsured single parent to apply for Medicaid or State Children's Health Insurance Program (see Centers for Medicare and Medicaid Services: www.cms.hhs.gov).

10. Express awareness that divorce or loss of a parent through absence or death can create severe emotional disruption for children of all ages. (21, 22)

21. Ask the single parent to discuss any immediate plans for change involving custody, visitation, or moving with the child and emphasize that consideration should be given to the effects of change on the child.

22. Assign the parent to read *Successful Single Parenting (*Richmond) or *Single Parenting for Dummies* (Peterson) to gain strategies for dealing with single-parent challenges.

11. Develop a cooperative plan with the co-parent for dealing with child management issues. (23, 24)

23. Advise the parent to establish regular communication with the co-parent to discuss child management issues, establish a bond of cooperation, and

present a united front to the child.

24. Develop a plan with the single parent in collaboration with the co-parent that sets clear expectations for the child in each home.

12. Verbalize a commitment to collaborate with the co-parent to resolve all problems and concerns involving the children. (25, 26)

25. Encourage the single parent to strongly advocate for custody and visitation arrangements that are conducive to the emotional stability of the children.

26. Offer to arbitrate disputes and differences between the co-parents to reduce their level of conflict and increase their sprit of cooperation.

13. Collaborate with the co-parent on major discipline issues. (27)

27. Instruct the single parent to discuss larger discipline issues with the co-parent, sharing individual perspectives, brainstorming solutions, and determining an approach that is acceptable to both parties.

14. Reassure the child about personal security, express an awareness and empathy for the child's fears, and commit to maintain a close, loving relationship. (28, 29, 30)

28. Assign the single parent to use active listening techniques and to express an awareness of and empathy for the child's fears, feelings, questions, and concerns.

29. Council the single parent to shield the child from arguments with the co-parent and to resist using the child as a messenger in their disputes.

30. Instruct the parent that a loving, positive relationship with both parents is in the best interest of the child and advise against making derogatory

comments about the other parent to the child.

15. Remain alert for signs and symptoms of the child's emotional distress and plan for addressing these problems. (31)

31. Advise the single parent to watch for signs that the child is experiencing severe emotional distress and to schedule counseling for the child if necessary.

16. Inform the child's school about the current family status and request their help in resolving school-related issues. (32, 33)

32. Instruct the parent to inform the child's teacher or the school counselor about the current family situation and develop a plan for the co-parents involvement in school-related issues (e.g., attendance at school functions, review of progress reports).

33. Advise the parent to request that supportive services be given to the child at school (e.g., divorce group counseling, individual counseling, academic support, peer mentoring) to help with adjustment to the family disruption.

17. Engage personal, family, and community resources to successfully meet the challenges of single parenting. (34, 35, 36, 37)

34. Encourage the single parent to join a faith-based or community group that supports single parents or to access support from an Internet site (e.g., *Single Parent Central*, www.singleparentcentral.com; *Single Mothers Online*, www.singlemothers.org; *Parents World*, www.parentsworld.com).

35. Assign the single parent to attend a parenting class that offers guidance for the challenges faced by single

parents (e.g., *Becoming a Love and Logic Parent* by Fay, Cline, and Fay or *The Parent Talk System* by Moorman and Knapp).

36. Council the single parent to join or form a children's playgroup to combine parent and child socialization while utilizing a low-cost and highly enjoyable activity.

37. Assist the single parent in reducing stress by scheduling some alone time or time with friends away from the children, and taking time for personal pampering (or assign the "Stress Reduction Strategies" activity from the *Parenting Skills Homework Planner* by Knapp).

—. ______________________ —. ______________________

______________________ ______________________

—. ______________________ —. ______________________

______________________ ______________________

—. ______________________ —. ______________________

______________________ ______________________

DIAGNOSTIC SUGGESTIONS

ICD-9-CM	*ICD-10-CM*	*DSM-5* Disorder, Condition, or Problem
309.24	F43.22	Adjustment Disorder, With Anxiety
309.0	F43.21	Adjustment disorder, With Depressed Mood
309.28	F43.23	Adjustment Disorder, With Mixed Anxiety and Depressed Mood
_____	_____	______________________
_____	_____	______________________

SPOUSAL ROLE AND RELATIONSHIP CONFLICT

BEHAVIORAL DEFINITIONS

1. Give attention and affection almost exclusively to the children, replacing the previous adult-centered, intimate spousal relationship.
2. Deprive the children of parental love, nurturing, and support due to a preoccupation with intimacy and attention given to each other.
3. Report feeling exhausted and overstressed by work, social, and family responsibilities, leaving little time and energy for maintaining intimacy in the marriage.
4. Create feelings of fear, intimidation, and resentment in spouse through abusive behavior.
5. Mother feels overburdened and father feels alienated due to rigid family role definitions.
6. Refusal or reluctance to use direct and open communication leads to triangulation, manipulation, and rivalry among family members.
7. Employ opposing parenting styles, creating conflict and confusion within the family.
8. Lack of commitment to family needs and responsibilities by one spouse, creates resentment, lack of self-esteem, and feelings of hostility in the co-parent and children.
9. Engage in addictive behavior preventing the fulfillment of family roles and responsibilities.
10. Lack constructive conflict-resolution strategies resulting in threats, anger, and emotional distancing among family members.

__. ____

____

LONG-TERM GOALS

1. Adapt and prioritize activities and strategies that support and nurture the spousal relationship.
2. Share the responsibility and workload required for managing family duties and child rearing.
3. Establish a cooperative, consistent and positive strategy for discipline and child nurturance.
4. Learn and utilize collaborative problem-solving and conflict-resolution strategies.

—. ____

____

SHORT-TERM OBJECTIVES

1. Verbalize realistic expectations for marital harmony and effective family functioning. (1, 2, 3)

THERAPEUTIC INTERVENTIONS

1. Assign the parents to describe and rate the current health of their marriage in various categories (e.g., parenting, shared responsibilities, intimacy or assign the "State of Our Marriage Report" activity from the *Parenting Skills Homework Planner* by Knapp).
2. Instruct the parents to set short-term goals for improving their relationship and family functioning that are specific and attainable (e.g., eat dinner together three times per week, reduce debt by 10 percent, engage in two family activities per week).
3. Assign the parents to read material to help them maintain a balanced perspective concerning marriage and family obligations (e.g., *Don't Sweat the Small Stuff with*

Your Family by Carlson or *The Seven Habits of Highly Effective Families* by Covey).

2. Negotiate and define spousal roles and responsibilities to one another and the family. (4, 5)

4. Instruct the parents to list all the jobs and duties necessary for effective functioning of the family for the following week; negotiate which parent is responsible for each assignment.

5. Ask the parents to evaluate which marital and family roles (e.g., income provider, household manager, disciplinarian, activity planner) could be shared more equally or reassigned to more evenly distribute the marriage and family responsibilities.

3. Identify and verbally affirm positive characteristics and behaviors in the marriage partner or co-parent. (6, 7)

6. Ask the parents to create a list of the strengths, assets, and positive behaviors they recognize in their spouse; assign each spouse to verbally acknowledge their appreciation of and admiration for one specific positive quality of their partner at least two times per day.

7. Assign each parent to support the co-parent by pointing out strengths during conversations with the children (e.g., "Your mom sure does love you; Your dad spends a lot of time supporting you.").

4. Identify and implement strategies to enhance a positive, supportive, and intimate relationship with the spouse. (8, 9, 10, 11)

8. Ask the parents to make a commitment to strengthen their marriage and to follow through by attending counseling sessions, completing homework assignments, and

implementing team-building strategies with the partner.

9. Assign the parents to read *The Five Love Languages* (Chapman) and identify their preferred methods of giving and receiving love (e.g., quality time, words of affirmation, gifts, acts of service, physical touch).
10. Instruct the parents to create intimacy by giving affection according to the love language most preferred by their partner at least once per day.
11. Recommend that the couple read *The Gift of the Magi* (Henry) as a preparation for creating ways to offer love and commitment to their spouse even though the effort may require some personal sacrifice.

5. Demonstrate techniques of effective communication that involve empathetic listening and clearly stated points of view. (12, 13, 14)

12. Teach the parents to clearly state their point of view using "I" statements (e.g., "I feel . . . When . . . Because . . .") that express personal feelings and reactions to a situation rather than blaming personal feelings on another person (see *Parent Effectiveness Training* by Gordon). Assign the spouses to use this strategy at least five times during the subsequent week.
13. Role play with the parents how to use active listening (e.g., listening with empathy and understanding without giving advice or rushing to solve the problem) during spousal discussions.

14. Council the parents to establish a private and distraction-free time and place to meet for one hour two times per week to communicate about shared goals, interests, and concerns.

6. List and resolve to modify addictions, habits, and behaviors that are detrimental to the marriage and family. (15, 16, 17)

15. Brainstorm with the parents a list of their habits, addictions, and marriage-defeating behaviors that cause pain and/or friction in the relationship and family (e.g., infidelity, alcohol abuse, excessive spending, workaholic).

16. Assist the parents in prioritizing their negative habits and behaviors and in choosing one or two to eliminate and replace with more productive, family-friendly activities.

17. Refer the parent or parents to community programs or services dedicated to addressing serious addictions (e.g., Alcoholics or Gamblers Anonymous, psychiatric hospital).

7. Participate in social activities that are family friendly and satisfying to both spouses. (18, 19, 20)

18. Assist the parents in brainstorming a list of activities that are mutually enjoyable; assign them to engage in one activity as a couple each week.

19. Instruct the parents to eliminate television, videos, and computer access for everyone in the family for one hour per evening and to use the time to interact with one another (e.g., talking, listening to music, playing a game,

working on a puzzle, participating in a hobby); invite the parents to increase the media-free time as they and the family adjust and discover the benefits of being together without media distraction.

20. Encourage the parents to plan a weekly family outing and to enlist the participation of each family member in the preparation.

8. Define parenting roles and responsibilities so that both parents share the joys and responsibilities of raising the children. (21, 22, 23)

21. Brainstorm with the parents a list of their parental responsibilities and assist them in assigning these obligations so that both parents engage equitably in providing for the children's physical, financial, and emotional needs.

22. Ask the parents to predict emerging future needs of the children and to commit to an ongoing relationship and personal involvement with them that includes nurturing and guidance.

23. Encourage the couple to predict how their spousal roles will change as the marriage and family evolves (or assign the "Our Evolving Marriage and Spousal Roles" activity from the *Parenting Skills Homework Planner* by Knapp).

9. Agree to work together to eliminate resistance, manipulation, and triangulation by the children. (24, 25, 26)

24. Advise the parents to avoid power struggles with their children by setting limits with controlled choices (e.g., "Would you rather clean your room on Saturday or

Sunday?") and using contingency management strategies (e.g., "You may watch television as soon as you homework is completed.").

25. Teach the parents the importance of administering discipline in a unified, even-handed, consistent, and logical manner to defuse manipulative efforts.

26. Direct the parents to avoid overprotective parenting by determining which problems belong to their child and then allowing the child to solve the problem alone or with guidance if necessary.

10. Back up the partner in issues of discipline and behavior management. (27, 28)

27. Advise the parents to form a cooperative alliance when addressing child management issues and to support each other on discipline decisions unless they are perceived as abusive.

28. Instruct the parents to discuss child management differences privately, come to an agreement that both can support, and then form a united front when presenting their decisions to the children.

11. Negotiate and agree on strategies for positively relating to and disciplining the children. (29, 30)

29. Teach the parents to use consequences designed to teach their children a more appropriate behavior and to eliminate overly punitive reactions to negative behavior (e.g., broken curfew, return home one hour earlier next time, failure to clean room, no fun activities until room is clean).

30. Encourage the parents to refrain from interfering when a natural consequence is available to teach their children to be more responsible (e.g., forgetting gym shoes and sitting out during play, refusing to eat lunch and getting hungry before dinner).

12. Utilize techniques of positive discipline to address all child-behavior concerns. (31, 32, 33)

31. Teach the parents to work together to offer frequent descriptive praise when recognizing positive behavior and to use constructive guidance when behavior requires redirection.

32. Encourage the parents to prioritize the discipline issues and to address them one by one rather than trying to solve all the behavior problems at once.

33. Advise the parents to remain involved in the lives and activities of their children; explain that careful monitoring of children's behavior is an essential responsibility of parents until the child is living independently.

13. Reinforce and affirm all efforts given to positive relationships and appropriate activities among the siblings. (34)

34. Instruct the couple to promote positive interaction by initiating family games, reinforcing attempts at mutual activities, and encouraging discussions during meals and family gatherings.

14. Agree on and utilize a problem-solving process for resolving marital and family disputes. (35, 36, 37)

35. Teach the parents a structured conflict-resolution process: (1) problem definition, (2) brainstorming for solutions, (3)

listing the pros and cons of each potential solution, (4) agreeing on a strategy, (5) implementation of the plan, and (6) evaluation of the outcome); ask them to resolve two conflicts during the following week.

36. Teach the parents to work toward win-win solutions when resolving conflict by agreeing to negotiate and identify potential strategies until both spouses are satisfied with the plan.

37. Instruct the parents to eliminate hostile and passive-aggressive behaviors (e.g., arguing, pouting, appeasement, leaving) when resolving conflict by substituting more assertive, proactive negotiation strategies (e.g., "I" statements, active listening, brainstorming).

__. ____________________ __. ____________________

____________________ ____________________

DIAGNOSTIC SUGGESTIONS:

ICD-9-CM	*ICD-10-CM*	*DSM-5* Disorder, Condition, or Problem
309.0	F43.21	Adjustment disorder, With Depressed Mood
309.24	F43.22	Adjustment Disorder, With Anxiety
309.28	F43.23	Adjustment Disorder, With Mixed Anxiety and Depressed Mood
300.4	F34.1	Persistent Depressive Disorder
V61.10	Z63.0	Relationship Distress with Spouse or Intimate Partner
______	______	____________________
______	______	____________________

STRATEGIES FOR PRESCHOOLERS (AGE BIRTH TO SIX)

BEHAVIORAL DEFINITIONS

1. Lack effective parenting techniques and rely on strategies learned from personal, family, and childhood experiences.
2. Exhibit a permissive approach to the child and a reluctance to set reasonable limits.
3. Waver between overly protective and overly demanding interactions with the child.
4. Become frustrated and confused when the child behaves in an oppositional manner.
5. Neglect the child's basic needs for nurturing by ignoring pleas for love and attention.
6. Rely too heavily on day care, nannies, babysitters, and relatives to provide love, nurture, and guidance to the child.
7. Develop a symbiotic relationship with the child by excluding outside interaction and childcare.
8. Allow the child to make decisions and receive privileges that are far beyond the child's level of maturity.
9. Child demonstrates an absence of age-appropriate self-control in various environments.
10. Child lacks respect for self, parents, and others.

__. ____

____

__. ____

____

__. ____

____

LONG-TERM GOALS

1. Establish a strong, loving, nurturing bond with the child while employing positive discipline strategies that set limits and encourage independence.
2. View parenting as a manageable challenge and an opportunity to learn and grow with the child.
3. Child demonstrates respect and regard for self and others.
4. Child develops a sense of security, self-confidence, and responsibility.

__. ____

____

__. ____

____

__. ____

____

SHORT-TERM OBJECTIVES

1. Engage in daily affectionate, nurturing, and playful contact with the child. (1, 2)
2. Verbalize the advantages of implementing positive discipline at an early age. (3, 4)

THERAPEUTIC INTERVENTIONS

1. Instruct the parents to initiate a strong bond with their baby through loving interaction (e.g., holding, rocking, talking, making eye contact,) and providing for essential needs (e.g., food, clean diaper, warmth).
2. Assign the parents to schedule daily playtime when they devote full attention to the child; turn off the television or radio and engage in an exclusively child-centered activity.
3. Advise the parents to provide a sense of security in the young child by establishing age-appropriate limits (e.g., bedtime, mealtime, play areas, clean up routine).

4. Brainstorm with the parents a list of characteristics they hope their child will develop (e.g., honesty, empathy, self-confidence, social skills); discuss the benefits of encouraging these traits when the child is very young because young children desire to emulate and please their parents.

3. Structure the environment to ensure the young child's safety. (5, 6)

5. Assign the parents to childproof their home by removing fragile or dangerous items and providing a safe eating, sleeping, and play area for the child.

6. Instruct the parents to combine a verbal inhibition (e.g., "No touch," when child pulls on glasses) with physical management (e.g., hold the child's hands) to teach the child not to engage in an inappropriate behavior.

4. Identify the developmental stages of the child. (7, 8)

7. Discuss the developmental stages of early childhood with the parents as outlined in current literature (e.g., *Touchpoints* by Brazelton).

8. Assist the parents in determining if their child's behavior is within normal developmental limits (or assign the "Charting Our Child's Developmental Stages" activity from the *Parenting Skills Homework Planner* by Knapp).

5. Read literature and/or attend a parenting class to learn effective parenting strategies for young children. (9, 10)

9. Assign the parents to read literature about implementing strategies of positive discipline with their young child (e.g., *Love and Logic Magic for*

Early Childhood by Fay and Fay or *The Gesell Institute's Child Behavior* by Ilg and Ames).

10. Refer the parents to a positive parenting class (e.g., *Parenting Young Children* by Dinkmeyer, McKay, and Dinkmeyer, *Becoming a Love and Logic Parent* by Fay, Cline, and Fay, or *The Parent Talk System* by Moorman and Knapp).

6. Verbalize an awareness of the problems created by being an overprotective parent. (11, 12, 13)

11. Assign the parents to listen to the audiotape, *Helicopters, Drill Sergeants, and Consultants* (Fay) to recognize the advantage of allowing their child to solve some problems alone or with limited assistance.

12. Teach the parents how over-protective parenting can contribute to the child's feelings of inadequacy and dependency (e.g., child relies on parents rather than developing problem-solving abilities); encourage them to allow age-appropriate tasks and responsibilities.

13. Assign the parents to watch the *Finding Nemo* video (Walt Disney Pictures) with their child and note examples of how an overprotective parent can interfere with the child's normal maturation and development.

7. Set age-appropriate limits using strategies of positive discipline. (14, 15, 16)

14. Role-play with the parents the use of "I" statements (e.g., "I feel . . . when you . . . because . . .") (see *Parent*

Effectiveness Training by Gordon).

15. Instruct the parents to use "Controlled Choices" (see *Parent Talk* by Moorman) to limit options according to the child's maturity and decision-making abilities (e.g., "Would you like hot dogs or grilled cheese?" versus "What would you like to eat?").

16. Advise the parents to use a short timeout when the child's behavior becomes defiant, or overly emotional, requiring that the child remain away until a cooperative attitude has been established.

8. Teach the child appropriate behavior through modeling and defining what is expected. (17, 18)

17. Instruct the parents to model a desired behavior for their child and verbally refer to the action (e.g., "When I come home I put my boots in the closet and hang my coat on the hook.").

18. Assign parents to use the "Next time . . ." technique (see *Parent Talk* by Moorman) to help the child replace inappropriate with appropriate behavior (e.g., "Next time you need my help please ask for it in a polite tone of voice.").

9. Initiate reinforcement strategies to help the child develop responsible behavior. (19, 20)

19. Assign the parents to teach responsible behavior by asking the child to act responsibly (child asked to turn off the television), using misbehavior as a learning opportunity (child refuses to complete the task), imposing a consequence to teach a more appropriate behavior (no television until

tomorrow), allowing the same opportunity to act responsibly (next day the child is allowed to watch a favorite show and then turn off television) (see "The Four Steps to Responsibility" in *Parenting with Love and Logic* by Cline and Fay).

20. Ask the parents to assign one new responsibility each month (e.g., leaving pacifier in the bedroom, putting on own coat) for which the child is reinforced (or assign the "Helping My Child Develop Responsible Behavior" activity from the *Parenting Skills Homework Planner* by Knapp).

10. Utilize logical consequences to re-direct inappropriate behavior. (21, 22, 23)

21. Brainstorm with the parents a list of situations in which they could allow their preschooler to learn from the consequences of poor decisions (e.g., kicks sister and earns a timeout, doesn't pick up toys and loses them for one day).

22. Assign the parents to allow the child to experience the consequences of an irresponsible personal choice (e.g., fooling around at bedtime leads to losing bedtime story) and to reassure the child by saying, "Next time you'll have a chance to make a different choice."

23. Help the parents design several logical consequences to deal with chronic misbehavior (e.g., wandering off at the store results in riding in the stroller,

throwing a temper tantrum results in a timeout).

11. Promote the child's efforts to become self-reliant using encouragement and support. (24, 25, 26)

24. Advise the parents to use the empowering statement, "I think you can handle it," when the preschooler is asking for too much assistance and to exclaim: "You did it!" when the child has successfully mastered a challenge.

25. Assign the parents to use "Act as if" in response to "I can't language" (see *Parent Talk* by Moorman) to encourage the preschooler to make an effort despite fear of failure, (e.g., "Act as if you knew how to draw that tree.").

26. Ask parents to use the "Check Yourself" technique (see *Parent Talk* by Moorman) (e.g., "Check your backpack to make sure you have what you need for school.") to help the child develop the ability to prepare successfully for upcoming events.

12. Verbally recognize and affirm the child's positive qualities. (27, 28)

27. Instruct the parents to affirm the child's positive assets and qualities whenever possible (e.g., "You're a good helper. You like different kinds of food.").

28. Council the parents to deal with negative behavior by separating the deed from the doer (e.g., "Biting is not allowed") and directing the child toward more positive behavior (e.g., "Use your words to tell others how you feel.").

13. Refrain from personal criticism while directing the child toward positive, desirable behavior. (29)

29. Encourage the parents to regularly refer to an ongoing list of the child's emerging positive characteristics as an encouragement for both themselves and the child.

14. Grant specific freedoms and privileges consistent with the child's demonstrated level of maturity and self-control. (30)

30. Council the parents to wait until the necessary self-control is acquired before granting specific privileges (e.g., allow walking independently in the store only when staying close to the parent has been demonstrated).

15. Report a reduction in power struggles resulting from strategies designed to enlist the child's cooperation. (31, 32, 33)

31. Instruct the parents to use the "broken record" technique by repeating the same phrase until the child complies (e.g., "It's time for you to take your nap." "It's time for you to take your nap.") to avoid arguing about a parental directive.

32. Assign the parents to use age-appropriate choices (e.g., "You may wear your red shirt or your green shirt. Turn off the television or I will.") to share control with the preschooler and direct the focus toward the choice.

33. Direct the parents to avoid power struggles with their preschooler by making a result desired by the child contingent upon a behavior desired by the parent (e.g., "You may watch television after your toys have been picked up.").

16. Express awareness that all behaviors have a social purpose and all

34. Teach the parents the four goals of children's misbehavior: attention, power,

misbehavior is goal oriented. (34, 35)

revenge, and overcoming feelings of inadequacy; determine how they may be reinforcing misbehavior by their reactions and brainstorm more appropriate responses (see *Children: The Challenge* by Dreikurs and Stoltz).

35. Assign the parents to involve the child in reciprocal activities that encourage a healthy self-esteem and a feeling of belonging (e.g., one-to-one chats, high fives, daily greetings, reciprocal smiles).

17. List and implement activities designed to maintain a strong couple-centered family environment. (36, 37)

36. Assign the parents to read *The Seven Habits of Highly Effective Families* (Covey) to learn strategies for attaining a positive family atmosphere.

37. Brainstorm with the parents ideas for strengthening their marriage and maintaining a couple-centered family (e.g., support each other during child interactions, keep a weekly date night).

18. Seek support, encouragement, and respite from co-parent, family, and friends. (38, 39)

38. Brainstorm with the parents a list of support people who can be relied on to babysit, console, listen, and help out in case of emergency or burn out.

39. Discuss with the parents the importance of cooperation in the co-parenting process and offer to mediate any current roadblocks.

__. ______________________ __. ______________________
______________________ ______________________
__. ______________________ __. ______________________
______________________ ______________________
__. ______________________ __. ______________________
______________________ ______________________

DIAGNOSTIC SUGGESTIONS:

ICD-9-CM	*ICD-10-CM*	*DSM-5* Disorder, Condition, or Problem
314.01	F90.1	Attention-Deficit/Hyperactivity Disorder, Predominately Hyperactive /Impulsive Presentation
300.02	F41.1	Generalized Anxiety Disorder
309.21	F93.0	Separation Anxiety Disorder
V71.02	Z72.810	Child Antisocial Behavior
V61.20	Z62.820	Parent-Child Relational Problem
________	________	______________________
________	________	______________________

STRATEGIES FOR CHILDREN (AGE 7 TO 12)

BEHAVIORAL DEFINITIONS

1. Lack effective parenting strategies and the ability to set reasonable limits for the child.
2. Verbalize unclear boundary definitions and fail to differentiate between the parent and the child's needs, interests, and problems.
3. Place pressure on the child to achieve or excel, creating an anxiety-ridden parent/child relationship based on conditional love.
4. Maintain low expectations of and fail to reinforce the child's abilities and achievements.
5. Neglect the child's basic needs for food, shelter, nurturing, and guidance.
6. Overprotect the child, leading to dependency, low self-esteem, and a lack of responsible behavior in the child.
7. Use harsh and punitive discipline resulting in fearful, manipulative, self-protective behavior, and/or retaliation from the child.
8. Implement polarized approaches to parenting, creating isolation, confusion, triangulation, and hostility among family members.
9. Child lacks the ability to function independently at home, school, and in the community.

__. ____

____

LONG-TERM GOALS

1. Acquire positive discipline strategies that set limits and encourage independence.
2. Agree to form a united parent front and cooperate on all issues of discipline and child management.

3. Demonstrate support and involvement in the child's interests, activities, and academic achievement.
4. Demonstrate unconditional love for the child.
5. Be a positive role model for the child in all areas of functioning.

__. ____

____

SHORT-TERM OBJECTIVES

1. Read parenting literature and attend classes that teach a positive approach to child management. (1, 2)

2. List the essential needs of an elementary aged child and create a plan for accommodating these needs. (3, 4)

THERAPEUTIC INTERVENTIONS

1. Assign the parents to read literature defining theories of positive discipline and child management strategies (e.g., *Parenting with Love and Logic* by Cline and Fay, *Kids Are Worth It!* by Coloroso, or *Children: The Challenge* by Dreikurs).

2. Refer the parents to a parenting class (e.g., *Systematic Training for Effective Parenting(STEP)* by Dinkmeyer and McKay, *Becoming a Love and Logic Parent* by Fay, Cline, and Fay, or *The Parent Talk System* by Moorman and Knapp) to acquire techniques of positive discipline to use with the child.

3. Brainstorm with the parents the essential requirements for the healthy development of their child (e.g., food, shelter, affirmation, discipline, character development); determine how these needs are being met.

4. Assist the parents in creating a definition of unconditional love (e.g., complete and

constant love given regardless of personal attributes or performance); brainstorm methods of sharing this nurturing form of love with all family members.

3. Establish limits for the child using "I" statements, choices, positive conditions, and timeout. (5, 6, 7, 8)

5. Discuss and role play with the parents the use of "I" statements (e.g., "I feel . . . , when . . . , because . . .") with the child as a first step in addressing inappropriate behavior (see *Parent Effectiveness Training* by Gordon).

6. Instruct the parents in using "Controlled Choices" (see *Parent Talk* by Moorman) to limit options according to the child's level of responsibility (e.g., "Would you like hot dogs or grilled cheese?" versus "What would you like to eat?").

7. Teach the parents to use positive conditions to make a privilege the child desires contingent on a behavior the parent requires (e.g., "Your friend may come over when you have picked up your room").

8. Advise the parents to use a short timeout when the child's behavior becomes defiant or overly emotional and to require that the child remain excluded from family interaction until the child adopts a cooperative attitude.

4. Utilize natural and logical consequences to redirect behavior. (9, 10)

9. Define natural (e.g., naturally occurring in the environment) and logical

(e.g., created by the parents) consequences and outline their effectiveness as part of a positive discipline strategy.

10. Assist the parents in designing several logical consequences to deal with the child's chronic, inappropriate behavior (e.g., forgets to make bed before school, is not allowed after school activities until the bed is made, procrastinates about doing homework, required to get up early to complete homework).

5. Implement strategies of discipline that teach responsible decision making. (11, 12)

11. Assign the parents to give the child an age-appropriate task or responsibility (e.g., completing homework); use misbehavior as a learning opportunity (e.g., child fails to complete the task); combine a logical consequence and empathy to teach responsible decision making (e.g., "So sorry, no television until the homework is complete."); give the same task again (e.g., child allowed to watch television next day after homework is completed) (see *Parenting with Love and Logic* by Cline and Fay).

12. Ask the parents to use the "Red Light, Green Light" technique to turn an irresponsible behavior into a responsible behavior: (1) Red light: Describe the inappropriate behavior to the child (e.g., trash overflowing); (2) Green light: Describe the

expected behavior (e.g., trash taken to dumpster) (see *Parent Talk* by Moorman).

6. Grant specific freedoms consistent with the child's maturity and level of self-control. (13, 14)

13. Describe to the parents the importance of extending freedoms to the child only after developmental maturity has been attained; brainstorm with the parents a list of acceptable and unacceptable privileges for an elementary-aged child (e.g., acceptable: later bedtime on weekends, riding bike in neighborhood, unacceptable: late bedtime on school nights, riding bike on highway).

14. Teach the parents to use the phrase "Soon you'll be on your own," to encourage the child to earn freedom from close parental supervision by demonstrating the ability to complete a task independently (see *Parent Talk* by Moorman).

7. Encourage the child to solve personal problems with guidance. (15, 16, 17)

15. Advise the parents to use the empowering statement, "I think you can handle it," when the child is asking for too much assistance in solving problems and to offer recognition when the child has successfully mastered a challenge.

16. Brainstorm with the parents strategies for assisting the child to complete tasks without taking over the child's responsibility (e.g., offer guidance on an as needed basis, ask the child to describe what type of assistance is needed).

17. Instruct the parents to assist their child in solving personal problems using an interactive process that allows the child to develop problem-solving skills: (1) Child states the problem; (2) parent assumes a supportive role using active listening and empathy; (3) child states potential solutions; (4) parent offers additional possible solutions; (5) parent and child consider the options and possible outcomes; and (6) child chooses a strategy and parent remains supportive.

8. Promote the child's efforts to become self-reliant and independent using encouragement and support. (18, 19)

18. Request that the parents use "Act as if" in response to "I can't" language to encourage the child to make an effort despite fear of failure (e.g., "Act as if you knew how to ride a bike") (see *Parent Talk* by Moorman).

19. Ask parents to use the phrase, "Check Yourself" (e.g., "You have basketball tonight, check yourself to make sure you have your uniform and equipment.") to help the child develop the ability to prepare successfully for upcoming events (see *Parent Talk* by Moorman).

9. Allow the child to learn from mistakes. (20, 21)

20. Instruct the parents to allow the child to revise an impulsive action that has created a negative parent reaction (or assign the "Rewind Game" activity from the *Parenting Skills Homework Planner* by Knapp).

21. Assign the parents to allow the child to experience the results

of questionable personal choices (e.g., homework incomplete results in a lower grade) and to reassure the child by saying, "Don't worry, next time you'll have a chance to make a different choice."

10. Express awareness that all behaviors have a social purpose and all misbehavior is goal oriented. (22, 23, 24)

22. Teach the parents the four goals of misbehavior: attention, power, revenge, and overcoming feelings of inadequacy; help them to identify the goals of their child's misbehavior (see *Children: The Challenge* by Dreikurs and Stolz).

23. Determine with the parents how they may be reinforcing the child's misbehavior by their reactions and brainstorm more appropriate responses to encourage appropriate behavior (or assign the "Record of Reinforced Behavior" activity from the *Parenting Skills Homework Planner* by Knapp).

24. Encourage the parents to involve the child in reciprocal activities which enhance self-worth (e.g., one-to-one chats, daily greetings, reciprocal smiles).

11. Differentiate between adult problems and those that belong to the child. (25, 26, 27)

25. Assign the parents to listen to the audio tape, *Helicopters, Drill Sergeants, and Consultants* (Fay) to recognize the advantage of allowing their children to problem solve.

26. Teach the parents to differentiate problems that belong to the child (e.g., friends,

homework) from problems that belong to the parents (e.g., messy kitchen, misplaced belongings of the parent).

27. Guide the parents in using pro-active discipline strategies (e.g., consequences, limit setting, choices) to modify behavior that is creating a problem for them and supportive interventions (e.g., active listening, empathy, brainstorming) when the problem belongs to the child.

12. Involve the child in developing strategies for correcting inappropriate behaviors. (28, 29)

28. Teach the parents the advantages of involving the child in creating a discipline plan for correcting inappropriate behaviors (e.g., teaches the child problem-solving skills, child plans for future appropriate behavior).

29. Instruct the parents to assign the child the "Problem-Solving Worksheet" activity from the *Parenting Skills Homework Planner* (Knapp) whenever a significant misbehavior occurs to encourage the child to plan for a more appropriate response in the future.

13. Convene weekly family meetings to discuss family issues, make family plans, and create a feeling of connectedness. (30, 31)

30. Assign the parents to read about "The Family Council" (see *Children: The Challenge* by Dreikurs and Stoltz) or "The Family Meeting" (see *Systematic Training for Effective Parenting (STEP)* by Dinkmeyer and McKay) to understand the process of family meetings.

31. Encourage the parents to initiate weekly family meetings to discuss concerns, reflect upon positive events, review responsibilities, and plan for positive interaction.

14. Report a reduction in power struggles resulting from strategies designed to enlist the child's cooperation. (32, 33)

32. Ask the parents to practice methods of sidestepping power struggles (e.g., broken record, "I" statements, choices, refusing to argue).

33. Assist the parents in analyzing the child's repetitive cycle of negative behavior (e.g., instigating event, child reacts negatively, adult criticizes the child, child escalates the negative reaction); brainstorm strategies for breaking the cycle by responding calmly and rationally (e.g., count to ten before responding, engage in positive self-talk).

15. Help the child recognize personal attributes and talents. (34, 35)

34. Instruct the parents to use "Attribute Awareness" to point out how the child's behaviors directly affect results (e.g., "You earned an A on this paper, what do you attribute that to?", "You can't find your rollerblades. What caused that?" (see *Parent Talk* by Moorman).

35. Assign the parents to assist the child in developing a list of positive personal attributes and to post the list prominently at home.

16. Teach appropriate behavior through modeling and defining what is expected. (36, 37)

36. Assign parents to use the statement, "Next time . . ." to help the child replace inappropriate with appropriate

behavior (e.g., "Next time you need my help please ask for it in a polite tone of voice") (see *Parent Talk* by Moorman).

37. Identify for the parents the power of using referential speaking (e.g., explaining while doing) while completing tasks to model and define for the child the importance of completing the tasks.

17. Work together to establish a loving, respectful, cooperative family atmosphere. (38, 39)

38. Explore for any triangulation or sabotaging that is occurring within the family; direct the parents to eliminate it through open discussions, mutual problem solving, and presenting a united parental front.
39. Discuss with the parents the importance of cooperation in the co-parenting process; offer to mediate any current roadblocks to supporting one another in all areas of child management.

DIAGNOSTIC SUGGESTIONS:

ICD-9-CM	*ICD-10-CM*	*DSM-5* Disorder, Condition, or Problem
314.01	F90.1	Attention-Deficit/Hyperactivity Disorder, Predominately Hyperactive /Impulsive Presentation
313.81	F91.3	Oppositional Defiant Disorder
300.02	F41.1	Generalized Anxiety Disorder
309.21	F93.0	Separation Anxiety Disorder
V71.02	Z72.810	Child Antisocial Behavior
V61.20	Z62.820	Parent-Child Relational Problem
______	______	______
______	______	______

STRATEGIES FOR TEENAGERS (AGE 13 TO 18)

BEHAVIORAL DEFINITIONS

1. Demonstrate an inability to communicate effectively with the teenager.
2. Lack trust in the teenager's decision-making abilities.
3. Lack the discipline skills necessary to set reasonable limits and encourage the teenager's independent functioning.
4. Worry about the negative influences of sex, violence, drugs, and peers on their teenager.
5. Reluctant to allow the teenager to accept adult responsibility and independence.
6. Push and pressure the teenager to excel academically, socially, artistically, or athletically.
7. Report high levels of stress and anxiety in the family.
8. Teenager lacks respect for self, parents, and others.
9. Teenager exhibits symptoms of anger, unhappiness, and depression.
10. Teenager withdraws from parents and seeks role models and nurturing outside of the family.

__. ____

____

__. ____

____

__. ____

____

LONG-TERM GOALS

1. Acquire positive discipline strategies that set reasonable limits on and encourage independence in teenagers.
2. Guide the teenager to develop effective problem-solving skills and strategies for success at home, school, and in the community.
3. Build a positive relationship with the teenager that can carry over into adulthood.
4. Demonstrate respect, regard, and unconditional love for the teenager.
5. Teenager develops independence, self-reliance, and a pattern of responsible behavior.

—. ______________________________

____

—. ______________________________

____

—. ______________________________

____

SHORT-TERM OBJECTIVES

1. Read literature and attend parent education classes to acquire strategies for effective parenting of teenagers. (1, 2)

THERAPEUTIC INTERVENTIONS

1. Assign the parents to read about strategies of positive discipline (e.g., *Between Parent and Teenager* by Ginott, *Parenting Teens with Love and Logic* by Cline and Fay, or *Children: The Challenge* by Dreikurs and Stoltz).
2. Refer the parents to a positive parenting class (e.g., *Systematic Training for Effective Parenting of Teens* by Dinkmeyer, McKay, McKay, and Dinkmeyer, *Discipline with Love and Logic* by Cline and Fay, or *The Parent Talk System* by Moorman and Knapp).

2. Initiate strategies that help the teenager develop responsible behavior. (3, 4, 5)

3. Teach the parents to use four steps to teach the teenager a responsibility (e.g., return car on time), use a mistake to create a learning opportunity (e.g., teenager fails to act responsibly), combine consequences and empathy to teach responsible decision making (e.g., "Sorry, but the car will be off limits for three days"), and give the same task again (e.g., teenager allowed to use car again after three days) (see *Parenting Teens with Love and Logic* by Cline and Fay).

4. Instruct the parents to use the phrase "Please make a different choice" when the teenager engages in an inappropriate behavior (e.g., using inappropriate language) to require that the teenager make a more appropriate choice. (See *Parent Talk* by Moorman.)

5. Assign the parents to teach the teenager skills important for future independence (e.g., washing clothes, performing car maintenance, doing yard care).

3. Verbalize the awareness that all teenage behaviors have a social purpose and all misbehavior is goal oriented. (6, 7)

6. Teach the parents the four goals of misbehavior (e.g., attention, power, revenge, and overcoming feelings of inadequacy); ask the parents to reflect upon how they are reinforcing this misbehavior by their reactions (see *Children: The Challenge* by Dreikurs and Stoltz).

7. Teach the parents to eliminate reinforcement of negative actions and to encourage appropriate behavior (e.g., ignore attention-seeking behavior and give attention for positive behavior; refuse to engage in power struggles and use problem solving; resist being hurt by revengeful behavior and treat the teenager with fairness and respect; don't criticize in areas of low self-esteem and use encouragement).

4. Utilize natural, logical, and delayed consequences to redirect inappropriate teenager behavior. (8, 9, 10)

8. Define natural (e.g., naturally occurring in the environment) and logical (e.g., created by the parents) consequences and outline their effectiveness as part of a positive discipline strategy.

9. Help the parents design several logical consequences to deal with chronic inappropriate behavior (e.g., teenager breaks weekend curfew, curfew reduced by one hour the following weekend).

10. Teach the parents to use a "delayed consequence" to address inappropriate teenage behavior when no consequence is immediately obvious or the misbehavior is extremely upsetting and creates anger (see *Parenting Teens with Love and Logic* by Cline and Fay).

5. Allow the teenager to learn from the results of mistakes. (11, 12)

11. Assign the parents to allow the teenager to cancel out an impulsive action by reformatting

it into a more acceptable action (e.g., teenager yells "You never help me with anything, I hate you!" then after some reflection reformats the statement as "I really need your help, when will you be available?") (or assign the "Rewind Game" activity from the *Parenting Skills Homework Planner* by Knapp).

12. Assign the parents to allow the teenager to learn the principle of cause and effect through experiencing the consequences of personal choices and to respond with the encouraging statement: "Don't worry, next time you'll have a chance to make a different choice."

6. Implement effective communication strategies with the teenager. (13, 14, 15)

13. Instruct the parents to focus on the inappropriate action rather than attacking the teenager's self-esteem when dealing with discipline issues (e.g., "Underage drinking is illegal and against the family rules" versus "When you drink you're a juvenile delinquent and an embarrassment to this family.").

14. Role play with the parents the use of "I" statements (e.g., "I feel . . . , when . . . , because . . .") as a first step in addressing teenager behavior which disturbs the parent (see *Parent Effectiveness Training* by Gordon).

15. Assign the parents to listen for and reflect feelings to communicate respect and

concern, and to strengthen the relationship through compassion and empathy (or assign the "Listening with Empathy" activity from the *Parenting Skills Homework Planner* by Knapp).

7. Set behavioral limits using choices, and enforceable parameters. (16, 17)

16. Instruct the parents to define the limited options for the teenager and to encourage responsible decision-making (e.g., "Would you rather do the dishes or drive your brother to soccer?" versus "Do you want to help me or not?").
17. Teach the parents to use enforceable statements (see *Parenting Teens with Love and Logic* by Cline and Fay) to direct behavior in a positive manner (e.g., "Feel free to go to the party as long as Justin's father assures me that he will be there to chaperone" versus "You're not going to that party until I know it will be chaperoned").

8. Grant specific freedoms consistent with the teenager's demonstrated level of maturity and responsible behavior. (18, 19)

18. Emphasize to the parents to extend freedoms only after responsibility has been demonstrated by the teenager and brainstorm a list of acceptable and unacceptable privileges (or assign the "Earning Privileges and Freedoms" activity from the *Parenting Skills Homework Planner* by Knapp).
19. Teach the parents to use the phrase "Soon you'll be on your own" to encourage the teenager to earn freedom from parental monitoring by

demonstrating the ability to complete a task independently and to respond with "When you show me you can handle it, you'll be on your own" when the teenager complains about too much supervision (see *Parent Talk* by Moorman).

9. Teach appropriate behavior through modeling and defining what is expected. (20, 21, 22)

20. Assign the parents to practice remaining firm yet kind when disciplining the teenager and to withdraw from the conflict by taking a short timeout when they feel themselves becoming angry.

21. Teach the parents to use the "Describe, Describe, Describe" technique to help the teenager replace negative behaviors with positive actions: (1) Describe the situation to the teenager, ("The gas tank is on empty"); (2) describe the parent's feeling ("I feel annoyed"); (3) describe what needs to be done ("Gas needs to be added when the tank reads below one quarter full") (see *Parent Talk* by Moorman).

22. Identify for the parents the power of using referential speaking (explaining while doing) while completing tasks to model and define for the teenager the importance of completing the tasks.

10. Convene weekly family meetings to discuss family issues, make family plans and create a feeling of connectedness. (23, 24)

23. Assign the parents to read about "The Family Council" (see *Children: The Challenge* by Dreikurs and Stoltz) or The " Family Meeting" (see *Parenting Teenagers* by

Dinkmeyer, McKay, McKay, and Dinkmeyer) to understand the process of meeting to discuss family issues.

24. Encourage the parents to initiate weekly family meetings to discuss concerns, reflect on and plan positive events, coordinate activities, and discuss responsibilities.

11. Differentiate between parent problems and those that belong to the teenager. (25, 26)

25. Teach the parents to differentiate problems that belong to the teenager (e.g., friends, homework) from problems that belong to the parents (e.g., messy kitchen, disrespectful behavior).

26. Instruct the parents to use proactive discipline strategies (e.g., "I" statements; describe, describe, describe; consequences; enforceable statements; choices) to modify behavior that is creating a problem for them and supportive interventions (e.g., active listening, brainstorming, problem solving) to assist when the problem belongs to the teenager.

12. Encourage the teenager to solve personal problems alone or with guidance. (27, 28, 29)

27. Advise the parents to use the statement, "I think you can handle it," when the teenager is asking for too much assistance in solving problems; suggest that they offer affirmations when a courageous attempt to problem solve has been made.

28. Brainstorm with the parents strategies for assisting the teenager to complete chores and homework (e.g., maintain eye

contact when delivering instructions; encourage questions; give specific, sequential directions; offer guidance on an as needed basis).

29. Assign the parents to manage problems with their teenager by exploring alternatives for possible solutions: (1) Understand the problem using empathy and reflective listening; (2) brainstorm possible solutions, (3) discuss the pros and cons of each idea; (4) help choose the best idea; (5) create a plan for implementation (see *Parenting Teenagers* by Dinkmeyer, McKay, McKay, and Dinkmeyer).

13. Actively involve the teenager in developing strategies for correcting inappropriate, self-defeating behaviors. (30, 31)

30. Advise the parents to deal with chronic inappropriate behavior by requiring that the teenager develop a "change in behavior plan" which must be implemented before the teenager may participate in any privileges or freedoms granted by the parents (e.g., television, computer time, car or phone use); urge them to reinstate privileges only as long as the plan results in a positive change in behavior.

31. Encourage the parents to empower the teenager to take ownership for both positive and negative outcomes by using "Attribute Awareness" (see *Parent Talk* by Moorman) to point out how the teenager's actions have created specific results (e.g., "You earned an A on this paper, what do you

attribute that to?" "You can't find your car keys. What caused that?").

14. Assist the teenager to identify personal strengths, attributes, and talents. (32, 33)

32. Assign the parents to collaborate with the teenager to create a list of personal strengths, attributes and talents that the teenager has.

33. Council the parents to affirm the teenager by pointing out or noticing cooperative or helpful behavior (e.g., "I noticed you walked and fed the dog." "You played with your sister this afternoon, thanks.").

15. Report a reduction in power struggles resulting from strategies designed to enlist the teenager's cooperation. (34, 35)

34. Assign the parents to collaborate with the teenager to create a list of mutually enjoyable activities (e.g., shopping, working on the car, attending a sports event); agree to participate in at least one interactive activity each week.

35. Assign the parents to practice methods of sidestepping power struggles (e.g., use broken record, "I" statements, choices, enforceable statements, time out, delayed consequences).

16. Promote independent behavior using encouragement and support. (36, 37)

36. Request that the parents use "Act as if" in response to "I can't" language (see *Parent Talk* by Moorman) to encourage the teenager to make an effort despite fear of failure (e.g., "Act as if you felt confident about inviting someone to the school concert.").

37. Instruct parents to use the statement, "Check Yourself" (e.g., "Tomorrow is your job interview, check yourself to

make sure you've revised and printed out your resume.") to help the teenager develop the ability to prepare successfully for upcoming events (see *Parent Talk* by Moorman).

17. Promote positive character development through family discussions, analyzing literature and media examples, loving interactions, spiritual training, and community involvement. (38, 39)

38. Discuss with the parents the significance of regular family attendance at the church, synagogue, or other spiritual organization of their choice for the teenager's character development, moral training, and awareness of the family values.

39. Assign the parents to read *The Seven Habits of Highly Effective Families* (Covey) to learn strategies for attaining a positive family atmosphere.

__. ______________________________ __. ______________________________

__. ______________________________ __. ______________________________

DIAGNOSTIC SUGGESTIONS

ICD-9-CM	*ICD-10-CM*	*DSM-5* Disorder, Condition, or Problem
314.01	F90.1	Attention-Deficit/Hyperactivity Disorder, Predominately Hyperactive /Impulsive Presentation
313.81	F91.3	Oppositional Defiant Disorder
300.02	F41.1	Generalized Anxiety Disorder
V71.02	Z72.810	Child Antisocial Behavior
V61.20	Z62.820	Parent-Child Relational Problem
________	________	____________________
________	________	____________________

SUBSTANCE ABUSE

BEHAVIORAL DEFINITIONS

1. Family members regularly use alcohol or drugs to become intoxicated or high.
2. Absence of a strong parental message for the child to abstain from alcohol and drugs.
3. Lack open and positive communication with the child.
4. Absence of positive, consistent, and effective discipline strategies.
5. Demonstrate a lack of awareness of or concern about the child's use of mind-altering substances.
6. Verbalize fear and confusion about the child's use of mind-altering substances and an unawareness of effective intervention strategies.
7. Express feelings of guilt and inadequacy resulting from the child's addiction to dangerous mind-altering substances.
8. Physical evidence of alcohol or drug usage found on the child's person or in personal areas at home or school.
9. The child lies or is evasive about plans, activities, friends, and use of illegal substances.
10. The child evidences oppositional behavior problems, mood swings, irritability, emotional distancing, and changes in physical appearance and health.
11. The child is involved in increased risk-taking behavior (e.g., sexual promiscuity, driving while under the influence, stealing, curfew violation, and/or defiance of authority).

__. ______________________________
____

__. ______________________________
____

__. ______________________________
____

LONG-TERM GOALS

1. Establish a healthy, drug-free lifestyle in all family members.
2. Cooperate with a treatment program designed to help the child and/or other family members achieve and maintain recovery from all mood-altering addictions.
3. Set firm, consistent, and loving discipline limits for the child.
4. Realistically evaluate personal substance use and determine the negative effects on the child.
5. Reduce co-dependency and establish ongoing encouragement for the child's abstinence from mind-altering substances.

__. ____

____

__. ____

____

__. ____

____

SHORT-TERM OBJECTIVES

1. Disclose the family's history of substance abuse and/or special concerns about the child's use of illegal substances. (1, 2, 3)

THERAPEUTIC INTERVENTIONS

1. Assist the parents in outlining their concerns about substance usage in the family; gather background information about the child's social/emotional functioning, symptoms of chemical dependency, and behavior problems at home or school.
2. Ask the parents to disclose their own level of substance use and describe its effects on their daily functioning and relationship with the child.
3. Collaborate with the parents to enlist the assistance of a drug intervention specialist if necessary.

2. Schedule time to communicate openly with the child about the negative consequence of substance abuse. (4, 5)

4. Stress the importance of maintaining open communication with the child about underage drinking and drug use; help the parents prepare for typical questions that might arise during a discussion (e.g., "How come you drink and I can't? How is marijuana harmful?").

5. Teach the parents effective communication techniques by role playing conversations using I-statements, active listening, not interrupting, and avoiding absolutes like "always" and "never."

3. Establish a zero tolerance policy for substance abuse. (6, 7)

6. Assign the parents to set a clear family rule of no drug use including tobacco, underage drinking, marijuana, ecstasy, or inhalants and to frequently communicate this standard to the child.

7. Assign the parents to brainstorm with the child the various ways to maintain a substance-free lifestyle (e.g., learning substance refusal strategies, connecting with a substance-free friendship group, learning about the harmful side effects of substance use, focusing on future goals and aspirations).

4. Set reasonable limits for the child which encourage responsible behavior and appropriate independent functioning. (8, 9)

8. Emphasize to the parents the importance of extending freedoms to the child only after responsibility has been demonstrated (or assign the "Earning Privileges and Freedoms" activity from the *Parenting Skills Homework Planner* by Knapp).

9. Teach the parents to use enforceable statements (e.g., "Feel free to go to the party as long as Justin's father assures me that he will be there to chaperone" versus "You're not going to that party until I know it will be chaperoned") and limited choices (e.g., "Would you rather do the dishes or drive your brother to soccer?" versus "Do you want to help me or not?") (See *Parenting Teens with Love and Logic* by Cline and Fay.)

5. Remain firm and calm and use logical consequences when the child breaks the rules. (10, 11)

10. Assign the parents to design several logical consequences to deal with chronic inappropriate behavior (e.g., child comes home intoxicated, child attends alcohol abuse classes and writes a paper about underage drinking).

11. Teach the parents to use delayed consequences (e.g., "This is a serious problem and I will need to do something about it. I will let you know when I decide what to do.") to address inappropriate child behavior when no consequence is immediately obvious and the misbehavior is extremely upsetting. (See *Parenting Teens with Love and Logic* by Cline and Fay).

6. Monitor outside of school activities and require clear information detailing where, when, and with whom the child is involved. (12, 13)

12. Instruct the parents to require that the child inform them about the "where, when, and with whom" details of all activities.

13. Instruct the parents to remain firm yet compassionate when the child argues about the rules combining empathy (e.g., "I know that you desire an unlimited curfew") with the rule or limit (e.g., "Right now your curfew is 11:30").

7. Create a supportive, compassionate bond by giving the child daily affirmations and unconditional love. (14, 15)

14. Assist the parents in creating a definition of unconditional love (e.g., complete and constant love given regardless of performance); brainstorm methods of sharing this nurturing form of love as an antidote to the child's temptation to use illegal substances.

15. Assign the parents to collaborate with the child to create a list of personal strengths that the child has; encourage them to refer often to the list especially when discouraged.

8. Verbalize an accurate understanding of child and adolescence substance abuse education occurring in the child's school. (16)

16. Assign the parents to contact their child's school to become informed about the substance abuse education programs being offered for students.

9. Assist the child in listing the devastating effects of substance abuse upon personal behavior, relationships, health, and future goals. (17, 18)

17 Council the parents to engage the child in a discussion about the devastating effect of substance abuse upon personal quality of life (e.g., loss of former friends, drop in grades, family problems, memory loss, legal problems).

18. Instruct the parents to explore the process of chemical dependency with the child by describing the initial exposure

to mind-altering substances, the gradual process of dependency, the awareness of the negative effects of addiction and the difficult recovery process.

10. Schedule a complete chemical dependence evaluation to determine treatment recommendations necessary to address any abuse of substances. (19, 20, 21)

19. Strongly encourage counseling for any family members with addiction problems that may be contributing to the child's oppositional behavior, feelings of despair, and attempts to escape through chemical dependence.

20. Refer the parents to a certified substance abuse therapist who will evaluate the child's use of mind-altering substances.

21. Review the results of the substance abuse evaluation with the child and the parents and discuss treatment options (e.g., inpatient treatment, outpatient therapy, family therapy, Alcoholic's Anonymous); enlist a firm commitment to a course of treatment.

11. Participate in an intervention in which family and other concerned relatives and friends confront the child's substance abuse and strongly advocate for appropriate treatment. (22, 23, 24)

22. Explain the intervention process and goals with the parents and other close associates (e.g., drug-free friends, teachers, clergy, relatives, coaches) who will participate.

23. Role play how each person will present their concerns during the intervention and have a treatment facility available to work with the child immediately after the intervention.

24. Help the parents and other participants prepare for maintaining a loving, yet strong and determined, approach in the face of the child's anger and denial during the intervention.

12. Arrange for the child to attend group sessions focused on increasing self-esteem, expressing feelings and developing social skills and problem solving abilities. (25, 26)

25. Council the parents to arrange group counseling sessions for the child at school or a community agency that focus on building social skills, healthy self-esteem, feelings expression, and refusal skills.
26. Assign the parents to enroll the child in a conflict management or assertiveness training program to develop interpersonal skills, appropriate assertiveness, and conflict-resolution abilities.

13. Gain a deeper understanding of the child's self destructive behavior, its causes and treatment strategies. (27, 28)

27. Direct the parents to informational resources offering interventions and treatments for preventing and treating adolescent chemical dependence (e.g., Partnership for a Drug-Free America, www.drugfreeamerica.org; Talking with Kids about Tough Issues, www.talkingwithkids.org; Teen Drug Use and Abuse Prevention, www.parentingteens.com).
28. Assign the parents to read and share with the child literature which describes adolescent substance abuse, it's causes and coping strategies (e.g., *Street Wise Drug Prevention* by Jalil or *Field Guide to the American Teenager* by DiPrisco).

14. Verbalize an increased recognition and encouragement of the child. (29, 30)

29. Teach the parents to recognize and affirm the child daily by noticing personal attributes and verbalizing an awareness of activities that promote recovery.

30. Help the parents plan for reassuring the child about personal security and expressing awareness and empathy for the child's fears during the recovery process.

15. Verbalize support the child's renewing interest in former healthy activities and increased social interaction with a substance-free peer group. (31, 32)

31. Assign the parents to support the student in joining a drug free extracurricular group sponsored by school, a religious group, or the community.

32. Instruct the parents to assist the student in planning for an after school or weekend activity or to attend a school-sponsored function with a substance-free friend or group.

16. Define the threats to the child's recovery and maintaining a substance-free lifestyle. (33, 34)

33. Assign the parents to brainstorm with the child the many factors that influenced the substance usage or addiction, list strategies that can combat these threats to recovery and discuss how to implement positive behaviors to prevent relapse.

34. Assign the parents to complete with the child the "Healthy Habits to Support Recovery" activity in the *Parenting Skills Homework Planner* (Knapp) to define positive behaviors and activities that can become antidotes to relapse.

17. Involve the child in creating a plan for long-term abstinence from all mind-altering substances. (35)

35. Instruct the parents to sign and require that the child sign a joint commitment to maintain a substance-free lifestyle which includes long- and short-term recovery goals, support people, and the lifelong personal consequences of recovery versus dependency (or assign the "Our Commitment to a Substance-Free Life Style" activity in the *Parenting Skills Homework Planner* by Knapp).

__. ____________________

__. ____________________

__. ____________________

__. ____________________

__. ____________________

__. ____________________

DIAGNOSTIC SUGGESTIONS:

ICD-9-CM	*ICD-10-CM*	*DSM-5* Disorder, Condition, or Problem
305.00	F10.10	Alcohol Use Disorder, Mild
303.90	F10.20	Alcohol Use Disorder, Moderate or Severe
305.20	F12.10	Cannabis Use Disorder, Mild
304.30	F12.20	Cannabis Use Disorder, Moderate or Severe
304.20	F14.20	Cocaine Use Disorder, Moderate or Severe
305.30	F16.10	Hallucinogen Use Disorder, Mild
313.81	F91.3	Oppositional Defiant Disorder
312.82	F91.2	Conduct Disorder, Adolescent Onset Type
______	______	____________________
______	______	____________________

SUICIDE PREVENTION

BEHAVIORAL DEFINITIONS

1. Demonstrate volatile family relationships, unrealistic expectations, and a lack of consistent emotional support for the child.
2. Exhibit aggressive and abusive behavior, including physical and sexual abuse of the child.
3. Have a history of unstable living conditions and frequent moves to different locations.
4. Family members are recovering from a recent divorce, separation, or death of a parent.
5. Members of the immediate or extended family have attempted or committed suicide.
6. One or both parents have a history of mental illness or have been diagnosed with a serious affective psychiatric disorder.
7. One or both parents have engaged in alcohol or drug abuse.
8. Child is diagnosed with depression, dysthymia, bipolar disorder, or suicidal ideation.
9. Child has verbalized the threat of suicide and/or made previous suicide attempts.
10. Child evidences recurrent themes of death, dying, and morbidity in conversations, writing, artwork, music, and selection of reading or video materials.
11. Child lacks personal problem-solving skills or the ability to seek support and assistance in dealing with personal loss, rejection, or humiliation.

—. ______________________________________

____

—. ______________________________________

____

LONG-TERM GOALS

1. Seek medical and psychological treatment to diffuse the child's suicidal ideation and eliminate the eminent danger of suicide.
2. Create a positive and supportive parent/child relationship.
3. Establish social and emotional stability among all family members.
4. Develop an understanding of the underlying factors contributing to the child's suicidal ideation,
5. Implement positive, effective, and consistent child management strategies designed to promote responsible behavior, healthy self-esteem, and feelings of optimism toward the future.

—. ______________________________

____

—. ______________________________

____

SHORT-TERM OBJECTIVES

1. Outline the family history and take steps to prevent any suicide attempt by the child. (1, 2)
2. Require the child to sign a contract to not engage in self-destructive behavior and to contact a counselor or other concerned adult if the urge to die becomes overwhelming. (3, 4, 5)

THERAPEUTIC INTERVENTIONS

1. Gather information about the family and the child's social/ emotional functioning, symptoms of depression episodes, and previous suicidal thinking or attempts.
2. Collaborate with the parents to develop a plan designed to prevent any suicide attempts (e.g., seeking immediate psychiatric intervention, remove all lethal weapons from the child's access, form a 24-hour suicide watch during the crisis period).
3. Assist the parents in eliciting a signed commitment from the child to control suicidal behavior and to contact a trained mental health professional, or a suicide prevention hotline if the desire

to commit suicide becomes overpowering.

4. Provide the parents with a 24-hour suicide prevention hotline number and other emergency access numbers; strongly recommend that these numbers be carried at all times by the child and other responsible family members.

5. Assign the parents to encourage the child to disclose to a mental health professional any thoughts of suicide including specific plans, availability of lethal materials, written suicide notes, and previous attempts.

3. Schedule an evaluation for the child at a psychiatric hospital or clinic to determine if hospitalization is needed to prevent a suicide attempt. (6, 7)

6. Facilitate the parents in scheduling a complete psychiatric evaluation for the child to assess the child's current suicidal thinking and to develop treatment recommendations.

7. Support the parents and the child in accepting hospitalization, if necessary, to prevent self-destructive behavior and return the child to emotional stability.

4. Seek medical intervention for the child to determine the need for antidepressant medication. (8, 9)

8. Advise the parents to consult with a physician to determine the need for medication or other medical intervention to treat the child's depression.

9. Encourage the parents to monitor the effects of antidepressant medication upon the child's social/emotional adjustment (e.g., be alert to any increase in strength of suicidal urge).

5. Communicate regularly with the child's treatment team and assist the child in implementing all treatment recommendations. (10, 11)

10. Assign the parents to attend appointments with the child's treatment team; review and process the recommended treatment strategies.

11. Assist the parents in accessing the level of care recommended for the child's suicidal behavior (e.g., inpatient, residential, partial hospital, or outpatient).

6. Verbalize a deeper understanding of the child's self-destructive behavior, its causes, and recommended interventions. (12, 13, 14)

12. Encourage the parents and the child to participate in a suicide support group.

13. Direct the parents and the child to informational resources offering interventions for preventing adolescent suicide (e.g., American Foundation for Suicide Prevention (AFSP): www.afsp.org; Suicide Prevention Advocacy Network (SPAN): www.spanusa.org).

14. Assign the parents and the child to read literature which describes adolescent suicide, its causes and coping strategies (e.g., *Out of the Nightmare* by Conroy, *Suicide: The Forever Decision* by Quinnett, or *Choosing to Live* by Ellis and Newman).

7. Explore the child's feelings related to suicide and depression and assist in identifying appropriate methods for expressing these feelings. (15, 16, 17)

15. Assign the parents to encourage the child to express feelings of frustration, anxiety, hopelessness and helplessness by drawing pictures, writing songs or poems.

16. Assign the parents to engage the child in creating a list of close personal relationships, including family members,

friends, teachers, mentors and role models as a network of caring people.

17. Council the parents to help the child reframe situations that trigger feelings of fear, anger, abandonment or sadness by discussing events rationally and logically with their child.

8. Attend drug rehabilitation or substance abuse group sessions. (18, 19)

18. Explore the family's history of substance abuse and encourage the parents to seek counseling and rehabilitation for any family members who are addicted.

19. Refer the parents to Alcoholics Anonymous, Alanon, a community drug rehabilitation program, or a school-sponsored class to deal with the child and/or other family members' problems with substance abuse.

9. Implement effective communication strategies with the child. (20, 21, 22)

20. Role-play with the parents the use of "I" statements (e.g., "I feel . . . when . . . because . . .") with the student as a first step in addressing behavior that disturbs the parent (see *Parent Effectiveness Training* by Gordon).

21. Meet with the parents and other supportive family members to teach them how to actively listen to the child's feelings (or assign the "Heart to Heart Smart Talks" activity from the *Parenting Skills Homework Planner* by Knapp).

22. Assign the parents to read *How to Talk so Kids Will Listen and Listen so Kids Will Talk* (Faber and Mazlish) or

Parent Talk (Moorman) to develop additional positive communication skills for use with the child.

10. Implement methods to show empathy for the child's feelings. (23)

23. Teach the parents or other family members how to express awareness of and empathy for the feelings of helplessness and hopelessness that are contributing to the child's suicidal ideation.

13. Encourage the child to participate in activities that promote healthy self-esteem. (24, 25)

24. Assign the parents to enroll the child in group counseling offered by the school, their faith-based organization or a community agency.

25. Instruct the parents to encourage and affirm the child's behavior that supports healthy self-esteem and positive goals for the future (e.g., engage in moderate exercise, connect with positive and upbeat friends, develop involvement in curricular and extracurricular activities).

12. Grant specific freedoms consistent with the child's demonstrated level of maturity and responsible behavior. (26, 27)

26. Emphasize to the parents the importance of extending freedoms only after responsibility has been demonstrated by the child; brainstorm a list of acceptable and unacceptable privileges (e.g., acceptable: watching television after homework is completed; unacceptable: becoming engrossed in television and forgetting about homework) (or assign the "Earning Privileges and Freedoms" activity from the *Parenting Skills Homework Planner* by Knapp).

27. Teach the parents to use the phrase "Soon you'll be on your own" to encourage the child to earn freedom from parental monitoring and to respond with "When you show me you can make healthy and safe choices, you'll be on your own until then I will need to monitor your progress" when the child complains about too much supervision (see *Parent Talk* by Moorman).

13. Monitor the child's daily participation in class and completion of daily academic assignments. (28, 29, 30)

28. Assign the parents to enlist the teacher(s) support in involving the child in compatible cooperative learning groups and projects and in monitoring the child's academic and social adjustment at school.
29. Instruct the parents to assist the child in creating a plan for completing all classroom assignments and to record weekly progress in a personal journal or an assignment planner.
30. Encourage the parents to reinforce the child's academic, family, and social successes by photographing completed projects that trigger personal pride and displaying the photos prominently in the home or in a family album.

14. Encourage the child to increase social interaction with classmates and friends. (31, 32)

31. Assign the parents to support the child in joining an extra-curricular group or club in an area of interest sponsored by school, a religious group, or the community.
32. Instruct the parents to assist the child in planning for an after school or weekend

activity or attending a school-sponsored function with a supportive friend or group.

15. Support the child in setting personal goals, describing personal hopes and dreams and expressing optimism for the future. (33, 34)

33. Assign the parents to brainstorm with the child the many factors that influenced the depression or thoughts of suicide; list strategies that can combat these threats to recovery and discuss how to implement positive behaviors to maintain the commitment to live a healthy, productive life.
34. Assign the parents to complete with the child the "Healthy Habits to Support Recovery" activity in the *Parenting Skills Homework Planner* by Knapp to define positive behaviors and activities can become antidotes to relapse into depression, substance abuse or suicidal ideation.

__. ________________________

__. ________________________

DIAGNOSTIC SUGGESTIONS

ICD-9-CM	*ICD-10-CM*	*DSM-5* Disorder, Condition, or Problem
296.xx	F33.x	Major Depressive Disorder, Recurrent Episode
296.89	F31.81	Bipolar II Disorder
296.xx	F31.xx	Bipolar I Disorder
309.0	F43.21	Adjustment Disorder, With Depressed Mood
311	F32.9	Unspecified Depressive Disorder
311	F32.8	Other Specified Depressive Disorder
309.81	F43.10	Posttraumatic Stress Disorder
V62.82	Z63.4	Uncomplicated Bereavement
____	____	____________
____	____	____________

Appendix A

BIBLIOTHERAPY REFERENCES

Abusive Parenting

Canfield, J., M. Hansen, and K. Kirberger (1993). *Chicken Soup for the Soul.* Deerfield Beach, FL: Health Communications.

Coloroso, B. (1994). *Kids Are Worth It!* New York: William Morrow and Company, Inc.

Dinkmeyer, D., and G. McKay (1989). *Systematic Training for Effective Parenting (STEP).* Circle Pines, MN: American Guidance Service.

Dreikurs, R., and V. Stoltz (1964). *Children: The Challenge.* New York: Plume Printing.

Moorman, C. (1996). *Where the Heart Is: Stories of Home and Family.* Merrill, MI: Personal Power Press.

Moorman, C. (1998). *Parent Talk: Words That Empower, Words That Wound.* Merrill, MI: Personal Power Press.

Attention-Deficit/Hyperactivity Disorder (ADHD)

Barkley, R. A. (1995). Taking Charge of ADHD: The Complete, Authoritative Guide For Parents. New York: Guilford Press.

Fay, J., F. Cline, and C. Fay (2000). *Becoming a Love and Logic Parent.* Golden, CO: The Love and Logic Press.

Hallowell, E., and J. Ratey (1994). *Driven to Distraction.* New York: Pantheon Books.

Richfield, S. (1998). *Parent Coaching Cards.* Blue Bell, PA: Parent Coaching Cards, Inc.

Shapiro, L. (1994). *Jumpin' Jake Settles Down.* Secaucus, NJ: Childswork/Childsplay.

Attention-Seeking Behavior

Dinkmeyer, D., and G. McKay (1989). *Systematic Training for Effective Parenting (STEP)*. Circle Pines, MN: American Guidance Service.

Dinkmeyer, D., and G. McKay (1996). *Raising a Responsible Child*. New York: Simon and Schuster.

Dreikurs, R., and V. Soltz (1964). *Children: The Challenge*. New York: Plume Printing.

Gordon, T. (2000). *Parent Effectiveness Training*. New York: Three Rivers Press.

Gardner, H. (1993). Intelligence Reframed: Multiple Intelligences for the 21st Century. New York: Simon and Schuster.

Moorman, C. (1998). *Parent Talk: Words That Empower, Words That Wound.* Merrill, MI: Personal Power Press.

Moorman, C., and S. Knapp (2001). *The Parent Talk System: The Language of Responsible Parenting.* Merrill, MI: Personal Power Press.

Blended Family

Fay, J., F. Cline, and C. Fay (2000). *Becoming a Love and Logic Parent*. Golden, CO: The Love and Logic Press.

Gorton, T. (2000). *Parent Effectiveness Training.* New York: Three Rivers Press.

Roosevelt, R., and J. Lofas (1976). *Living in Step*. Blue Ridge Summit, PA: McGraw-Hill, Inc.

Shomberg, E. (1999). Blending Families: A Guide for Parents, Stepparents, and Everyone Building a Successful New Family. Berkley, CA: Berkley Publishing Group.

Wisdom, S., and J. Green (2002) Stepcoupling: Creating and Sustaining a Strong Marriage in Today's Blended Family. New York: Three Rivers Press.

Bonding and Attachment Issues

Barkley, R. (1998). Your Defiant Child: Eight Steps to Better Behavior. New York: Guilford.

Cline, F. (1991). *Hope for High Risk and Rage Filled Children*. Evergreen, CO: EC Publications.

Dinkmeyer, D., and G. McKay (1989). *Systematic Training for Effective Parenting (STEP)*. Circle Pines, MN: American Guidance Service.

Schooler, J. (1993). *The Whole Life Adoption Book*. Colorado Springs, CO: Pinon Press.

Thomas, N. (1997). *When Love Is Not Enough*. Glenwood Springs, CO: Families by Design.

Welch, M. (1988). *Holding Time*. New York: Simon and Schuster.

Career Preparation

ACT Inc. (1994). *ACT Career Planning Program*. Iowa City, IA: The American College Testing Program.

Fiske, E. (2004). *The Fiske Guide to Colleges 2005*. Naperville, IL: Sourcebooks Inc.

Holland, J. (2001). *The Career Interest Game*. Tampa Bay, FL: Psychological Assessment Resources Inc. (http://career.missouri.edu/Holland/).

Michigan Occupational Information System (MOIS; 2004). Mason, MI: Ingham Intermediate School District. (www.mois.org).

Character Development

Cline, F., and J. Fay (1990). *Parenting with Love and Logic*. Colorado Springs, CO: Navpress.

Gordon, T. (1989). *Teaching Children Self-Discipline*. New York: Random House.

Greer, C., and H. Kohl (1997). A Call to Character: A Family Treasury of Stories, Poems, Plays, Proverbs and Fables to Guide the Development of Values for You and Your Children. New York: HarperCollins

Pipher, M. (1995). Reviving Ophelia: Saving the Selves of Adolescent Girls. New York: Ballantine Books.

Children with Physical Challenges

Chapman, G. (1992). The Five Love Languages: How to Express Heartfelt Commitment to Your Mate. Chicago: Northfield Publishing.

Hickman, L. (2000). Living in My Skin: The Insider's View of Life with a Special Needs Child. San Antonio, TX: Communication Skill Builders.

Lavin, J. L. (2001). Special Kids Need Special Parents: A Resource for Parents of Children with Special Needs. New York: Berkley Books.

McHugh, M. (2002). Special Siblings: Growing Up with Someone with a Disability. Baltimore: Paul H. Brookes.

Meyer, D. (1997). Views from Our Shoes: Growing Up with a Brother or Sister with Special Needs. Bethesda, MD: Woodbine House.

Naseef, R. (1997). "Journaling Your Way Through Stress: Finding Answers Within Yourself." (article available at www.specialchild.com/family.html) Santa Clarita, CA: The Resource Foundation for Children with Challenges.

Conduct Disorder/Delinquent Behavior

Barkley, R. (1998). Your Defiant Child: Eight Steps to Better Behavior. New York: Guilford Press.

Dinkmeyer, D., and G. McKay (1989). *Systematic Training for Effective Parenting (STEP)*. Circle Pines, MN: American Guidance Service.

Dreikurs, R., and V. Stoltz (1964). *Children: The Challenge*. New York: Plume Printing.

Forehand, R., and N. Long (1996) *Parenting the Strong-Willed Child.* New York: NTC Publishing Group.

Greene, R. (1998). *The Explosive Child.* New York: HarperCollins

Koplewicz, H. (1996). It's Nobody's Fault: New Hope and Help for Difficult Children. New York: Random House.

Dependent Children/Overprotective Parent

Cline, F., and J. Fay (1990). *Parenting with Love and Logic.* Colorado Springs, CO: Navpress.

Dreikurs, R., and V. Stoltz (1964). *Children: The Challenge.* New York: Plume Printing.

Fay, J. (1986). *Helicopters, Drill Sergeants, and Consultants.* Golden, CO: The Love and Logic Press. (Audiotape)

Fay, J., F. Cline, and C. Fay (2000). *Becoming a Love and Logic Parent.* Golden, CO: The Love and Logic Press.

Moorman, C. (1998). *Parent Talk: Words That Empower, Words That Wound.* Merrill, MI: Personal Power Press.

Depression

Cline, F. and J. Fay (1990). *Parenting with Love and Logic.* Colorado Springs, CO: Navpress.

Dubuque, S. (1996). *Survival Guide to Childhood Depression.* Secaucus, NJ: Childswork/
Childsplay.

Faber, A. and E. Mazlish (1982). How to Talk so Kids Will Listen and Listen so Kids Will Talk. New York: Avon Books.

Fassler, D., and L. Dumas (1998). 'Help Me I'm Sad': Recognizing, Treating, and Preventing Childhood and Adolescent Depression. New York: Penguin USA.

Divorce/Separation

Baris, M., and C. Garrity. (1988). Children of Divorce: A Developmental Approach to Residence and Visitation. Dekalb, IL: Psytec Corp.

Baris, M., and C. Garrity (1997). *Caught in the Middle.* San Francisco, CA: Jossey-Bass.

Fay, J., F. Cline, and C. Fay (2000). *Becoming a Love and Logic Parent.* Golden, CO: The Love and Logic Press.

Faber, A., and E. Mazlish (1982). How to Talk so Kids Will Listen and Listen so Kids Will Talk. New York: Avon Books.

Gordon, T. (2000). *Parent Effectiveness Training.* New York: Three Rivers Press.

Moorman, C., and S. Knapp (1998). *The Parent Talk System: The Language of Responsible Parenting.* Merrill, MI: Personal Power Press.

Stern, Z., E. Stern, and E. Stern (1997). Divorce Is Not the End of the World: Zoe's and Evan's Coping Guide for Kids. New York: Tricycle Press.

Teyber, E. (1992). *Helping Children Cope with Divorce.* San Francisco, CA: Jossey-Bass Publishers.

Eating Disorder

Faber, A., and E. Mazlish (1982). How to Talk So Kids Will Listen and Listen So Kids Will Talk. New York: Avon Books.

Siegel, M., J. Brisman, and M. Weinshel (1997). Surviving an Eating Disorder: Perspectives and Strategies for Family and Friends. New York: Perennial Press.

Waterhouse, D. (1997). Like Mother, Like Daughter: How Women Are Influenced by Their Mother's Relationship with Food and How to Break the Pattern. New York: Hyperion Press.

Gifted/Talented

Brown-Miller, A. (1994). Learning to Learn: Ways to Nurture Your Child's Intelligence. New York: Plenum Press.

Cline, F., and J. Fay (1990). *Parenting with Love and Logic.* Colorado Springs, CO: Navpress.

Dinkemeyer, D., and G. McKay (1989). *Systematic Training for Effective Parenting (STEP).* Circle Pines, MN: American Guidance Service.

Galbraith, J. (1996). *The Gifted Kid Survival Guide: A Teen Handbook.* Minneapolis, MN: Free Spirit Publishing.

Galbraith, J. (1998). *The Gifted Kid Survival Guide: Ages 10 and Under.* Minneapolis, MN: Free Spirit Publishing.

Moorman, C., and S. Knapp (2001). *The Parent Talk System: The Language of Responsible Parenting.* Merrill, MI: Personal Power Press.

Rimm, S. (1990). *How to Parent so Children Will Learn.* Watertown, WI: Apple Publishing Company.

Grandparenting Strategies

Cline, F., and J. Fay (1994). *Grandparenting with Love and Logic.* Golden, CO: The Love and Logic Press.

Coloroso, B. (1994). Kids Are Worth It! Giving Your Child the Gift of Inner Discipline. Toronto: The Penguin Group.

Coloroso, B. (1999). *Parenting with Wit and Wisdom in Times of Chaos and Loss.* New York: William Morrow and Company.

Fay, J., R. Cline, and C. Fay (2000). *Becoming a Love and Logic Parent.* Golden, CO: The Love and Logic Press.

Linsley, L. (1997). Totally Cool Grandparenting: A Practical Handbook of Tips, Hints, Activities for the Modern Grandparent. New York: St. Martin's Press.

Wiggin, E., and G. Chapman (2001). The Gift of Grandparenting: Building Meaningful Relationships with Your Grandchildren. New York: Tyndale House Publishers.

Grief/Loss

Bissler, J. (1997). *The Way Children Grieve*. www.counselingforloss.com: Counseling for Loss and Life Changes.

Buscaglia, L. (1985). *The Fall of Freddie the Leaf*. Chatsworth, CA: AIMS Media.

Clayton, J. (1997). *Lessons from Geese*. www.counselingforloss.com: Counseling For Loss and Life Changes.

Coloroso, B. (1999). Parenting with Wit and Wisdom in Times of Chaos and Loss. Toronto, Ontario: Penguin Group.

Faber, A., and E. Mazlish (1982) How to Talk so Kids Will Listen and Listen so Kids Will Talk. New York: Avon Books.

Gardner, R. (1973). *The Talking, Feeling, and Doing Game.* Cresskill, NJ: Creative Therapeutics, Inc.

Grollman, E. (1967). *Explaining Death to Children*. Boston: Beacon Press.

Metzgar, M. (1996). *Developmental Considerations Concerning Children's Grief.* Seattle WA: SIDS Foundation of Washington (www.kidsource.com).

Maberly, K. (1993). *The Secret Garden.* Los Angeles, CA: Warner Studios (DVD)

Moser, A. (1996), *Don't Despair on Thursdays*. Kansas City, MO: Landmark Editions.

Walt Disney Home Entertainment. (2003). *The Lion King.* Burbank, CA: Buena Vista Home Entertainment, Inc. (Video)

Zakich, R. (1989). *The Ungame.* New York: Talicor.

Oppositional Defiant Disorder (ODD)

Abern, A. (1994). *Everything I Do You Blame on Me.* Plainview, NY: Childswork/Childsplay, LLC.

Barkley, R. (1998). Your Defiant Child: Eight Steps to Better Behavior. New York: Guilford.

Fay, J., F. Cline, and C. Fay.)2000). *Becoming a Love and Logic Parent.* Golden, CO: The Love and Logic Press.

Forehand, R., and N. Long. (1996). *Parenting the Strong-Willed Child.* New York: NTC Publishing Group.

Greene, R. (1998). *The Explosive Child.* New York: HarperCollins.

Koplewicz, H. (1996). It's Nobody's Fault: New Hope and Help for Difficult Children. New York: Random House.

Mannix, D. (1996). Life Skills Activities for Secondary Students with Special Needs. New York: Jossey-Bass.

Moorman, C. (1998). *Parent Talk: Words That Empower, Words That Wound.* Merrill, MI: Personal Power Press.

Moorman, C. and S. Knapp (2001). *The Parent Talk System: The Language of Responsible Parenting.* Merrill, MI: Personal Power Press.

Moser, A. (1988). *Don't Pop Your Cork on Mondays!* Kansas City, MO: Landmark Editions.

Peer Relationships/Influences

Abern, A. (1994). *Everything I Do You Blame on Me*. Plainview, NY: Childswork/Childsplay, LLC.

Giannetti, C., and M. Sagarese (2001). *Cliques: 8 Steps to Help Your Child Survive the Social Jungle.* New York: Broadway Books.

Gordon, T. (1989). Teaching Children Self-Discipline at Home and at School. New York: Random House.

Meyers, W. (1992). *Mop, Moondance, and the Nagasaki Knights.* New York: Delacorte Press.

Ogen, S. (2001). *Words Will Never Hurt Me.* Los Angeles, CA: Elton-Wolfe Publishing.

Thompson, M., C. O'Neill, and L. Cohen (2001). *Best Friends, Worst Enemies: Understanding the Social Lives of Children.* New York: Ballantine Books.

Posttraumatic Stress Disorder

Faber, A., and E. Mazlish (1982). How to Talk so Kids Will Listen and Listen so Kids Will Talk. New York: Avon Books.

Gordon, T. (2000). *Parent Effectiveness Training*. New York: Three Rivers Press.

Manassis, K. (1996). *Keys to Parenting Your Anxious Child.* New York: Barrons Educational Series.

Schmidt, F., A. Friedman, E. Brunt, and T. Solotoff (1996). *Peacemaking Skills for Little Kids.* Miami, FL: Peace Education Foundation.

Spencer, E., R. DuPont, and C. DuPont (2003). *The Anxiety Cure for Kids: A Guide for Parents.* New York: John Wiley and Sons.

Poverty-Related Issues

Alliance for Children and Families (1998). *FAST: Families and Schools Together.* Milwaukee, WI: Alliance for Children and Families.

Cline, F., and J. Fay (1990). *Parenting with Love and Logic*. Colorado Springs, CO: Navpress.

Fay, J., R. Cline, and C. Fay (2000). *Becoming a Love and Logic Parent*. Golden, CO: The Love and Logic Press.

Moorman, C. (1998). *Parent Talk: Words That Empower, Words That Wound.* Merrill, MI: Personal Power Press.

Payne, R. (1998). *A Framework for Understanding Poverty*. Highlands, TX: RFT Publishing Co.

Schmidt, F., A. Friedman, E. Brunt, and T. Solotoff (1996). *Peacemaking Skills for Little Kids.* Miami, FL: Peace Education Foundation.

Prenatal Parenting Preparation

Brazelton, B. (1992). Touchpoints: Your Child's Emotional and Behavioral Development. Reading, MA: Addison-Wesley.
Churchill Films (1992). *Expect More Than a Baby!* Los Angeles, CA. (Video)
Curtis, G., and J. Schuler (2000). *Your Pregnancy Week by Week.* Cambridge, MA: Fisher.
Eisenberg, A., H. Mrukoff, and S. Hathaway (1996). *What to Expect When You're Expecting.* New York: Workman Publishing.
Lifestart Multimedia Corp. (1997). *The Baby System: Pregnancy and Birth* (Video and Book). Salt Lake City, UT: Lifestart Multimedia Corp.
Moorman, C., and S. Knapp (2001). *The Parent Talk System: The Language of Responsible Parenting.* Merrill, MI: Personal Power Press.

School Adjustment Difficulties

Cline, F., and J. Fay (1990). *Parenting with Love and Logic.* Colorado Springs, CO: Navpress.
Darcey, J., L. Tiore, and G. Ladd.(2000). Your Anxious Child: How Parents and Teachers Can Relieve Anxiety in Children. San Francisco, CA: Jossey-Bass.
Dinkmeyer, D., and G. McKay (1989). *Systematic Training for Effective Parenting (STEP).* Circle Pines, MN: American Guidance Service.
Fay, J. (1988). *Helicopters, Drill Sergeants, and Consultants.* Golden, CO: Cline/Fay Institute, Inc. (Audiotape)
McEwan, E. (1998). When Kids Say No to School: Helping Children at Risk of Failure, Refusal or Dropping Out. Harold Shaw Publishing.
Moorman, C. (1998). *Parent Talk: Words That Empower, Words That Wound.* Merrill, MI: Personal Power Press.
Moorman, C., and S. Knapp. (2001). *The Parent Talk System: The Language of Responsible Parenting.* Merrill, MI: Personal Power Press.

Sexual Responsibility

Alfred Higgins Productions (1989). *Sex Myths and Facts* (rev.) Los Angeles, CA. (Video)
Alfred Higgins Productions (1995). *Teens at Risk: Breaking the Immortality Myth.* Los Angeles, CA. (Video)
Bell, R. (1998). Changing Bodies, Changing Lives: Expanded Third Edition: A Book for Teens on Sex and Relationships. New York: Three Rivers Press.
Copperfield Films (1981). *Dear Diary.* Boston: Copperfield Films. (Video)

Gordon, S., and J. Gordon (1989). Raising a Child Conservatively in a Sexually Permissive World. New York: Fireside Books.

Hansen, G. (1996). *Sexual Integrity for Teens.* Lexington, KY: Kentucky Cooperative Extension Service. www.agnr.umd.edu/nnfr/adolsex/fact/adolsex_integ.html.

Mercer, R. (2001). *Adolescent Sexuality and Childbearing.* Sunnyvale, CA: Video Productions. (Video)

M.L. Video Productions. (1997). *Everyone Is Not Doing It.* Durham, NC: M.L. Video Productions. (Video)

Scott, S. (1997). *How to Say No and Keep Your Friends.* Highland Ranch, CO: HRC Press.

United Learning. (1990). *Matter of Choice: A Program Confronting Teenage Sexual Abuse.* Niles, IL: United Learning. (Video)

Sibling Rivalry

Blume, J., and I. Trivas (1984). *Pain and the Great One.* New York: Simon and Schuster.

Covey, S. (1997). The Seven Habits of Highly Effective Families: Building a Beautiful Family Culture in a Turbulent World. New York: Golden Books Publishing Co.

Crary, E., and M. Katayama (Illustrator) (1996). *Help! The Kids Are at It Again: Using Kids' Quarrels to Teach "People" Skills.* Seattle, WA: Parenting Press.

Faber, A. and Mazlish, E. (1982). How to Talk so Kids Will Listen and Listen so Kids Will Talk. New York: Avon Books.

Faber, A., and Mazlish, E. (1998). Siblings Without Rivalry: How to Help Your Children Live Together so You Can Live Too. New York: Avon Books.

Mario, H. (1998). *I'd Rather Have an Iguana.* Watertown, MA: Charlesbridge Publishing.

Single Parenting

Fay, J., F. Cline, and C. Fay (2000). *Becoming a Love and Logic Parent.* Golden, CO: The Love and Logic Press.

Moorman, C., and S. Knapp (2001). *The Parent Talk System: The Language of Responsible Parenting.* Merrill, MI: Personal Power Press.

Noel, B., A. Klein, and A. Klein (1998). *The Single Parent Resource.* New York: Champion Pr. Ltd.

Peterson, M. (2003). *Single Parenting for Dummies.* New York: For Dummies.

Richmond, G. (1998). *Successful Single Parenting.* New York: Harvest House.

Teyber, E. (1992). *Helping Children Cope with Divorce.* San Francisco, CA: Jossey-Bass.

Spousal Role and Relationship Conflict

Carlson, R. (1998). Don't Sweat the Small Stuff with Your Family. New York: Hyperion.
Chapman, G. (1995). The Five Love Languages: How to Express Heartfelt Commitment to Your Mate. Chicago: Northfield Publishing.
Covey, S. (1997). The Seven Habits of Highly Effective Families. New York: Golden Books.
Gordon, T. (2000). *Parent Effectiveness Training*. New York, NY, Three Rivers Press.
Henry, O. (1988). *The Gift of the Magi.* New York: Simon and Schuster.
McGraw, P. (2001). *Relationship Rescue.* New York: Hyperion Press.

Strategies for Preschoolers (Age Birth to Six)

Brazelton, T. (1992). *Touchpoints: The Essential Reference*. New York: Addison-Wesley.
Cline, F., and J. Fay (1990). *Parenting with Love and Logic*. Colorado Springs, CO: Navpress.
Covey, S. (1997). The Seven Habits of Highly Effective Families: Building a Beautiful Family Culture in a Turbulent World. New York: Golden Books Publishing Co.
Dinkmeyer, D., G. McKay, and Dinkmeyer (1989). *Parenting Young Children*. Circle Pines, MN: American Guidance Service.
Dreikurs, R., and V. Stoltz (1964). *Children: The Challenge*. New York: Plume Printing.
Fay, J. (1988). *Helicopters, Drill Sergeants, and Consultants.* Golden, CO: Cline/Fay Institute, Inc. (Audiotape)
Fay, J., and C. Fay (2002). *Love and Magic for Early Childhood.* Golden, CO: The Love and Logic Press.
Fay, J., F. Cline, and C. Fay (2000). *Becoming a Love and Logic Parent.* Golden, CO: The Love and Logic Press.
Gordon, T. (2000). *Parent Effectiveness Training*. New York: Three Rivers Press.
Ilg, F., and L. Ames (1985). The Gesell Institute's Child Behavior: From Birth to Ten. New York: HarperCollins.
Moorman, C. (2003). Parent Talk: How to Talk to Your Children in Language That Builds Self-Esteem and Encourages Responsibility. New York: Fireside.
Moorman, C., and S. Knapp (2001). *The Parent Talk System: The Language of Responsible Parenting.* Merrill, MI: Personal Power Press.
Walt Disney Pictures. (2003). *Finding Nemo.* Burbank, CA: Buena Vista Home Entertainment. (Video, DVD)

Strategies for Children (Age 7 to 12)

Cline, F., and J. Fay (1990). *Parenting with Love and Logic*. Colorado Springs, CO: Navpress.

Dinkmeyer, D., and G. McKay (1989). *Systematic Training for Effective Parenting (STEP)*. Circle Pines, MN: American Guidance Service.
Fay, J. (1988). *Helicopters, Drill Sergeants, and Consultants.* Golden, CO: Cline/Fay Institute, Inc. (Audiotape)
Fay, J., F. Cline, and C. Fay (2000). *Becoming a Love and Logic Parent.* Golden, CO: The Love and Logic Press.
Gordon, T. (2000). *Parent Effectiveness Training*. New York: Three Rivers Press.
Moorman, C. (1998). *Parent Talk: Words That Empower, Words That Wound.* Merrill, MI: Personal Power Press.
Moorman, C., and S. Knapp (2001). *The Parent Talk System: The Language of Responsible Parenting.* Merrill, MI: Personal Power Press.

Strategies for Teenagers (Age 13 to 18)

Cline, F., and J. Fay (1992). *Parenting Teens with Love and Logic*. Colorado Springs, CO: Navpress.
Covey, S. (1997). The Seven Habits of Highly Effective Families: Building a Beautiful Family Culture in a Turbulent World. New York: Golden Books Publishing Co.
Dinkmeyer, D., G. McKay, J. McKay, and D. Dinkmeyer (1998). *Parenting Teenagers: Systematic Training for Effective Parenting of Teens*. Circle Pines, MN: American Guidance Service.
Dreikurs, R., and V. Stoltz (1964). *Children: The Challenge*. New York: Plume Printing.
Ginott, H. (1985). *Between Parent and Teenager.* New York: Avon.
Gordon, T. (2000). *Parent Effectiveness Training*. New York: Three Rivers Press.
Moorman, C., and S. Knapp (2001). *The Parent Talk System: The Language of Responsible Parenting.* Merrill, MI: Personal Power Press.
Tainey, D., B. Rainey, and B. Nygren (2002). Parenting Today's Adolescent: Helping Your Child Avoid the Traps of the Preteen and Teen Years. Nashville, TN: Thomas Nelson.

Substance Abuse

Cline, F., and J. Fay (1992). *Parenting Teens with Love and Logic*. Colorado Springs, CO: Navpress.
DiPrisco, J. (2000). Field Guide to the American Teenager: A Parent's Companion. New York: Perseus Book Group.
Jalil, G. (1996). *Street Wise Drug Prevention*. Reading, PA: No More Drugs Inc.
Moorman, C. (1998). *Parent Talk: Words That Empower, Words That Wound.* Merrill, MI: Personal Power Press.
Wachel, T., D. York, and P. York (1982). *Toughlove*. Garden City, NJ: Doubleday.

Suicide Prevention

Arena, J. (1996). Step Back from the Exit: 45 Reasons to Say No to Suicide. New York: Zebulon Press.

Blauner, S. (2003). How I Stayed Alive When My Brain Was Trying to Kill Me: One Person's Guide to Suicide Prevention. New York: Quill.

Conroy, D. (1991). Out of the Nightmare: Recovery from Depression and Suicidal Pain. New York: New Liberty Press.

Ellis, T., and C. Newman.(1996). *Choosing to Live: How to Defeat Suicide Through Cognitive Therapy.* Oakland, CA: New Harbinger Publications.

Faber, A., and Mazlish, E. (1982). How to Talk so Kids Will Listen and Listen so Kids Will Talk. New York: Avon Books.

Gordon, T. (2000). *Parent Effectiveness Training*. New York: Three Rivers Press.

Moorman, C. (1998). *Parent Talk: Words That Empower, Words That Wound.* Merrill, MI: Personal Power Press.

Quinett, P. (1989). *Suicide: The Forever Decision.* New York: Continuum.

Appendix B

RECOVERY MODEL OBJECTIVES AND INTERVENTIONS

The Objectives and Interventions that follow are created around the 10 core principles developed by a multidisciplinary panel at the 2004 National Consensus Conference on Mental Health Recovery and Mental Health Systems Transformation, convened by the Substance Abuse and Mental Health Services Administration (SAMHSA, 2004):

1. **Self-direction:** Consumers lead, control, exercise choice over, and determine their own path of recovery by optimizing autonomy, independence, and control of resources to achieve a self-determined life. By definition, the recovery process must be self-directed by the individual, who defines his or her own life goals and designs a unique path toward those goals.
2. **Individualized and person-centered:** There are multiple pathways to recovery based on an individual's unique strengths and resiliencies as well as his or her needs, preferences, experiences (including past trauma), and cultural background in all of its diverse representations. Individuals also identify recovery as being an ongoing journey and an end result as well as an overall paradigm for achieving wellness and optimal mental health.
3. **Empowerment:** Consumers have the authority to choose from a range of options and to participate in all decisions—including the allocation of resources—that will affect their lives, and are educated and supported in so doing. They have the ability to join with other consumers to collectively and effectively speak for themselves about their needs, wants, desires, and aspirations. Through empowerment, an individual gains control of his or her

own destiny and influences the organizational and societal structures in his or her life.

4. **Holistic:** Recovery encompasses an individual's whole life, including mind, body, spirit, and community. Recovery embraces all aspects of life, including housing, employment, education, mental health and healthcare treatment and services, complementary and naturalistic services, addictions treatment, spirituality, creativity, social networks, community participation, and family supports as determined by the person. Families, providers, organizations, systems, communities, and society play crucial roles in creating and maintaining meaningful opportunities for consumer access to these supports.
5. **Nonlinear:** Recovery is not a step-by-step process but one based on continual growth, occasional setbacks, and learning from experience. Recovery begins with an initial stage of awareness in which a person recognizes that positive change is possible. This awareness enables the consumer to move on to fully engage in the work of recovery.
6. **Strengths-based:** Recovery focuses on valuing and building on the multiple capacities, resiliencies, talents, coping abilities, and inherent worth of individuals. By building on these strengths, consumers leave stymied life roles behind and engage in new life roles (e.g., partner, caregiver, friend, student, employee). The process of recovery moves forward through interaction with others in supportive, trust-based relationships.
7. **Peer support:** Mutual support—including the sharing of experiential knowledge and skills and social learning—plays an invaluable role in recovery. Consumers encourage and engage other consumers in recovery and provide each other with a sense of belonging, supportive relationships, valued roles, and community.
8. **Respect:** Community, systems, and societal acceptance and appreciation of consumers—including protecting their rights and eliminating discrimination and stigma—are crucial in achieving recovery. Self-acceptance and regaining belief in one's self are particularly vital. Respect ensures the inclusion and full participation of consumers in all aspects of their lives.
9. **Responsibility:** Consumers have a personal responsibility for their own self-care and journeys of recovery. Taking steps toward their goals may require great courage. Consumers must strive to understand and give meaning to their experiences and identify coping strategies and healing processes to promote their own wellness.

10. **Hope:** Recovery provides the essential and motivating message of a better future—that people can overcome the barriers and obstacles that confront them. Hope is internalized, but can be fostered by peers, families, friends, providers, and others. Hope is the catalyst of the recovery process. Mental health recovery not only benefits individuals with mental health disabilities by focusing on their abilities to live, work, learn, and fully participate in our society, but also enriches the texture of American community life. America reaps the benefits of the contributions individuals with mental disabilities can make, ultimately becoming a stronger and healthier Nation.[1]

The numbers used for Objectives in the treatment plan that follows correspond to the numbers for the 10 core principles. Each of the 10 Objectives was written to capture the essential theme of the like-numbered core principle. The numbers in parentheses after the Objectives denote the Interventions designed to assist the client in attaining each respective Objective. The clinician may select any or all of the Objectives and Intervention statements to include in the client's treatment plan.

One generic Long-Term Goal statement is offered should the clinician desire to emphasize a recovery model orientation in the client's treatment plan.

LONG-TERM GOAL

1. To live a meaningful life in a self-selected community while striving to achieve full potential during the journey of healing and transformation.

SHORT-TERM OBJECTIVES

1. Make it clear to therapist, family, and friends what path to recovery is preferred. (1, 2, 3, 4)

THERAPEUTIC INTERVENTIONS

1. Explore the client's thoughts, needs, and preferences regarding his/her desired pathway to recovery (from depression, bipolar disorder,

[1] From: Substance Abuse and Mental Health Services Administration's (SAMHSA) National Mental Health Information Center: Center for Mental Health Services (2004). *National consensus statement on mental health recovery.* Washington, DC: Author. Available from http://mentalhealth.samhsa.gov/publications/allpubs/sma05-4129/

posttraumatic stress disorder [PTSD], etc.).

2. Discuss with the client the alternative treatment interventions and community support resources that might facilitate his/her recovery.
3. Solicit from the client his/her preferences regarding the direction treatment will take; allow for these preferences to be communicated to family and significant others.
4. Discuss and process with the client the possible outcomes that may result from his/her decisions.

2. Specify any unique needs and cultural preferences that must be taken under consideration during the treatment process. (5, 6)

5. Explore with the client any cultural considerations, experiences, or other needs that must be considered in formulating a mutually agreed-upon treatment plan.
6. Modify treatment planning to accommodate the client's cultural and experiential background and preferences.

3. Verbalize an understanding that decision making throughout the treatment process is self-controlled. (7, 8)

7. Clarify with the client that he/she has the right to choose and select among options and participate in all decisions that affect him/her during treatment.
8. Continuously offer and explain options to the client as treatment progresses in support of his/her sense of empowerment, encouraging and reinforcing the client's participation in treatment decision making.

4. Express mental, physical, spiritual, and community needs and desires that should be integrated into the treatment process. (9, 10)

9. Assess the client's personal, interpersonal, medical, spiritual, and community strengths and weaknesses.

10. Maintain a holistic approach to treatment planning by integrating the client's unique mental, physical, spiritual, and community needs and assets into the plan; arrive at an agreement with the client as to how these integrations will be made.

5. Verbalize an understanding that during the treatment process there will be successes and failures, progress and setbacks. (11, 12)

11. Facilitate realistic expectations and hope in the client that positive change is possible, but does not occur in a linear process of straight-line successes; emphasize a recovery process involving growth, learning from advances as well as setbacks, and staying this course toward recovery.

12. Convey to the client that you will stay the course with him/her through the difficult times of lapses and setbacks.

6. Cooperate with an assessment of personal strengths and assets brought to the treatment process. (13, 14, 15)

13. Administer to the client the *Behavioral and Emotional Rating Scale (BERS): A Strength-Based Approach to Assessment* (Epstein).

14. Identify the client's strengths through a thorough assessment involving social, cognitive, relational, and spiritual aspects of the client's life; assist the client in identifying what coping skills have worked well in the past to overcome problems and what talents and

abilities characterize his/her daily life.

15. Provide feedback to the client of his/her identified strengths and how these strengths can be integrated into short-term and long-term recovery planning.

7. Verbalize an understanding of the benefits of peer support during the recovery process. (16, 17, 18)

16. Discuss with the client the benefits of peer support (e.g., sharing common problems, receiving advice regarding successful coping skills, getting encouragement, learning of helpful community resources, etc.) toward the client's agreement to engage in peer activity.
17. Refer the client to peer support groups of his/her choice in the community and process his/her experience with follow-through.
18. Build and reinforce the client's sense of belonging, supportive relationship building, social value, and community integration by processing the gains and problem-solving the obstacles encountered through the client's social activities.

8. Agree to reveal when any occasion arises that respect is not felt from the treatment staff, family, self, or the community. (19, 20, 21)

19. Discuss with the client the crucial role that respect plays in recovery, reviewing subtle and obvious ways in which disrespect may be shown to or experienced by the client.
20. Review ways in which the client has felt disrespected in the past, identifying sources of that disrespect.

21. Encourage and reinforce the client's self-concept as a person deserving of respect; advocate for the client to increase incidents of respectful treatment within the community and/or family system.

9. Verbalize acceptance of responsibility for self-care and participation in decisions during the treatment process. (22)

22. Develop, encourage, support, and reinforce the client's role as the person in control of his/her treatment and responsible for its application to his/her daily life; adopt a supportive role as a resource person to assist in the recovery process.

10. Express hope that better functioning in the future can be attained. (23, 24)

23. Discuss with the client potential role models who have achieved a more satisfying life by using their personal strengths, skills, and social support to live, work, learn, and fully participate in society toward building hope and incentive motivation.

24. Discuss and enhance internalization of the client's self-concept as a person capable of overcoming obstacles and achieving satisfaction in living; continuously build and reinforce this self-concept using past and present examples supporting it.